GUNSMITHING the AR-15

VOLUME 2

- Field-stripping
- Detailed disassembly
- Step-by-step instructions

PATRICK SWEENEY

Published by

Gun Digest® Books, an imprint of F+W Media, Inc.
Krause Publications • 700 East State Street • Iola, WI 54990-0001
715-445-2214 • 888-457-2873
www.krausebooks.com

To order books or other products call toll-free 1-800-258-0929
or visit us online at www.gundigeststore.com

Cover photography by Yamil Sued

ISBN-13: 978-1-4402-3848-2
ISBN-10: 1-4402-3848-0

Designed by Dane Royer
Edited by Corrina Peterson

Printed in United States of America

10 9 8 7 6 5 4

DEDICATION

As always, and ever, to Felicia. Center, partner, team-mate, the best.

And also, to my father. Dad was born with exquisite timing. A kid during the great depression, he graduated from high school just in time to be drafted (like there was any doubt, or choice), get trained and be sent over to Europe. He wasn't airborne, but if you want to know what he did over there for seven months, just watch Band of Brothers "Last Patrol." Night raids is what he did, night after night.

He then came back home, got married, raised a family, sent us to college and lived a good, long life. I learned from him a balance of practical and theoretical, research and "good enough," and how to last over the long haul.

Thanks, Dad.

TABLE OF CONTENTS

ACKNOWLEDGMENTS

I could not have done this book, or the ones leading up to this one, without the knowledge gained from other people's experiences.

From my customers, through a couple of assault weapons panics and the marginally-assembled rifles they brought in. From the competitors I've locked horns with in matches, from basic club matches, to 3-gun national championships, to barrel-melting bowling pin matches.

And from the classes, learning, teaching, fixing, with my friends Jeff Chudwin and Ned Christiansen. In the space of a three- or five-day class, we get to see 25-30 or more officers thrashing ARs of various vintages, manufacturers and level of maintenance, through at least a thousand rounds and often more. As the late, great Yogi Berra once said, "You can observe a lot by just watching." The most cost-effective way to learn is from others' mistakes, and the classes afford us that boon.

And, the various manufactures who have loaned me gear to test, abuse, break, repair and report on, chief of which is Mark Malkowski and Stag Arms. Thanks, Mark.

PREFACE

For a rifle that has been around for as long as the AR-15/M16, there is not a lot known for sure. Well, there is, but it is locked up in the safe of the various manufacturers who make good gear. Or on the shelf of the nearest Regular Army or NG training NCO, in training manuals that are hardly ever read.

On the other hand, there is a huge amount of information to be had, known, digested and used for decision making, but every bit of it is a small tidbit, a scattered data point, known to the guy or guys who tested/learned it, and not disseminated further. Mix in all the "a buddy told me" or information that "everyone knows" that is spread as gospel in guns shops and strewn all over the internet, and you have a real mess.

This book is for the new AR-15 owner (and the not-so-new owner as well) who is not interested in building a dozen different ARs, each with a perfectly-matched set of options, parts, features and goodies. If you are simply looking for info on how to keep your AR-15 running, how to de-bug it if it gets to acting cranky, or need to set right some minor error that the factory/builder didn't tend to, this is the book for you. If you pay attention, your AR 15 will be reliable, accurate, properly sighted-in, and all the parts and accessories on it will stay tightly attached. Plus, for those who just have to have it, this will have detailed assembly instructions, with the assumption that you have somehow acquired a box 'o parts and want to turn them into a working AR-15.

I wrote a lot of the first edition of *Gunsmithing the AR-15* from the perspective that readers knew a lot more than they actually knew. It wasn't basic enough. This second volume takes a step back and covers many of those very basic things.

Those with a bit more experience will be tempted to skim over some sections. I'd ask you not to do that, because there may well be some tidbit or gem, some detail not previously known, from which you could benefit. And those who "know" something that isn't true will benefit from reading the correct information. I'm not one to brag, but I can say with more than a little certainty that if you know something and that fact is in disagreement with what I'm telling you, that other "fact" is wrong. If you disagree, don't just shrug it off and declare me to be a fraud, ignorant or terminally dense. Do your homework. Do some testing. Find me on an internet forum someplace and ask how I know, what I know, that disagrees with your knowledge. That's the only way we'll all learn.

Let's get to it.

INTRODUCTION

YOUR CURRENT, black aluminum, hated-by-politicians rifle differs from previous military rifles in, oh, just about every way possible. The AR-15/M16/M4 (let's just keep it simple, and refer to all of them as the "AR") is a self-loading rifle that feeds from a box magazine and uses the direct-gas impingement operation system (aka, DI system). In most instances, it isn't a machine gun and it isn't an assault rifle, even though it gets called that by many.

And, just to get things on the correct footing, nowhere in any book I ever write on the AR will you ever read of me describing it as a weapon, unless it is so-used. That is, a weapon is what you use in a fight. In legal terms, it is the tool you use in any action under legal scrutiny. You do not shoot in a match with a weapon. You do not go hunting, or varmint plinking, with a weapon. Can it be a weapon? Yeah, sure, you betcha. But to describe it always as "a weapon" is to be sloppy with the English language, and I try very hard not to be sloppy. And where I do use that term, it is a deliberate choice.

The AR was not developed, like the M1 Garand or the M14, by the military, which tested, re-tested and modified as the process continued. It was a far messier process than that. The M1 Garand took almost twenty years to come to fruition, and its inventor, John Garand, had to be fast on his feet several times in that process to keep his baby from being killed. Post-WWII, the US Army Ordnance department spent a decade and millions of dollars "improving" the Garand, ending with the M14.

While the US Army was laboring to disgorge the M14, itself a barely-modified M1 Garand, an aerospace company by the name of Armalite (not the same company that today bears the name) was working on lightweight alloys and space-age designs. The designer there, Eugene Stoner, came up with an amalgam of design highlights and assembled them into a rifle with lightweight aluminum receivers. The result was a .308 rifle that weighed significantly less than then-current .308 rifles: the M14, G3 and the FAL.

Alas for Armalite, the militaries of the world, dragged along kicking and screaming by the US Army, had settled on .308, and since they had to use .308 they insisted on going with their own designs. They could not fight off being strong-armed into caliber, but by god they were going to make the rifle at home, and not depend further on Uncle Sam's largesse.

Armalite then shopped the prototype around, and also down-sized it. Colt picked up the option to make the rifle for the sum of $75,000 and a small percentage of future profits.

The new Armalite was shown around the world, demonstrated anyplace someone showed interest, until someone managed to get it into the hands of General Curtis LeMay. LeMay was in charge of SAC, and was a WWII combat veteran. As an Army Air Force General in WWII, he was responsible for basically burning Japan to the ground in the last

The M14 was supposed to replace everything. The selector switch would go right where the button is on the one you see here.

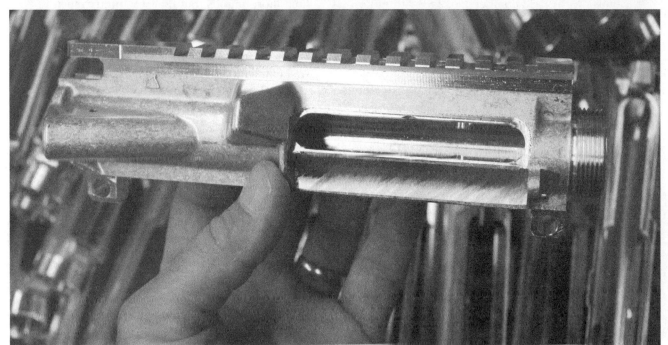

The AR receiver is carved out of an aluminum forging, and is just the shell that holds the parts. It does not work like the receiver of an M1 Garand or M14.

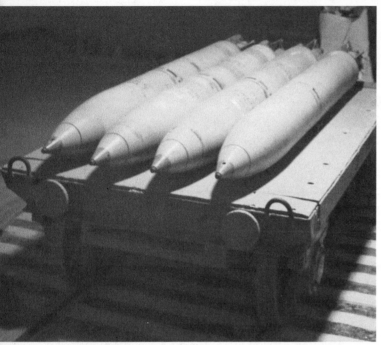

When it comes to waging war, rifles are way down the list of important tools to the planners. Here is a display of torpedoes, ready to be loaded into Soviet subs, in a sub base carved out of a mountain. They said there were never any nukes there, but you gotta wonder.

year of the war. SAC in the late 1950s and early 1960s meant B-52 bombers, loaded with nukes, waiting on runways to be flown north and at the Soviets. And B-52s loaded with nukes required armed guards.

The Air Force had been created as a separate arm after WWII, and was still very prickly about their newly-won independence from the Army. However, the small arms the SAC guards used, primarily M1 and M2 carbines, had to be serviced by the Army. Not that the Air Force didn't have the skill to do it, but the Army had kept hold of all the parts, tools, armorers classes and institutional knowledge, and they weren't giving it up. LeMay, shown the AR-15 rifle at a barbeque, shot the new Armalite, liked it, and immediately ordered enough to arm his base guards.

This, and the subsequent history, is all covered in great detail in a number of books. If you really want the blow-by-blow of how it all happened, they are available for your education. In this book, we will cover use and maintenance, but in order to do that well, it will help to have a grasp of the history, messy and messier, that got so much mis-information in print.

Colt was very happy. Once the Air Force bought the AR-15s, the company was "in the system." That is, it now had an official government stock number, and if someone else wanted some, they could apply for Armalite rifles made by Colt by using the stock number and sending a payment.

Enter Robert McNamara. A successful engineer, salesman and President of Ford Motor Company, he was brought into the government as the Secretary of Defense. (Oh, and he had been an analyst in WWI, working under General LeMay. Not that that influenced the AR-15/M16 situation.) He immediately began applying business practices to defense habits, one focus being the Ordnance department. The Ordnance department had, as I mentioned, labored to design the M14. In the process of developing, testing, and adopting the M14, the Ordnance department and the Army had over-promised and under-delivered. By the early 1960s, the M14 was proven to not be less expensive to produce than the M1 Garand, as had been promised. Also, it provided no advantage over the Garand in recoil, weight, ammunition payload or size. It did have a shorter cartridge, and it did hold more rounds, but that was pretty much it.

In fact, it was also horribly behind schedule in procurement. At the time of the Berlin Blockade in 1961, it was discovered that the Berlin Brigade was not armed with the new rifle, and was still using M1 Garands. In an earlier work, I looked into manufacture and issue rates of the time and calculated that, at the rate the Army was getting M14s, they would have had the entire Army switched over to M14s by 1976. This, with a rifle officially adopted in 1957.

The problem was that we were by the mid-1960s in an increasingly hot war. The Army needed rifles, and they did not need long-range rifles, capable of delivering a killing blow at 1,000 yards. In Vietnam, the locations where you could see 1,000 yards were limited, and the VC and NVA became quite aware that standing in the open was asking to get shot. So they didn't.

The lightweight, compact, low-recoiling and reliable Armalite was just the thing for a close-range war. So, the Army was ordered to adopt

An original Colt, here an early SP1, lacking a forward assist, fences and a push-pin takedown front pin. This was state of the art, ca. 1967.

The first tele-stocks had two positions - open or closed. We got intermediate stops later.

it. The resulting cluster-bleep would have been comical, except there was a war on. The Army said, "Fine, but we need Ordnance to de-bug it first." To which the smart young guys, the whiz-kids, the ones McNamara had brought in, remembered the debacle of the M14 and said "No way, you'll just stall it until you can kill it." Which was true. Referring to the demo, round-the-world tour of the AR-15, they countered, "The prototype went 40,000 rounds without a malfunction, it is perfect, use it as-is."

Every time the Army suggested a change, an upgrade, an improvement, they were nixed. Why? According to the "whiz kids" in Defense, "It was perfect as it was." And, they knew the Army wanted to kill it, and figured every excuse was just that, an opening to nix the change.

The Army tried to kill it by claiming the useful range it had was too short, in effect moving the goalposts, until they insisted on a minimum level of retained energy at 500 yards. The ammo companies improved the round, and Colt altered the rifle to match.

And then it went off to combat, where at first it seemed to do OK. Then, reality raised its ugly head.

The Army had a bazillion .30 cleaning kits in warehouses across the country. After all, for over half a century, through two World Wars, a police

The earliest AR-15s were so-marked, regardless of semi or select-fire. That's right, the first batch of these that were machine guns were not marked as M16s.

action and countless firing ranges and barracks, they had used .30 rifles, light, medium and heavy machine guns, so they had a multi-war supply of rods, brushes and patches on hand. And none of them would fit an AR.

The earliest rifles were AR-15, and marked so, even when they were select-fire. I've seen a lot of AR 15 marked rifles that were, for all intents and purposes, M16s, but they were made too early in the process to be marked "M16".

As a result, grunts in Vietnam were writing home for .22 cleaning kits, since the Army had none.

NEVER TO BE TRUSTED?

Then, volume production and use began to show problems, big time. The original ammunition had used a special powder, one with a burn rate that worked properly with the direct-gas system. (Since the system ports the gas directly back into the receiver, it can be quite sensitive to the pressure remaining in the bore when the bullet passes the port, known as the "port pressure.") That powder maker could not produce the powder used in developing the rifle and cartridge, not in the volume needed for wartime needs. So, the Army asked a different powder maker to provide a suitable powder. The replacement powder had a different burn rate, one not suited to the DI system. The port pressure was too high. The cyclic rate of the rifles with the old ammo was 700-750 rpm. Driven harder by the new powder, the rifles when given a final test before shipping cycled at over 900 rpm. Colt had to ask for continual variances from the specifications, in order to ship the needed rifles.

I can just imagine the phone calls. "Look, you guys sent us the ammo to use and test. The rifles are cycling over 900 rpm with your ammo. Either give us a variance to ship as-is, or ship us the old ammo to test with." There was a war on, and no more of the old ammo to be had, so the rifles got a variance, and got shipped.

Adding to the problems, the new powder was basically the same old powder used in 7.62X51 cartridges. It had a chemical in it to reduce flash, known as a flash retardant. In loading cartridges for the M14 and machine guns in 7.62, two percent of this chemical in the powder mix was no big deal, and reduced visible flash very nicely. The gas system of the M14 and the M60 shrugged it off as if it wasn't even in there. In the AR, two percent was too much. It hardened the powder residue to a hard scale, a scale difficult to clean off if not scrubbed immediately, and if not cleaned off, one that caused difficulty in function.

The Army had suggested using hard-

In the early days, barrel markings were easy. There was only one twist (1/12) and your choices were chromed or not.

The AR is now common, so common that manufacturers who would not have previously considered it are in the market.

chrome plating on the chambers and bore, as Stoner had done with his original .308 rifle. The whiz kids had turned that down, assuming it was more Army stalling, and the resulting rust (gee, bare steel in a jungle environment, who could predict rust?) caused even more function problems. In all fairness, the M1 Garand had been used in jungles, and it did not have a chrome-plated chamber or bore. But it was a .30 rifle, with big, heavy moving parts that didn't care about a little powder residue.

The Army had to de-bug the rifle while combat was going on, and the resulting problems gave the AR a reputation for unreliability and fragility it was a long time getting over. In some minds, it still has not overcome that early rep.

You will still hear and read people recounting those problems as if they had happened yesterday, and that the Army, the manufacturers, and the politicians have done nothing to change them. Not true, although we can't give a lot of credit to the politicians. However, and to the great distress of those using or building ARs, the minor problems that remained were not viewed as minor. They were swamped by the overwhelming attitude of, "These things failed their owners in the jungle, they are never to be trusted."

LATER CHANGES

By 1971, the Army had solved all the big problems. The barrels had the bore and chamber hard-chromed. The powder problem had been addressed, at least as far as the flash retardant was concerned, and the cyclic rate was down to where it worked better. They had done so without making the rifle heavier or larger, and it was still a lightweight, handy rifle. It was never going to satisfy the .308 lovers, but it would do its job.

Then, after we had extricated ourselves from Vietnam, the spectre of the Soviets rose again. By the mid-1970s we were out of the jungles and back to the plains, forests and cities of Europe. And the Soviets were going to have body armor. (Cue ominous drum roll, and eerie music.) We needed ammo that would reach through armor. Meanwhile, the Marine Corps, never happy with the M16, was agitating to have a rifle that could

The M16 replaced the M14, mightily annoying many marines at the time. Two CH-46Es unload Marines off into combat north of Phu Bai, South Vietnam, during Operation Hastings, 1966.

The bolt of the AR locks directly into the rear of the barrel, in the barrel extension. The barrel locks onto the receiver by means of the barrel nut, the black part in this photo. The receiver doesn't hold the pressure of firing.

actually allow them to post "proper" scores on the qualification course, one that went out to 500 meters.

Now, again, you have to keep this in context. In the 1970s, there was no GPS, there were no JDams, no digital trickery of any kind. Marines who hit the beach (and that was their job) still depended on naval gunfire and air support, both of which were done by voice, over radio frequencies.

Directing naval gunfire or air support was, "Two hundred meters from the wrecked white building, on a bearing of one hundred and thirty five degrees magnetic north from violet smoke. Fire and wait correction." To solve their problems, soldiers in a Marine rifle company that hit the beach pretty much had only what they hauled off the landing craft themselves. A rifle squad might be tasked with the job of keeping the enemy machine gun in a building ahead of them busy until the company commander could get the mortar team on it. Or until the off-loaded tank got un-stuck from the mud.

The M16A1, with barely-adjustable sights, a light bullet with a sucky ballistic coefficient, and thus a poor trajectory, was unsuited to a fire team hammering a machine gun position with aimed semi-auto fire, keeping it busy until a bigger hammer could be brought to bear. So in the early 1980s, the M16 was tested for improvements and the new rifle was produced to "solve" those problems.

The resulting M16A2 had a heavier barrel, to allow the USMC to use a sling as an aiming aid, which the skinny barrel of the M16A1 objected to. The stock was lengthened (and also made of a more durable material, an actual good thing) again, to permit proper marksmanship methods. The rear sight was made user-adjustable both for range and windage, another marksmanship upgrade.

And, the barrel twist was changed, from one turn in 12 inches, to one in seven. This stabilized heavier bullets, allowing for great retained energy, potentially greater accuracy, and the use of bullets suited to military use.

One of those new bullets was the M855, a 62 grain bullet (compared to the 55 grains of the M193, the original load) which contained a steel penetrating tip inside the jacket. The M855 was the American-made version of the original test bullet, known in European circles as the SS-109. While the originals were accurate, the early versions of the M855 were much less so, causing a certain amount of heartburn during the transition.

The steel tip, all ten grains of it, allowed the bullet to work better on body armor. It also removed, almost entirely, the wounding effectiveness

A beautiful, almost idyllic scene. And one in which a thousand-yard rifle would be of no use. More power can be good, but more reach isn't always useful.

Helicopters created a new mode of warfare, and light and fast were its hallmarks. Old rifles were not needed or desired, at least not by those at the top.

The first M16s to arrive came to Vietnam lacking cleaning equipment. Grunts figured out how to cope.

The big advantage of the M16 was that a soldier could carry many more rounds than he could of 7.62. Dropped off in the middle of nowhere, and with resupply uncertain, lots of bullets is a good thing. US Army photo.

of the original load. The other new round to go with it was the new tracer bullet, the M856. This bullet, in order to contain enough chemical to burn through the full effective distance desired (more of a problem with machine guns than rifles, but what can you do?) is so long it requires the 1/7 twist, where lead-core bullets did not have to be spun that quickly. At least, not for another twenty years.

I have wondered if the cause and effect is the reverse of what we have long thought. After all, the testing that produced the 1/7 twist rate was ongoing, and the ballisticians who produced the M856 could well have known that, and used every bit of its stabilizing effect, to produce a tracer round that burned "all the way out there."

But, we need to move on.

The result, in the late 1980s, was a service rifle that was not at all like the one issued in 1971. The M16A2 was longer, heavier, balanced differently, and had a sighting system that fairly begged to be used at ranges well beyond what was considered the new normal; infantry doesn't generally shoot people with rifles past 300 meters. That, too, took another twenty years.

The first wake-up call came in Somalia, the running gunfight in Mogadishu, where our troops reported repeatedly shooting people with "green tip" (the M855 has a green-painted tip to identify it) and having those people keep running or keep fighting, or not really pay much attention. In ballistic parlance, the bullet was so stable it passed through without overturning, and thus created wounds not unlike being stabbed with a sharp knitting needle. Not that that is any fun (I do not speak from experience) but it certainly does not greatly discourage the motivated armed combatant.

But, ballistics is both a science and an art, and the prevailing ethos in the military, for the most part, has been managerial for a couple of generations now. (Some branches, more than others.) People practice, train and do what they are graded on, and no-one was being graded on small arms effectiveness. So it should not have come as a surprise when, almost a decade later, the same complaints were voiced in Iraq and Afghanistan.

COLT'S EXCLUSIVE DESIGN

Meanwhile, Colt was still trying to move things forward. They realized by the early 1990s that the M16A2 was too long, too heavy and too bulky for some end-users. But they could not convince the Army to do anything. So they did it themselves. They spent their own money, and did the work on their own time, to produce a de-bugged, reliable, carbine version of the M16A2, which Colt called the M4.

The repercussions of that course of action are still being felt, twenty years later. You see, the M16A1, and the A2, having been government-initiated and developed, belonged to the government. If the Department of Defense wanted to source the M16A2 from an extra, replacement, or competitive manufacturer, Colt had one choice – suck it up and compete for the bid. That's why, if you get a chance to see some M16A1s up-close, don't be surprised if you see some marked "Hydramatic." Yep, made by the division of GM, during the Vietnam war, as an additional source to Colt. Later, M16A2, 3, and 4 models can be found marked by FN, out of South Carolina. DoD invited bids, and FNH-USA has won some. A lot, in fact. But the Technical Data Package (TDP in mil-speak) of the M4 was not paid for, nor developed by DoD. It was paid for by Colt, and thus belonged to them.

Colt offered the M4 to the military as an individual product, not a weapons system as part of a request for proposal, etc., and some units jumped on it, because it was a good thing to have. When it became known, more units had to have it, but budgets and TO&E limited adoption. (More mil-speak: TO&E, Table of Organization and Equipment. If the TO&E says your unit needs/uses/gets M16A2s, it doesn't matter that in a rational world, the better-tool-for-you M4 would be a no-brainer decision. You get M16A2s.)

FNH USA entered the bid for M16A2/A3/A4 contracts, won, and became a competitor to Colt for those products. But, the M4 was a sole-Colt product, since the TDP was Colt's. If the DoD wanted to get other bidders for M4 contracts, they would first have to buy the TDP from Colt. (Now

that would have been an interesting discussion to watch.)

Further complication: The government screws up. In the process of letting out bids for accessories to go onto M4 carbines, the DoD sent copies of the Colt-owned M4 TDP along with the accessory descriptions that the Army wanted. Ooops. While the government was within its bounds asking other companies to bid on extras, they did not own the TDP, and could not hand out copies of it to third parties.

This is where having good attorneys on hand is a good thing. Colt got the copies back, and the requirement that any knowledge those third parties might have gained, not be used. And more, Colt got exclusive use of the TDP for a specified period of time (up to 2009 as I recall) and afterwards, the government could use it and issue it.

But here's the fun part – any third party who uses the TDP post-2009 can use it only for a government contract (they can't improve their own civilian-market product, using the TDP) they can't make an M4-based product for non-DoD sale, and when the contract is done, they have to destroy all copies of the TDP they possess.

And as a capper, Colt also collects a royalty for all M4 production by third parties, to government sales, for a time period (don't know the time, but I'd bet twenty years from 2009) in the future. Colt could very well give up M4 production for the government, focus solely on civilian sales, and still make money on each M4 that goes to the DoD or overseas. Damn, that Colt attorney earned his yearly bonus.

DEMAND RISES

Meanwhile, back at the end of the 20th century the failed Assault Weapons Ban of 1994 was causing all kinds of consternation.

Colt, by this time, was basically out of the non-military firearms production business. The ban caused more interest in ARs than had existed before. As a result, a lot of people jumped in to make them. After all, unlike the traditional firearms manufacturing process, the AR was much more of an industrial product than many firearms

The gov mandates a flash hider not just to hide flash. Rifles get a lot of abuse in real-world use, and a smart designer knows that. Lance Cpl. Jaime J. Sweeney (no relation to author), radio operator for the 26th Marine Expeditionary Unit's Ground Sensor Platoon, checks the field of view from a camera

Colt made the M4, they own it, and they now can collect royalties from other makers who supply M4s in the future to the government. Nice work, if you can get it.

Fashion and need may dictate desire, but you use what you have. Everyone wants an M4, but the government has warehouses full of M16A2s. U.S. Army 1st Lt. Spencer Tadken reviews aiming techniques with an Afghan soldier during training at Forward Operating Base Shank.

designs had previously been. Plus, with receivers made of aluminum, it was possible to re-program a CNC machining station to machine the forgings. Unlike traditional firearms production, where a part that required twenty machine cuts, and thus twenty mills, each set up for its one cut, one CNC machine could do all twenty. Or forty, a hundred, or more.

A brief bit of background on forgings. The process involves heating aluminum bar stock, of a specified alloy, of a given diameter, to a certain temperature, and then holding it in place (with long tongs, obviously) while a big steel die slams down on it. The hot, plastic metal is forced into the shape of the inside of the die, and the grain of the metal is aligned according to the shape of the die.

The temperatures involved and the amount of force slammed down depend on the particular alloy. The amount of grain change induced depends on force, alloy, temperature and shape. The production rate depends on operator experience and investment in proper machines.

The forge machines are heavy, and require huge power to work. (Slamming a multi-ton piece of steel up and down in a controlled manner is not something you do with a 5-hp gasoline engine.) A forge company wants to keep the machines running 24/7. The only way they make money is by forging metal. So, let's say Colt has a government contract, and needs "X" number of upper and lower forgings a year. If that does not represent full utilization of the forge shop's output, the forge company will look for more work. That is the nature of heartless capitalism; the company has to pay its bills, and the fact that Colt doesn't need all their output is the problem. And that Colt does not want others to be making AR rifles is not the forge company's problem.

If you want to make ARs, you can walk in, checkbook in hand, and buy the time to make forgings. However, what you can't do is have your forgings made with the dies Colt paid for. You have to either use the shop's dies (which they paid to have made, for just such an occasion) or pay for your own dies. Dies can be "cheap" and only cost $10,000. Or they can cost more, a lot more.

Well, with everyone wanting ARs, and Colt not in the business, really, in the 1990s, there were several someones who were willing to pony up the money for dies. Some forge companies made their own, to sell to anyone who wanted to buy forgings, and some AR manufactures paid to have their own dies made, for their own forging supply.

Ten years from the enactment of the AWB/94, when it expired (and don't think we can ever trick the anti-gunners into that again), there were

A rifle good to a thousand yards wasn't of much use when the expected engagement distance was barely more than a stone's throw away.

more AR makers than there had ever been, and the quality was higher than ever. They were not, however, mil-spec. A clever engineer could copy a mil-spec part (without the drawings, the plus-or-minus dimensions, the testing protocols), and they

A rifle isn't just a bullet-launching tool these days, it is an observation optics rest, a laser guidance stick, a ten-pound burden when your real weapon is a radio. U.S. Army Staff Sgt. Mark Scott uses his weapon's scope to scan the area while providing security from his battle position during an escort detail at Forward Operating Base Farah.

could come close, but they could not be mil-spec. But in many instances, they were better than mil-spec.

In the same timeframe, a new type of sport burgeoned: 3-gun. I had been shooting 3-gun matches at my home club since the very early 1980s. I had shot in the second USPSA 3-Gun Nationals in 1995. That match was well-attended for a new event, in a strange (Long Island, NY) location. It grew so fast that by the time the 2002 3-Gun Nationals came about, the match was full long before it even started. Today there are TV shows devoted to 3-gun (and its evolution, multi-gun) but the time between the rise and the fall of the AWB got a lot of people interested. Plus, because they were interested in the competitive use of the AR, they were not bound by the traditional mil-spec limits.

With the sunset of the AWB/94, and with every political twist since, AR sales have increased.

An interesting parallel happened in the US Army Marksmanship Unit. Until the mid-1990s, the Army had been using M14s for High Power competition. A new commander came in and basically said, "That isn't the issue rifle any more, we're going to use what we're issued." Where civilian competitors had been testing ARs, and tuning them for High Power for a few years, the Army had to undergo a crash course in making them accurate to 600 yards. They succeeded. Within a couple of years, it was rare to see anything but an AR on the course at Camp Perry. In an interesting reversal, the .30

Soldiers and Marines have a lot of gear to haul, keep track of and use. And some of them even have more. Personally, I'd see that dog handlers were all issued suppressors, but that's just me. U.S. Marine Corps Lance Cpl. Brandon Mann uses his rifle's scope to scan the area while providing security with his military working dog, Ty. Ty is an improvised explosive device detection dog.

rifles became so sparse the NRA created a new, retro division competition, and set up matches just for.30 rifles.

THE ULTIMATE DIY RIFLE

Through it all, tales of failed M16s in the jungle have haunted the AR. And lousy accuracy, and fragile parts. And it is no longer true. A properly-built AR, using good (and not even the gold-plated best) parts is as reliable as any other self-loading rifle made. A recent test (not done by me, but I was not surprised by the results) had an array of AR carbines (16" barrel, telestock, more-or-less mil-spec) firing ten thousand rounds, each one of them one doing so without a failure. The one that did not fail was fed top-grade, commercial, new ammo in brass cases. The ones fed various steel-cased surplus had malfunctions, induced by the ammo. By then the bores on all were worn to the point that they were no longer accurate enough to pass anyone's acceptance test, but they still worked. I've had similar results.

In other titles from Gun Digest, I have shoveled dirt, sand and snow into and onto ARs, and they worked. Dunked them in water, shot them dripping with oil or bone dry, and they worked. The rifle works.

The biggest cause of malfunctions in the AR? You. That is, you building it wrong, assembling it wrong, treating it wrong, or feeding it crappy ammo, or good ammo from cheap, crappy magazines. If your AR doesn't work, the likely problem is staring at you from the nearest mirror.

A cheerful thought, yes?

And, the AR-15 now stands as the most popular rifle in America, for reasons not just political. Not that politics are excluded from its popularity. Oh, and if someone objects to the characterizations as "most popular" consider this: Winchester has been selling the M-1894 rifle and carbine since, oh, 1894. Most in .30-30, and as such considered the premier and traditional deer rifle in America for the entire 20th century. In various calibers, design variants and production changes, it has, in (as of this typing) sold over seven million units in 120 years.

The AR-15 has been around less than half that

time. And for several decades it was a marginal seller in many gun shops. Sales have now exceeded six million, most of that in the last two decades, a million of those in the last five years, perhaps.

Why, besides politics?

Simple. Unlike earlier rifles, the AR-15 is the ultimate do-it-yourself rifle, a rifle that can reflect the owners character and desires. Do you want to own an AR that is done all in pink, with Hello Kitty decals on it? You can have it. (And yes, you can have it, I don't need it.) Do you want a small caliber or large, a short rifle or a long and heavy one? Do you want a short-range, quick-handling rifle, or something stable for long-range target and varmint control? You can build it.

Oh, and here's another measure of just how popular the AR-15 has become: the Brownells catalog. Brownells offers parts, accessories and tools for gunsmithing, gunsmiths and the home gun-plumber. I first encountered a Brownells catalog in 1985. I don't remember how big it was in total, but it did not have an AR-15 section. What it had were a few offerings of AR receivers, barrels, parts and such, each in the "appropriate" section. That is, you'd have to pore through the Barrel section to find AR barrels. Then switch to the Receivers section for receivers. Ditto magazines, scope mounts and so-on.

The latest Brownells catalog thumped onto my doorstep as I was wrapping up this book. The first 89 pages are devoted to nothing but AR-15 parts, tools, accessories and extras, in the AR-15-only section. 89 pages. In 1985 you could improve your AR a bit by shopping in the catalog. Now, you can build an entire AR from scratch, just ordering from the catalog. (FFL required for the lower, of course.) That's how far we've come.

In that regard, the AR-15 is much like the personal computer of the late 1980s and early-to-mid 1990s. At the time I was going to both gun shows and computer shows. And the parallels of attendees poring over specs, purchasing parts, and building the AR-15/PC to just the specs they wanted, were interesting. PC gamers would get smoking fast hard drives (measured in megabytes back then, not gigabytes) video cards and hulking cpus, all driven by power systems with fans, heat exchangers and more. CAD/CAM people would get less-speedy cpus, but spend more on bigger hard drives, and buy the power system that was rated as most stable, since the PC would be running all night, crunching data.

At the gun shows, buyers would be finding the accessories that Colt could not or would not make, and plan on building their ARs into configurations that weren't in the Colt catalog. (Which was pretty sparse back then.)

All that exploded after the AWB/94 expired, driven by the expansion of smaller companies who offered the accessories, and by the pent-up demand of shooters to build their rifles the way they wanted, not hampered by nonsensical cosmetic restrictions.

Oh, and in an interesting aside, the military actually caught up, some. It was not unusual in the 'aughts to see photographs from Iraq and Afghanistan with soldiers and marines (and Airmen, too) packing M4s, M16s that would have been pretty useful 3-gun rifles from the mid-1990s. You know, back in the 1990s, when all optics were "too fragile for combat" and real men shot iron sights? When bolting a light to a handguard was the height of mall-ninja-tomfoolery (although the mall ninja would not be invented for a decade). It is sometimes amusing to have an ex-service person teaching me how to use gear I helped invent, by competing with the guys who were developing it.

But, the ad-hoc nature of the change meant that many of the old myths, the "everybody knows" things that weren't true, were not addressed. Even as shooters were fine-tuning, problem-solving and building reliable, accurate ARs, no-one was in a position to point out that this was happening.

So, this volume is aimed primarily at the million or so new users, the shooters who haven't had a lot of time to get familiar with the AR-15. And also at the experienced users – shooters who know some, but have been working in a fog of "everybody knows" and "it has always been".

Along the way, this volume will correct the misconceptions you may have about the AR. It will also tell you how to inspect, test, correct and maintain your rifle, your new investment.

You see, in the anti-gun battle, there are a whole lot of people who are in the middle, who don't care, and want to be left alone. However, every time someone who was otherwise in the middle buys an AR, they've made a choice. Where before they could be moved by rhetoric, mere or soaring, now they have made a thousand-dollar investment on one side. Sometimes more, even a lot more. And if the law changes, they will lose that investment. So, for all of you who have newly made that investment, here's how to properly treat your new investment, your new stake, your new AR-15.

The arithmetic is simple: M1 Garand, 8.5 ounces for eight shots; M14, 24 ounces for 20 shots. The M16? 19 ounces for 30 shots. A load of seven magazines and an M16 weighed less than an M1 Garand and seventeen clips. The M14? It could do the rifle, a mag in the rifle and four spare magazines. No contest.

CHAPTER 1
TERMINOLOGY

BEFORE WE CAN get to work, we all have to speak the same language. We can agree that for many things, there is more than just one "perfect" word. You'd be surprised at the things that will out you as a newbie or someone who does not know the subject, and not just in firearms. Something as simple as using "break" instead of "brake" in *muzzle brake* can get you hounded mercilessly on an internet forum. Hey, words matter, and this matters, but you don't have to be a real pain in the butt when you correct someone, OK? One means to halt something and the other means to damage it. I figure that we all make spelling errors from time to time, and this is one of those homophones that no spell-check software could ever catch. Take it with a grain of salt, because the internet is one of the greatest forces for moronic obsession that man has ever invented. But, it can also be a useful source of information. However, usefulness happens only if you're careful.

The AR-15 is a rifle, a carbine, a self-loading rifle or a modern sporting rifle. What it *isn't* is an assault rifle, a weapon (except in the actual, used-as-a-tool-weapon sense) a spray-and-pray bullet stick, or a useless collection of aluminum parts that shoots an underpowered cartridge. It is a rifle, and you need to know the parts in order to work on it.

Suppressors are the best flash hiders. Just don't believe the PR about their being the best muzzle brakes. They do that, but they aren't the best at that.

SBRs are lots of fun, but you pay for them with less muzzle velocity, more muzzle blast and a $200 tax stamp.

Keep in mind the fact that the AR is a collection of interrelated parts. What one does, or has to do, is often influenced by the part it works with, or rests next to. So, in any description of what is what, a certain amount of jumping around is needed. You need to know what a part does to understand how it works with the parts next to it. This can get a bit convoluted at times, so stick with me. It can also lead to a certain amount of what seems like repetition. However, covering the same part or operation from several different perspectives can be useful, and also can serve as a reminder. After all, if you "parachute in" to a chapter, and are looking to fix something, not having read (or recently read) some other part that bears on it, could lead to problems. So, I cover what is needed, where and when it is needed, even if it has been covered before. And not just in this chapter, but in others as well.

Working from front to back, and then under and back, we'll start on the right-hand side view.

FLASH HIDER

Screwed on to the end of the barrel, the flash hider dissipates muzzle blast and flash in such a way as to make it less obvious in firing. It also protects the crown of the barrel, the end of the bore where the bullet exits. The crown must be uniform, or accuracy suffers; uneven jetting of gas on the bullet's release from a damaged crown disrupts bullet stability. The flash hider comes in for more than it's fair share of dislike, and that goes so far as to include the threaded section of the barrel that the flash hider screws on to.

A muzzle brake is a device that replaces the flash hider but, instead of dissipating the gases, it re-directs them. By jetting the gases in desired

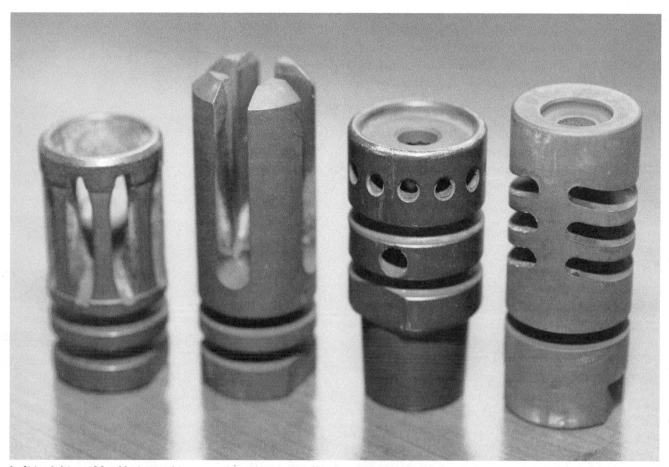

Left to right, an A2, a Vortex and two muzzle brakes, both effective and obnoxious.

directions, the designer can use those gas jets to reduce the muzzle rise in recoil, or even dampen the felt rearward thump of recoil.

This does not come without a cost. Re-directed gases have to go somewhere, and that place is usually at the shooter on the next bench. This is why muzzle brakes are roundly hated in some circles, mostly the guys who do all their shooting seated at benches. In all fairness, the most efficient muzzle brakes can jet so much gas and particulate matter to the sides that they will strip paint off of a wall. They can shove objects off of the shooting bench, even the bench next to yours. They can hurt you.

Flash hiders, as hiders, come in two original types and endless variants. The two originals are the A1 and the A2. The A1 (aka, birdcage) is the classic Vietnam-era flash hider. It is a short section of steel cylinder, with slots around the full circumference. The A2 is that A1 but with the slots on the bottom closed, so when you are firing prone you won't kick up too much dust.

The basic cylinder with slots or holes in it, to create turbulence in the muzzle blast and mix the hot exit gases with cooler ambient air, is legion in the aftermarket realm.

Some flash hiders or muzzle brakes are also mounting devices. Those who own suppressors need a way to attach them. Yes, you can simply unscrew your flash hider and screw on a suppressor, but some shooters like to have something a bit handier than that. (If you are

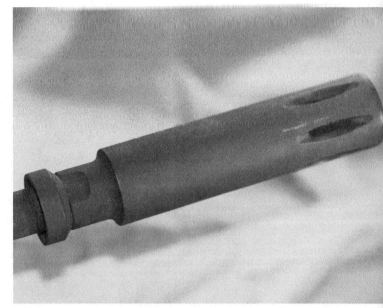

The old **XM-177** grenade launcher/flash hider/suppressor. Or at least, a close copy of one.

going to park a suppressor on your rifle and pretty much leave it there, then a threaded interface works just fine.)

With rare exceptions, you can have either a flash hider or a muzzle brake, but you can't have something that does both. The basic laws of physics don't permit it, and the designs that attempt to do both are compromises, doing some of each, but

◄ An A2 flash hider on an SBR. Short barrels need as much flash-hiding as they can get.

The pronged flash hider has made a comeback. The modern ones are often both flash hiders and suppressor mounts.

The flash hider or muzzle brake needs a locking system to hold it tightly in place. You can use a split washer or a peel washer.

neither as well as a unit designed to do just one of the tasks.

And finally, you'll see rifles that do not have a flash hider, muzzle device or even threads. Some of these are barrels made back in the bad old days of the assault weapons ban, and also rifles made currently for some states where such moronic laws still exist. There are also some shooters, such as varmint shooters, who do not feel the need for a flash hider. (Really, will prairie dogs notice an occasional muzzle flash, up on the ridge line?) The extra cost of cutting threads is one they do not feel the need to pay, and when gilt-edged accuracy is the ideal, anything that might create problems is first to be jettisoned.

This does, however, leave the muzzle bare and the crown unprotected. The muzzle is the exit end of the barrel, and the crown is the angle between the bore, the exit hole of the barrel, and the front face of the barrel. Again, a damaged crown, due to things such as wear, over-eager cleaning, or damage due to impact, has an adverse effect on accuracy.

The flash (in broad daylight, no less) that flash hiders work to dampen.

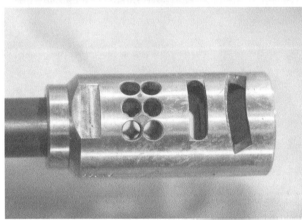
This is a McArthur comp, one of the most effective and heinously blasty comps in existence.

BARREL MARKINGS

The markings are typically on the top of the barrel, between the flash hider (or muzzle) and the front sight housing. (The very earliest Colts had no markings, and the next gen had but a capital "C" on the underside.) Some are on the underside. Since the AR design allows for easy barrel swaps, marking the receiver with the caliber is not smart

or convenient. So, each barrel gets marked instead. The markings can be simple, like very early Colts, which would have had a single "C" stamped on them, or involved, with nearly a paragraph, describing barrel composition and coatings, chamber dimensions, twist rate and company of manufacture.

One important detail to be aware of: the caliber marking, while it indicates generally what the chamber is, is not absolute proof. Oh, if you have a barrel marked "223" or "5556" it most certainly is not one bored and chambered for, say 6.8 RemSPC. However, barrels may be marked 5.56 that are actually more like (or exactly) .223, and that can be a problem. It is unlikely, but possible, for a barrel to be marked .223 and to be more like a 5.56 chamber in dimension. This is a situation we'll go into in some detail later, just be aware that of the markings, that one is not absolute.

That said, twist rate markings can be taken as being pretty darned close to the markings. If a barrel is marked "1/7" for example, it will be

One turn in nine inches is the modern compromise twist rate. It will work with just about everything, but might be a bit touchy with the heavies, the 75/77 grain match loads.

Most barrels these days are marked to let you know what twist rate and chamber they have. The twist rate is probably pretty close, the chamber not always so much.

a one-turn-in-seven-inches twist rate, and not something else. It may actually be a 1/6.9, or a 1/7.1, but it will not (unless someone at the barrel makers had an "oops") be a 1/9 or 1/12, when it is marked 1/7.

FRONT SIGHT

The standard sight housing is known as the front sight assembly, and is a solid piece, casting, forging or, rarely, a billet-cut housing.

On the AR-15, the front sight proper can be part of the gas system, it can be a separate mechanism bolted to a gas block, and it can be a sighting system bolted to the upper handguard. When it is a solid piece, it holds the gas tube in place and it is always in view. When it is a folding design, it is known as the front sight of a Back Up Iron Sight, or BUIS. A typical BUIS setup will have both front and rear sights that fold, to get them out of the way of the optics.

If the front sight is on the handguard, then the gizmo that is attached to the barrel out at the end of the handguard, which the silver tube attaches to, is known as the gas block. Block or sight housing, it is the attachment point for the gas tube, which you can see running along the top of the barrel, underneath the handguards.

The front sight itself, the little post that you use to aim, is adjustable, but only for elevation and only for zeroing purposes. Once set, it might be that you never touch the front sight again to adjust it.

The solid and upright front sight housing can be a casting, a forging, or machined from billet. The mil-spec mavens will tell you that if your front sight housing is not made from a forging, it is worse than useless, some day it will catastrophically fail, and in so-doing sterilize/kill everyone in your zip code. (OK, slight exaggeration.) In reality, if well-made it doesn't matter how it was made, as long as it is the correct

The gas block holds the gas tube and covers the gas port. Here is a railed block, with a folding front sight attached.

Front sights, old and new. Left to right, An A1, an A2, another A1 and a night sight front.

The front sight, its plunger and spring, in a standard front sight housing.

height and straight. If a forging, it may have markings on it. For the forgings, the marks will be the forge marks. (The upper receiver may also have a forge mark on it, we'll cover that when we get there.) The forge marks are usually a code for which machine or forging blocks were used, and do not necessarily indicate which company. However, if you had the insider's insider access to the codes, you could tell/know that a particular forge/forge block number or letter indicates this or that company.

Barrels typically come with front sight housings already firmly attached, so you may have little need to remove or replace them. Also, since the replacement barrel will likely have its own front sight housing attached, you won't need to remove the old to put it on the new barrel.

One detail that can be a source for obsession: F markings. When Colt made the M4, they made it with a removable carry handle. In the back-and-forth of testing and engineering, they ended up making the top deck of the M4 flat-top receiver slightly higher than had been originally planned. This parked the clamp-on carry handle, and its sight, a little higher than on previous R&D rifles. To correct this, Colt made a new front sight housing, and marks them with the letter "F."

You only need an F-marked front sight housing if

the barrel it is on is plugged into an upper receiver that merits it. It is not an improvement to install an F sight housing otherwise. In fact, you will be creating a problem if you mis-match the front sight housing and the receiver.

The combo is simple. If you have a flat-top receiver, you need an F-marked front sight. If you have a fixed carry handle upper, A1 or A2, you do not need an F.

Simple question: does your rifle properly zero? Then your front sight housing is the correct height. If, on the other hand, you have to bury the sight post deep into the housing or perch it high above the housing to correctly zero your rifle, then you have the wrong barrel/receiver combination, regardless of what the guy at the gun shop told you.

And just to make things clear for the next step, on the bottom of the front sight housing there is a steel loop, the sling swivel mount.

FRONT SIGHT HOUSING ATTACHMENT

Here is your first absolute pronouncement: it matters how your front sight housing is attached. There are four methods – pinned, set-screws, hoop-clamp and piece-clamp. If you are building/buying a rifle that may be used for defense,

A gas block, with the set screws being tightened. If you tighten them without making sure the block is square, your front sight will be tilted.

you need to only consider a barrel that has the front sight housing pinned. (That is for the standard, one-piece housing.) To attach it, the manufacturer slides the housing over the barrel, clamps everything into a holding fixture, and drills through the housing and the bottom edge of the barrel. The drilled hole is then reamed with a taper reamer, and a tapered pin, matching the reamer, is pressed into place.

This is the most secure method. A less-secure but acceptable method is to drill and press in non-tapered pins. This was something we saw in the old days (along with roll pins used to hold things together) but not so much anymore. My guess is that once people gained knowledge of the front sight system, they shied away from straight pin and roll pin barrels. And the barrel makers, since they were drilling anyway, could easily take the extra step of taper-reaming the drilled hole.

The second method is to drill and tap the front sight housing or, more often, a low-profile gas block that lacks a front sight, and use set screws to clamp it to the barrel. This can be good and it can be bad.

It is good, and acceptable, when it is a low-profile gas block, one that is not designed to accept a front sight. Typically, such a setup goes underneath a free-float handguard (more on those in a bit) and all the gas block has to do is stay in place and hold the gas tube.

It is bad when it is a regular front sight. The front sight is large enough, and banging it against objects has enough leverage, that the set screws can't hold and it slides. In the old days it was not uncommon to see these, and they always showed up for repairs when "the rifle won't work." Remember, the front sight is also the gas tube holder, and when the front sight housing shifts, it loses alignment with the gas port. No alignment, no gas.

One fix (the real fix is to replace the barrel) is to drill "dimples" in the barrel, locations where the set screws can gain greater purchase.

Hoop-clamp front sight housings are typically

This front sight housing is held on by means of four screws that clamp the assembly to the barrel. While it works, it is the weakest of the designs, and some avoid it because of that.

Some gas blocks are held on by means of set screws. Once they are tight (and the sight is properly aligned) paint the screws so you can tell if they ever move.

This front sight is an egregious one, with tiny little set screws to "hold" it in place. It doesn't really work very well, which is why it will be changed.

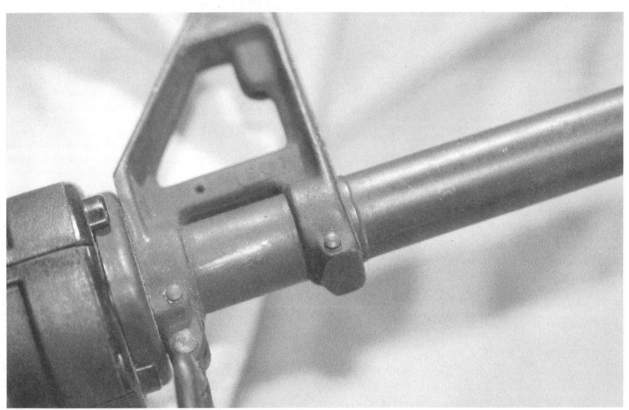

One of the things Colt has done in the past is remove the bayonet lug, to sooth the hurt feelings of the hoplophobes.

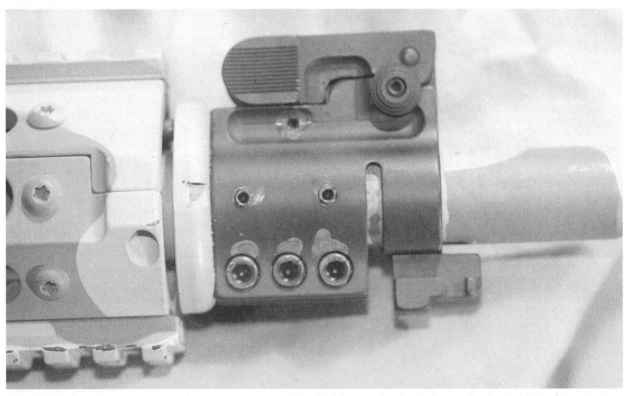

This folding sight/gas block uses screws, but is robust. This **GG&G** not only pinch-clamps the front sight in place, but has extra setscrews to keep it in place. The real belt-and-suspenders guys will use wicking Loctite, too.

folding front BUIS setups. The design is a drilled-through clamp. With screws internally on the bottom, screws that tighten the hoop around the barrel. One I have used with success is the GG&G, which has a large bearing surface, and side-drilled setscrews as well as the clamping screws.

The piece-clamp design uses a separate clamping parts, and two screws (sometimes four) per piece. This is the least-sturdy of the designs. However, this does not mean it is useless. As a folding sight, it can be compact. And if used on a training/practice rifle, or a .22LR conversion upper, it can serve you well.

But for something to be used for defense, I'd use only a pinned, or a low-profile gas block with dimples for the setscrew.

HANDGUARDS

The handguards give you a place to hold, and keep your hands off the smoking-hot barrel you've created with your afternoon of plinking.

Handguards can be plastic, old or new style, they can be aluminum replacements, and they can be aluminum "free-float" handguards.

The regular handguards are held in place by the rear aluminum hoop. On newer rifles the shape is an angled circular wedge known as the "delta ring." On the older rifles, the ring is a circle; it is called a "slip ring" and that one is a part builders of "retro" rifles are eager to find. The wedge shape of the delta ring is an A2 addition/upgrade, meant to make the ring easier to move, which you have to do against its spring tension, in order to remove the handguards.

The plastic handguards are wedged in place, hooked under the front plate that is directly behind the front sight housing, and held in by the spring action of the delta ring. They do not often need to come off, which is good, because it can be a two-man, four-handed job to wrestle them off.

Aluminum replacement handguards install the same way, but provide rails on which to mount lights, lasers and other gear.

The A2 delta ring is a wedge shape, unlike the cylindrical A1 design.

M4 handguards are fatter than the old **CAR** handguards, and oval, top to bottom.

The back of the front sight housing, and the handguard retaining ring. On the top is the hole for the gas tube.

The delta ring is actually three parts: ring, spring and retainer.

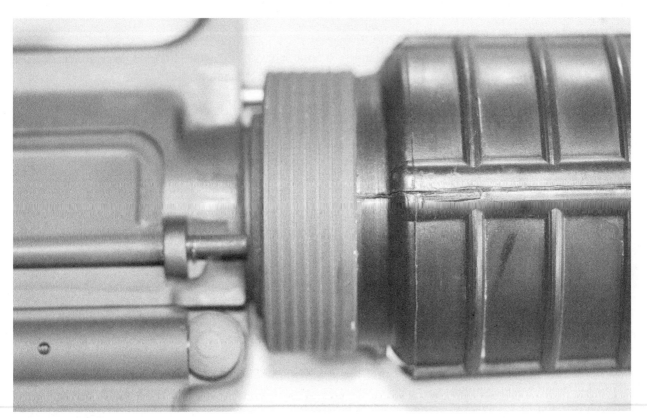

The correct slip ring, pre-delta ring, for a pre-A2 rifle or carbine.

This front cap is cut so it will work with any set of handguards, including the ones for the M203 grenade launcher.

The original, A1 handguards were triangular and tapered to the front. They are comfortable, but they are also, because of their design, paired as right and left handguards. The original design and plastic was somewhat fragile. For the A2, the government made them sturdier, and changed it to a ribbed cylinder, and they are all the same. They are assembled as top and bottom, but both are the same and can be swapped or replaced without concern about "which was top last time?" Retro builders want the triangular ones.

The ribbed handguards come in three flavors: CAR-15, M4 and A2. The originals, the CAR-15, are round, ribbed, short (they went on carbines) and have a single heat shield inside. The heat shield is simply a metal shield held in place to reflect heat off the handguards and back at the barrel.

Yep, that's right, they save your hands by cooking your barrel.

The A2 handguards are longer versions of the CAR-15, including the heat shield.

The M4 handguards are like the CAR-15, except the M4s are oval, taller top and bottom than side to side, and the heat shield is two layers of metal with an air space in-between them. If you are building a period-correct clone, you'll want to know what was in use there and then, and source the correct handguards.

Interestingly, the M4 and A2 handguards will fit inside of the triangular handguard retaining caps, common on older ARs such as the Colt SP1 or M16A1. This despite the later retaining caps being circular, to hold the rounded handguards. Clever design, that.

And why free-float? What are they? Simple. Free-float handguards are typically aluminum handguards that clamp around or replace the barrel nut, and do not touch the barrel except at the barrel nut. Older designs did two things: they kept the handguards from touching the barrel, and they provided a large amount of picatinny rail onto which you could attach extra equipment. Thus pressure on the handguards cannot influence the barrel. Without the vibrational changes caused

The M4 handguards have two heat shields in them.

by contact of the handguards, the barrel is free to demonstrate all the accuracy it can. Rifles with free-float barrels tend to be more accurate than those without.

The latest designs have deleted the rail sections and replaced them with slim tubular handguards, drilled and tapped to hold rail segments. Thus, instead of a handguard that is bulky, with a couple of feet of rail on it, you have an easier hand-hold, and rails just where you want them to mount just enough gear.

There is a special class of free-float handguard, a design that looks just like the normal, plastic standard handguards. They are used in NRA High Power shooting in the Service Rifle division. While a competition rifle meant for Service Rifle can have many internal improvements, regardless of those improvements it must appear to be a normal rifle. If you take a normal AR, and you "sling up" as the long-range competitors do, you will be putting a lot of lateral tension on the rifle. (And turning your fingertips blue, from the tension of the

Carbine handguards will fit carbine barrels, regardless of being M4 (this one) or the old **CAR** handguards. You can build with what works, what looks right or what feels good to you. That's the beauty of the AR.

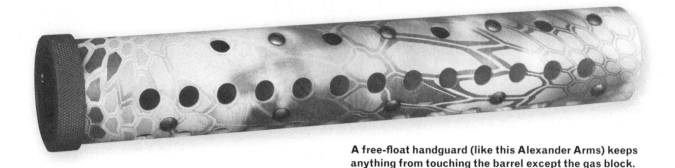

A free-float handguard (like this Alexander Arms) keeps anything from touching the barrel except the gas block.

sling.) With regular handguards that tension can flex the barrel, regardless of how thick a barrel you have, and that flex will change the point of impact at 600 yards. So competitors use a special free-float tube that is hidden inside of the regular handguards, and the sling swivel is attached to the tube, not the barrel. Sling up, and the tube takes the tension, not the barrel.

If you are shooting NRA High Power and your scores will benefit from it, this is a useful addition. If not, then it is extra weight, cost and complexity that you do not need.

GAS TUBE

Down inside the handguards is the gas tube. The normal operating system of the AR is "direct gas impingement" and that method simply ports some of the gases out of the barrel, back through the tube, and essentially blows the carrier back off the bolt.

This system has worked very well for the 50+ years the AR has been in use, and for the several decades before that where it was used on earlier rifles. (Not ARs, in case you were wondering.) The system offers the benefits of being light, simple, and not influencing the barrel.

The drawbacks are that it spurts combustion gases into the receiver, splattering them all over the bolt, carrier and interior of the upper receiver. The buildup of carbon is not good, but can be

controlled with lubrication and maintenance. It also jets some heat (the gases are still quite hot) into the receiver, which some complain about. I have tested ARs for this, and my testing showed me that, long before you have to worry about heat in the upper receiver, you will have over-hot barrels and gas tubes to worry about.

The competing, and newer, system to run ARs is a piston system. Here, the gases are used to shove a rod, which then pushes/slaps/bangs the carrier back to cycle the rifle. The supposed advantage is that it does not splatter the receiver. True, but you are still using gas to cycle the rifle, and the gas has to go somewhere. So you end up with a really hot gas block/piston mount, which will raise blisters if you touch it, and carbon buildup on that block instead of in the receiver.

The piston also adds weight, and that weight bears on the barrel somewhere. While piston makers work hard, there is always the potential that the piston system will be an adverse influence on accuracy.

This is one of the newer arguments over the AR system. Advocates of each will extol the virtues of theirs, and regale you at length with the shortcomings of the other. What I have found is that both work, and if advantage there be, it is with piston systems, when using an SBR or a suppressor.

Feeding the tube is the gas port, mentioned earlier. One of the raging controversies, and

The front of the barrel nut, showing the clearance for the gas tube.

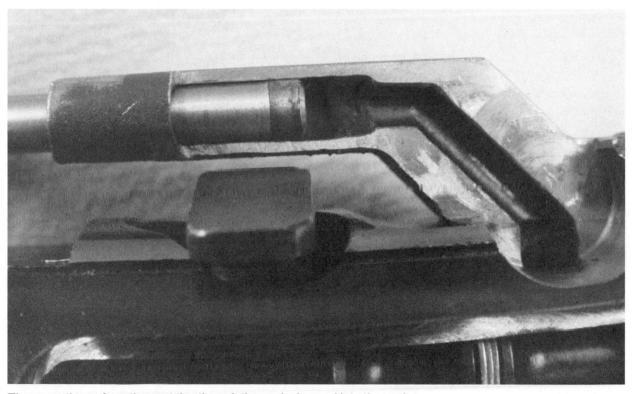

The gas pathway, from the gas tube, through the carrier key and into the carrier.

a subject that will turn sane, normal shooters into raving, spit-splattering orators, is gas port diameter. There are those who approach gas port diameter as a near-religious subject. Any mention of the subject will get you paragraphs of discussion, name-dropping like there's no tomorrow of who makes what, and what guns are "over-gassed" and if caught in the torrent of rant you will be lucky to escape in anything approaching a short time period.

My take on it is simple. The barrel maker has a pretty good idea of what it takes to run a gun. They'll drill the port big enough to run all of them, with any normal ammo that may be on the market, which may (and I emphasize *may*) mean some get more gas than they need. If your rifle is over-gassed, taming that is simple enough. Basically, move up to the buffer weight that is next-heaviest. But we'll cover that in a bit. Don't get so wrapped up in "what is right" that you lose sight of "does the rifle work?" And "Am I having fun?"

UPPER RECEIVER

The upper receiver of the AR has changed, perhaps more than any other part, since the mid-1960s. The original upper, even before the AR became famous in Vietnam, was the "A1 slickside" or just "slickside." This is a fixed carrying handle upper, with a barely-adjustable (and only for windage) rear sight. It has no forward assist, and no ejector "lump" aka spent brass diversion device (known officially as the "spent brass deflector"). As the bump on the upper deflects both spent brass and ejected live ammunition, I simply refer to it as the "ejector lump."

The slickside upper was replaced by a later A1, the most common style of the pre-A2 rifles, which has a forward assist but still lacks the ejector lump. This, starting in about 1966, was the only upper offered until the mid 1980s. And even after that, it rightfully retained popularity.

These two are both extremely durable and

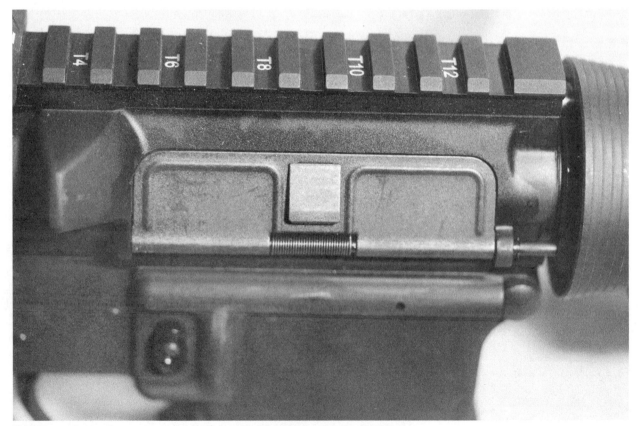

M4 upper rail, ejection port cover, takedown pin fence and magazine button.

useful uppers, but they lack a certain panache desired by many shooters today. Those looking to build a Retro rifle or carbine seek them out. The advantages are that they are simple, and the rear sight, once adjusted, requires a tool to change, and thus is almost impervious to idle hands. The drawback is that the ejected, empty cases are thrown vigorously to the right and back. Left-handed shooters find the empties skimming their right check and arm if they are lucky, or hitting their shoulder, face and arm if they are not.

The next upper to be created was the A2, a design in which the rear sight is click-adjustable for both windage and elevation. It is, essentially, a target sight machined into the carrying handle of a practical/defensive/combat rifle. This was done primarily at the behest of the USMC, who wished the new and improved service rifle to be suitable for posting suitable/higher/manly scores on their qualification course. In this, they succeeded. It did, however, make the rear sight more complex,

and also prone to idle hands. Where it takes a tool to adjust the sight setting on an A1 upper, on the A2 it just takes your fingers. Unless you mark your sights once you zero, you may find someone with time and a lack of social grace has been idly spinning your sight settings about. (Paint can give you some solace, a subject we'll cover later.)

The rear elevation dial allows you to click-adjust elevation on the sights up to 800 meters (600 on carbines) and for competition this is great. In the field, at least in modern use, not so much. Oh, and the target shooters are also prone to rebuilding the rear sight for greater precision. This involves changing the sight shaft threads and the threads of the adjustment wheel so they have more clicks per MOA of sight movement. They also drill the upper handle for an extra spring and plunger, to reduce "slop" or unwanted movement of the sight assembly.

The A2 upper retained the forward assist, but it also gained an extra attribute: the ejector "lump"

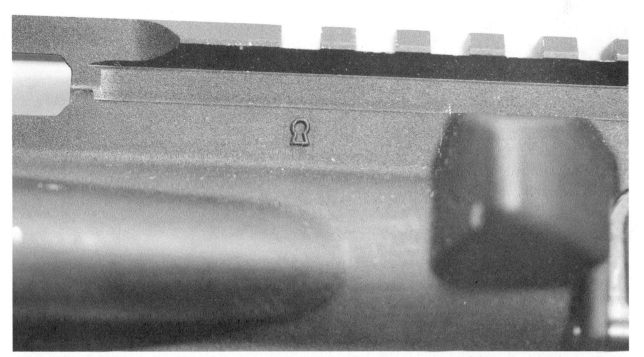

Some obsess over forge codes. This is a **Keyhole** mark, and it simply indicates who forged the upper. It tells you nothing about who machined it.

Left: Here is a retro upper and lower. The upper is a "slickside" lacking the forward assist and deflector. The lower has a fence only for the takedown pin, not the magazine button. Right: Not all fence-free lowers are retros. This is a Colt, when they were doing the two-headed screw as takedown design.

The rear sight need not be just a small and large aperture, it can be large and large.

mentioned before. So an A2 is a rather "bumpy" or "knobby" upper, compared to the original, slim and slick rifle. The A2 also came with a new cartridge, or loading of the existing cartridge, the M855, with a heavier bullet of 62 grains, versus the 55 of the M193. And that new load required a new barrel twist (the spin of the rifling). Using the new ammo in old rifles with their slower twist caused mediocre accuracy at best. Old ammo (M193) in new barrels was fine.

When the Canadians adopted the M16 some years ago now, they asked for a special upper, one that had both the simple rear sight of the A1 and its forward assist, but also had the ejector lump of the M16A2. Known as the "C7" model, and thus the "C7" upper, it is a style favored by those who wish to build a bare-bones, minimalist defensive rifle. If you are going to stick with iron sights, but don't feel the need to have one click-adjustable to 6 or 800 meters, then the C7 is a good choice.

Last is the "flat-top." Here, Colt took the regular A2 upper, and basically milled off the carry handle and sight, and installed a rail. (And the R&D models were exactly that. This was not new, gunsmiths and competitive shooters had been doing it for some years before Colt did it. I still have an upper around here someplace, with the Weaver rail section held on with screws and epoxy.)

Colt provided a removable carry handle that clamped on, with a rear sight built into it, and if you wanted you could simply leave the handle in place. But, if you unbolted it and took it off, you now had a convenient place to clamp optical sights, lights, lasers, whatever. This is the upper you will most likely see on an AR these days, as it was the design Colt used when they created the M4.

An A1 rear sight adjustment plate. Clockwise is Right.

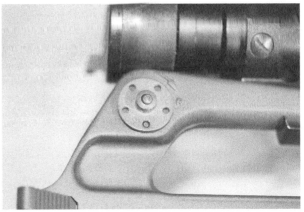

The A1 rear sight adjustment plate is a real hassle to use, which can be a good thing. Once set, it takes real effort to mess around with it.

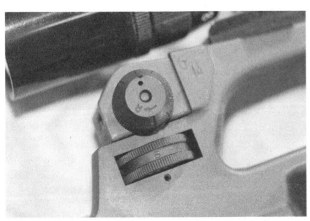

The A2 rear sight, seen from the right. The knob is finger-adjustable, and you can easily crank it back and forth. That could mean trouble, paint it once you are zeroed.

Not only a folding sight, but one with a bayonet lug as well.

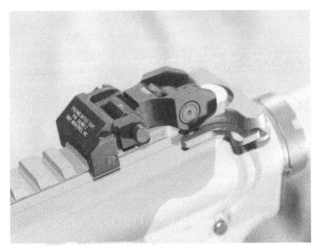

A folding rear sight, this one from Troy.

The A2 sight, front he left. The wheel is marked for range, in this case 300 to 800 meters. The protective wing reminds you which way is which.

One persnickety detail: the milled-off handle left a rather thin top deck on which to attach the rail on the original R&D models. (We had no choice back when we were doing mods such as this, so we just lived with it.) So, along the way, Colt made the top of the upper receiver thicker, in order for it to be stronger. Alas, the team that was making it thicker apparently didn't tell the team that was making the carrying handle. The carrying handle was made to the dimensions that worked with the original, thinner-top R&D models. The end result

If the rear sight is this much to the side, it isn't a big deal. This is the small aperture

The large aperture on an A2 sight.

was that the rear sight on the flat-tops, the M4s, was now a smidgen higher from the bore than the rear sight had been on previous, permanent-handle rifles. And that is why Colt had to come up with the "F" marked front sight housing, to get it equally higher, match the rear sight, and keep rifles zeroed.

Should Colt have gone back and re-designed the carry handle/sight for the M4, to avoid this? Yes. They chose not to, and now we're stuck with the "F" marked and non-F front sights quandary.

Colt also made a change on the interior of the upper receiver. Inside, the receiver doesn't do anything but guide the carrier back and forth. It is not a structural component, at least not insofar as the bolt is concerned.

The M1 Garand, and its descendants and evolutionary heirs, such as the M14, M1A and Mini-14, have receivers that are also structural components of the rifle. When the bolt of a Garand rotates closed, it rotates into notches milled into the receiver. When you fire a Garand, the receiver takes the brunt of the force generated, and thus must be quite strong. The cartridge back-pressure causes thrust, which the bolt lugs transfer to the recess shoulders in the receiver.

The AR does not work that way. The bolt lugs lock into a cylindrical part called the barrel extension. The barrel extension is permanently screwed to the barrel, and when the barrel is installed into the upper receiver, all the barrel nut does is hold the barrel in place. The bolt, in closing, locks into the barrel extension, not the receiver, and thus the receiver can be but an aluminum shell. (As a simple part to hold the receiver parts, the upper could be made of paper maché and still function, at least for a few magazines.) When the round fires, the thrust is transferred from the bolt to the barrel extension, and the upper receiver does not take any of that load. That is how the AR upper can be made of aluminum, and not steel. (Although I have seen steel uppers.)

All the AR upper receiver does is hold the barrel in place, and guide the carrier back and forth.

Now, when the bolt and carrier go forward, the bolt shoves a round ahead of it to be chambered. When Colt was working on the M4,

Thus cutaway barrel shows you the chamber, locking lugs and the barrel extension screwed onto the barrel proper.

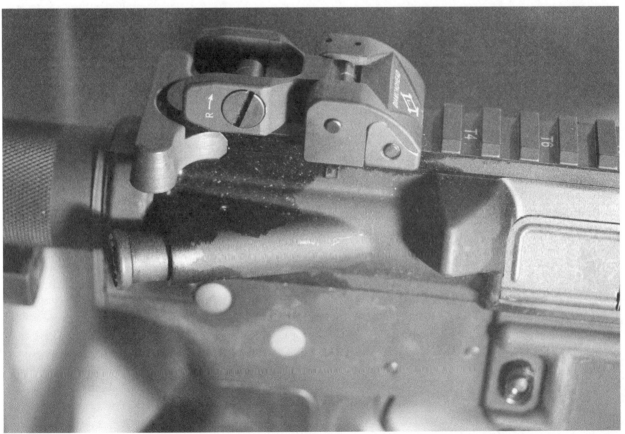

The A2 upper gained the ejector lump (brass deflector) ahead of the forward assist.

Left: The old-style, teardrop forward assist. The newer one is the "button" as it is a bit less bulky. Right: The pin in the receiver holds the forward assist assembly

they discovered that the carbine had occasional problems with the then relatively new cartridge, the M855. The speed of cycling in full-auto fire, and the shape of the new bullet, occasionally caused a round to drive forward with the point lower than was intended in the 1950s. The tip of the round would strike the inside of the front receiver and barrel extension too low, below the feed ramp machined into the barrel extension, and thus come to a stop.

Colt solved the problem by extending further downward the feed ramps, the grooves machined into receiver and barrel extension. Again, this was not new; gunsmiths had been doing it for some time. It also happened in semi-auto shooting, with rifles built from parts. Gunsmiths had been carefully machining the ramp down to solve this problem. I have an upper to which I had to alter this way, done sometime around 1987.

Receivers to which Colt has made this modification will be marked "M4" on the front face of the receiver, above the hole drilled for the gas tube. They intend these for carbines only, not for full-length rifle barrels.

Colt didn't just decide out of the blue to apply the feed ramp modification to the M4, and not do it to the M16A2/3/4. They did so for a very good,

and rational, reason: the Army wouldn't let them. You see, the M4, as we've explained before, was an all-Colt affair. Within reason, Colt could do whatever it wanted to the M4 and the Army had to go along. But, to make the same feed ramp change to the M16 that they had done to the M4, Colt would have to have the permission of the Army.

The Army, being the quintessential government bureaucracy that it is, could not make the change without proving that it was both beneficial, and would not have drawbacks in any other use. The first would be quick to do but expensive, and the second would be a years-long and expensive effort. So Colt made the change, the Army did not, and everyone is happy, more-or-less.

Do you need M4 feed ramps? Only if it's really necessary. It can cause problems. Since both the receiver and barrel extension have to be altered, you have to make sure you match the two. Three of the four combinations are not a problem: M4 upper & M4 barrel extension, regular upper & M4 barrel extension, and regular upper & regular extension are all good. The bad combo is an M4 upper and a regular barrel extension, as the long extension ramp overhangs the M4 ramp in the receiver, and creates a pocket to trap bullet tips on feeding.

Iron sights can come as folding units, like this one on an M4 upper.

The upper receiver also contains the dust cover. This is a spring-loaded cover that you can press closed, that will pop open and stay open when the bolt cycles. Some consider it superfluous, and others obsess over keeping it closed when you aren't actually shooting.

If the upper is a flat-top and you plan on having or using iron sights, you'll have to have some sort of iron sight system bolted onto it, as it does not have a sight system built in. This sight can be a solid, "fixed' sight (but one that can still be adjusted) or it can be a folding sight, part of the folding front-and-rear combo known as the Back Up Iron Sight, or BUIS. In Field manuals and Training manuals, the Army assumes it will be an iron sight, and simply calls them BUS.

Underneath the rear sight is the charging handle. This is the part you grasp and pull to retract the bolt, to charge it, unload it, or check to see if it is loaded or not.

STOCK

We have two general designs of stocks to consider here: fixed and telescoping. (There are some folding stocks, but the AR design makes them really rare.)

A fixed stock is just that, it doesn't move, slide, adjust or do anything but give you a place to put your face. There are two of them; the A1 and the A2. The A1 is the original Vietnam era design. It is shorter than the A2 by 5/8" and is also a bit more rounded on the edges. It is/was also made of a less-durable synthetic than the A2s have been. That change was a good one, as the old stocks had a deserved reputation for fragility.

Now, lest you think that means they will fall apart in your hands, "fragile" in a military context means you can't beat doors down with it and still use it afterwards as a shooting support. They are plenty sturdy enough to be used as shooting supports. The A1 and A2 stocks are also referred to as "rifle" stocks, and the telescoping stock is called a "carbine" stock. However, this designation is complicated by the mechanical quirk of the AR, one where you can have a rifle-length barrel upper installed on a carbine-stocked lower, and vice-versa, and if they are properly assembled, they will both work just fine.

The A2 was made longer for one reason: target shooting. Again, this can be laid directly at the doorstep of the Marines. The offhand portion of the qualification course for the USMC calls for a rather odd and involved stance, and one where the rifle is almost directly across the chest. In order to park the rear sight the correct distance from the shooter's eye, the Marines insisted that the stock be made longer.

This length worked against them, a decade-plus later, when Marines were trying to use A2-stocked rifles while wearing body armor, load-bearing vests and the other gear that had been developed since 1985.

The fixed stocks, except for the very earliest ones (and once again, desirable to retro builders) also have a storage compartment that you get to through a hinged door in the buttplate. This is intended to be a storage compartment for a cleaning kit, and you can, indeed, force-fit a cleaning kit in there. But hardly anyone does so.

The other stock design is the telescoping stock, as seen on the M4. This carbine stock adjusts from open to closed in increments. The very first carbine, the XM-177 series, had a telescoping stock with two positions: open or closed. That was it. Now, the standard is six positions, but I've seen custom stocks with seven or even eight. (The adjustments are actually in the tube, which we'll cover next.)

The whole back part of the carbine, behind the lower receiver, is the "stock assembly" while the part that actually moves is the stock, or the slider.

To open or close the slider, compress the lever you see on the bottom. That pivots the locking bar out of the circular recesses in the fin and allows

Before the flat-top upper, there wasn't a lot you could do to mount a scope. The only place was on the carry handle, and that meant an egregious stock addition like this Colt, to raise and support your head.

you to slide the stock forward or back. If you want to remove the slider from the tube, instead of squeezing the lever, grab the lever and pull it directly away from the fin. You can then slide the stock off the back of the tube.

BUFFER TUBE

Or, to be absolutely correct, pedantic, and a pain in the pants, "receiver extension" or, worse, "lower receiver extention." If you use "buffer tube," someone who wants to sound important, or one-up you, will say, "The correct part designation is receiver extension." You are allowed to give them a dirty look, and ignore all further information coming from that direction. You are not authorized to flip them the bird, unless continued application of the "I know more than you do, newbie" attitude is directed at you.

The buffer tube is the mounting point for the stock, but it does more than that. Before we jump inside, though, let's cover the outside.

The rifle stock, A1 or A2, requires a rifle buffer tube. The rifle buffer tube is a plain cylinder with a threaded end, and a rim, or shoulder, behind the threaded portion. You don't normally notice it for the simple reason that the stock almost completely covers it, from tube end to receiver.

The A1 or A2 stocks are held on by means of a screw in the buttplate, the top one of the two you see. A curious detail: the A1 and A2, despite being different lengths, use the same-length buffer tube. And, just to make things more complicated, the A2 stock, while having a tunnel in it long enough for a longer tube, also has a space inside that fills the tunnel, making it as short as the tube.

Why? Well, it seems that when it came time to present the A2-upgraded M16 for approval, the plan was to have two A2 stocks in inventory, the new longer one, and a replacement that was the same length as the old A1 but made of the stronger plastic. This would allow the Army and Marines to adjust stock length so that shorter service members could still use the otherwise-longer rifle.

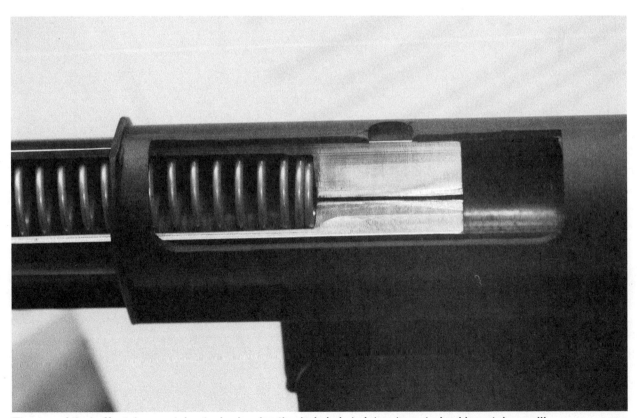

The rear of the buffer tube on a tele-stock, showing the drain hole to let water out, should you take a spill.

In order that they both fit, the longer A2 needed the filler adapter. (Why they didn't just make the A2 stock the correct internal length, I have never been able to find out.)

Well, when it came time to create the presentation, it turned out the presentation was too long. So they left off the last page of the presentation to make it fit, that page being the one describing the short A2 stock. (Don't believe me? Could I make stuff like this up?) So the rifle was adopted with the long stock only.

The real problem is the screw. The A2 stock, being longer, requires a longer attachment screw. If you mix up the parts and fit the A2 screw into an A1 stock, assembling an A1 rifle, the screw may stick into the tube long enough to get smacked by the back end of the recoiling buffer weight. And, the A1 screw won't reach to the buffer tube threads when you have an A2 stock on.

Sigh.

The carbine requires a different buffer tube than that of the rifle. Since the carbine stock does not butt up against the rear of the lower receiver, it has to have some way to stay in place. To keep it from spinning around the tube, the carbine tube is manufacture with a spine on the bottom. (Can we call it a "spine" if it is on the bottom? I prefer that, as dorsal fin gets to be cumbersome.)

The spine is also the location of the locking stops for the telescoping stock. If you have a carbine, turn it over and look at the spine/dorsal fin of your buffer tube. See the slot? In that slot are the circular depressions into which the locking bolt of the tele-stock latch. Squeeze the latch and move the stock back and forth. Where you stop, it may snap into a spot. If it doesn't, a push one way or another allows it to line up and snap into place.

Now, the design of the tele-stock requires a couple of extra parts – parts not seen on, or used on, the rifle. Up at the front of the tube, against the rear of the receiver, is a plate. Locking the plate into place is a ring on the threads of the

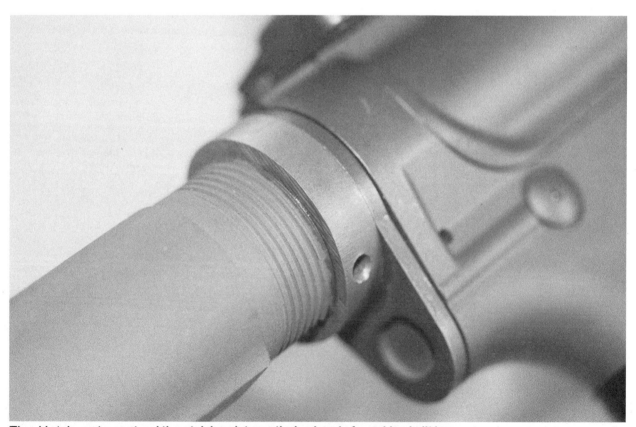

The old style capture nut and the retaining plate, on the back end of a carbine-built lower.

tube. The plate is the retaining plate, and the ring is the castle nut. The plate holds in the parts holding the rear takedown pin in the lower receiver. The castle nut locks the retaining plate in place. See the oval depression on the retaining plate? The obverse of that is a raised portion, and rides in a depression milled into the receiver, one that keeps the retaining plate from rotating out of alignment.

The castle nut keeps the retaining plate locked to the receiver.

BUFFER INTERNALS

Once you get to the point of disassembly, you'll have a chance to see the internals of the buffer tubes. In advance of that fun time, we'll take a look, if only because they can be the subject of more than a little confusion.

The inside of the buffer tube contains the buffer weight and recoil spring. Again, you'll have people "correct" you by telling you it is the "action spring" and yada-yada-yada. "Weight" and "spring" are clear enough that everyone understands.

The rifle tube and carbine tube each have their own weights and springs. And, since the rifle tube is longer than the carbine tube, you would be correct in your assumption that the weights and springs differ, and the rifle is longer for each.

In the rifle, there is no problem with extra details. The weight of the rifle buffer is the rifle weight, and the rifle spring is longer than the carbine spring. (For those who have to know right now, the rifle spring is 40-41 coils long, while the carbine spring is 37-38 coils.)

Unfortunately, for the carbine, a buffer weight is not just a buffer weight.

While shorter, the buffer weight is available in a surprising number of mass variations and, also, composition. One in particular was common for a while some years ago: a plastic weight, with lead shot in it. You could hear the shot when you shook the weight. If you have one of these, do not use it. It will certainly cause malfunctions, if not now, then soon, and for the rest of your life. It may also cause premature baldness, halitosis, high interest rates, and deductions from your man-card. Buy a proper one, and toss the crappy one.

Which, much to my displeasure, brings us to another one of the raging controversies of the AR world: what is the "proper" carbine buffer weight?

The buffer weight, either rifle or carbine, is an aluminum cylinder with a synthetic cap closing it. Inside are a series of steel weights, steel cylinders, that have more room than they need. As a result, they slide back and forth. There are also plastic washers in-between to keep them from clanging too loudly, but their weight is inconsequential. This is to turn the buffer weight into a dead-blow hammer, to deal with "carrier bounce." Something we will cover in detail later.

The original carbine buffers proved to be too light for heavy-duty use, to deal with hot loads, or to manage carbines that are over-gassed. As a result, the internal weights have been replaced with tungsten weights. A buffer with a single steel weight replaced with a tungsten one is marked with an "H" on the face of the buffer. Two weights, "H2" and so-on.

The increased mass of the buffer weight acts to slow the speed of shuttling of the reciprocating mass, and thus the cyclic rate of the carbine involved. If you have a select-fire AR (you lucky dog, you) and you swap the weights, you'll be able to measure the change in cyclic rate with a PACT timer.

The question is, what is the "right" weight/mass?

A lighter weight will cycle faster, and the decreased weight will cause less felt recoil, until the weight becomes so little that the resulting bolt speed and bottoming-out at the back end of the recoil stroke increases felt recoil, or the speed causes reliability problems. Problems? Detailed in the Troubleshooting chapter.

At the other end, increasing weight slows the rate and decreases felt recoil by preventing the cycling mass from bottoming out. However, increase the cycling mass too much, and at some point taken to extremes the greater mass can reduce cycling distance so much that is causes the rifle to not lock open when empty.

The simple test: does the carbine work? Is the brass not mangled on the trip out? Then what you have is within a useful range. Too much thinking on this can lead to obsession, and that is not good. My approach is to run the heaviest buffer weight with which the rifle or carbine runs smoothly, and not worry too much more about it.

SLING SWIVEL

Actually, in the case of the standard AR, it's not a swivel, not the one on the stock, as it doesn't move. On the rifle the sling loop is held on by the bottom screw you see in the buttplate. In carbines, the sling loop is often just a slot in the molded plastic slider, and you stick the sling through and secure it somehow. There are also designs that have a fixed sling loop, similar to that of the rifle, if you wanted to use a traditional-type sling.

Also, some aftermarket stocks have a round socket in the stock, typically anywhere from several to a slew of them. These are "QD" or quick-detach sling swivel sockets. To use them you must have a QD sling plug on your sling.

A last possible sling swivel location is the retainer plate on the carbines. The retainer plate can have loops or slots made on it (it is, after all, simply a steel stamping) and you then hook a clip-on sling adapter into the circle or hoop.

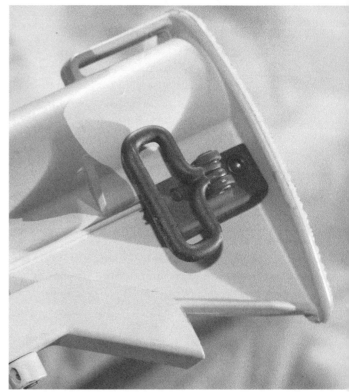

An add-on sling swivel, this from **GG&G**, one that increases the utility of the carbine.

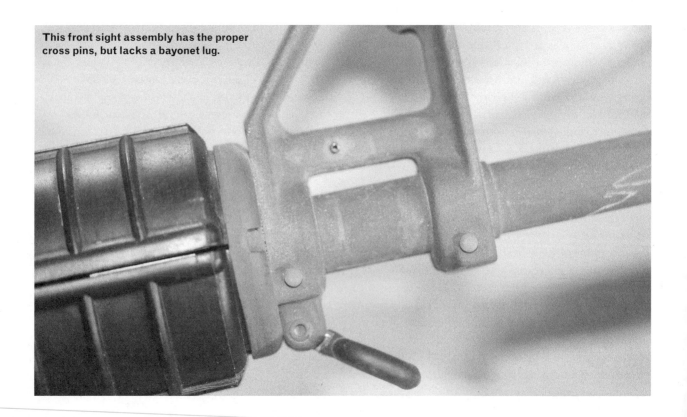

This front sight assembly has the proper cross pins, but lacks a bayonet lug.

Side-mounted sling swivels are so much more useful than the bottom-mounted ones.

PISTOL GRIP

This is one of those "evil" features that the anti-gunners get so exercised about. It is a place for your firing hand to hold on, and to position your hand so you can reach the trigger properly. It is held on by means of a single screw and is easily changed. You can change to one bigger, smaller, differently-shaped, differently-colored, or pretty much anything your imagination can come up with (or that the marketing department can dream up and wave in front of you).

Does it matter which one you use? Mostly not. If you can measure a difference in your scores or shooting times with one pistol grip over another, then by all means change. If one feels better than another, and the better-feeling one does not hurt your scores/times, go for it.

The pistol grip is a good point to demonstrate the inter-related nature of the AR design. Not only is it a place to hold, it also secures the spring and detent that actuate your safety/selector lever. You do not want your pistol grip to come loose, as it won't then be able to properly control the safety spring and plunger.

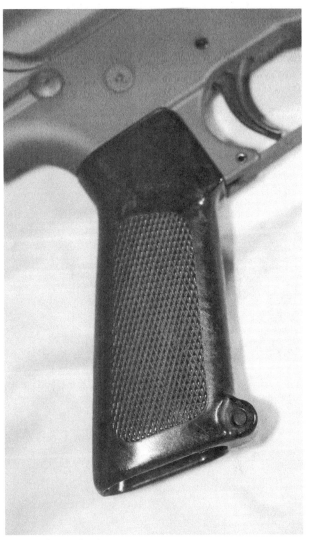

A pre-A2 pistol grip.

WINTER TRIGGER GUARD

On mil-spec rifles, the trigger guard is hinged. By pressing in the little detent, you can hinge it down against the pistol grip, and thus in wintertime fire your rifle while wearing mittens. A lot of "newer-than-mil-spec" designs dispense with that and make the trigger guard a fixed piece, but big enough that you can reach in with gloves on.

Some do so by making the guard larger, that is, curve it away from the lower face of the receiver. Other designs do away with the separate trigger guard and simply machine the guard as an integral part of the lower receiver.

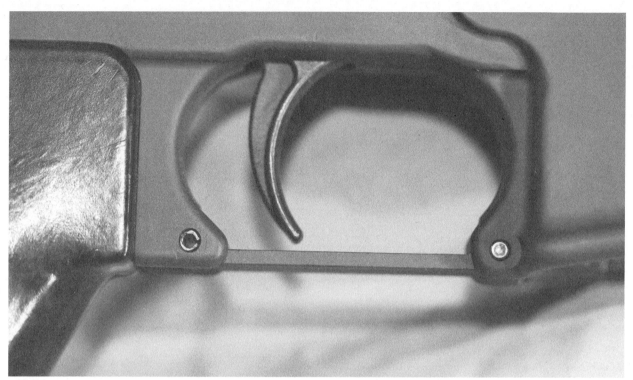

The winter trigger guard. Spring-loaded retainer at the front, that you push in with a bullet tip. Hinge down the guard and you can use mittens.

MAGAZINE WELL

The big rectangular opening is where the magazines go. As I remarked to one of our club members, a few decades ago, when he was a bit flustered in the middle of a 3-gun match "shiny end up, pointy ends forward."

Magazines, their selection, care and upgrades, are subjects all to themselves, and cannot be covered in a paragraph here.

The magazine well is created in the receiver by one of two methods; broaching or wire EDM. Broaching uses what amounts to a file, an eight-foot-long steel bar with teeth in it. The start end is just small enough to fit through the access hole in the receiver forging. The bar gets larger with each cutting tooth, until the last ones are as large as needed, and the exact shape of the magazine well. The manufacturer simply pulls the broach through the receiver (held in a fixture) and in one pass creates the opening. This is fast, but broaches cost a lot of money.

Wire EDM uses a "cutting" wire. The wire has a huge electrical charge pumped through it, and when the wire gets close enough to aluminum, the resulting spark erodes the aluminum. To cut, the wire is moved around the interior of the forging, burning a slot through the aluminum.

You may run into a lower receiver that has a tight fit. From time to time, someone on the internet will attempt to compile a list of "what receivers have tight fits." This is an exercise in futility. Yes, some will be tight fits. And when a manufacturer realizes that the latest receivers are tight, they will pull the new broach out of storage, or see what has gotten wonky with the EDM guide path software.

If the receiver truly is a tight fit, send it back for a replacement. If it is "tight" because you are too cheap to discard your ancient magazines, stop whining to the rest of us.

We now go from the magazine well, past the underside of the handguards, all the way to the front sight assembly again. On the bottom you will find two things of interest: the front sling swivel and the bayonet lug.

The magazine well is where the magazines go.

FRONT SLING SWIVEL

The sling swivel on a mil-spec rifle is held on by means of a rivet, one end of which is peened over after the rivet is inserted through the two front sight housing loops. On a non-mil-spec rifle, the swivel may be held on with a roll pin driven through, or there may not be a sling swivel. If you want a sling in the traditional location and design, you need the swivel. If you don't care how it is held on, then you're set with whatever is there.

BAYONET LUG

This is another "evil" feature that the anti gunners get all in a flutter over. On the rifle, the military bayonet has a loop on the top of the guard, and that loop goes over the flash hider. The lug on the front sight housing is what the bayonet clips to, and what holds it on.

Curious fact: the bayonet will not fit on your sixteen-inch carbine barrel. The distance from flash hider to bayonet lug is too great.

The distance of the grip, the guard-to-lug reach, is the entire reason that military M4 carbines have 14.5" barrels. I kid you not, that was what the first

buyer of the M4 asked Colt to make, so they would not need two different bayonets in inventory.

Once the first customer had to have it that way, that was that, and the design was fixed in stone.

Do you need it? No, but the insistence on the part of anti-gunners that it be removed makes it all the more appealing.

A rifle has more than a top and a bottom. So we'll have to consider the sides as well.

RIGHT SIDE

With the sights up, and the muzzle to the right, we'll look at the right side. On the upper, we have the forward assist and ejector lump. The very first ARs lacked both the forward assist and the ejector lump. The earliest ARs are thus known as "slickside" models, and those who wish to build a Vietnam-era clone search out the slickside uppers. The M16A1 and the Colt semi-auto model known as the SP1 have the forward assist, but not the ejector lump. The Lump comes to us courtesy of the A2 upgrade.

You'll also see the ejection port cover on most rifles. The cover is spring-loaded, and locks shut. When you fire the rifle, or work the action, the carrier acts to unlock the cover and the cover flips open. Some custom ARs lack this. If the upper is made from a billet of aluminum, instead of a forging, it was common in years past to simply not machine the dust cover details into the upper. (And also not the forward assist or ejector lump.) These are not so common today, although the S&W M&P15 Sport model lacks the dust cover, for economic reasons.

MAGAZINE CATCH

The magazine catch is the button below the ejector lump. By pressing it, you allow the magazine to come free, to fall out or be pulled out. The design is simple and it is non-adjustable. You can (when we get there) screw the button tighter onto the shaft, but that doesn't increase magazine catch engagement on the magazine shell. It just makes the spring tension marginally greater.

TAKEDOWN PINS

Near the top edge of the lower receiver, front and rear, are round-headed pins. These are the captured pins that hold the upper and lower together, "captured' in that even when you press them all the way across (out from the left) they will stay attached to the lower receiver. The very first design was not like that for the front pin, anyway, and losing the front pin (the rear was captured) was a real concern.

The spring and retainer of the front pin are in the ridge that runs along the top edge of the lower receiver. The rear pin is retained by the spring and plunger, held in by the stock or retaining plate we discussed earlier.

FENCED, NON-FENCED AND FREE-RANGE

The ridge that contains the front takedown pin retainer and spring is part of an addition called a "fence." The first ARs lacked fences, and the takedown pin wasn't captured, and the magazine button was not protected. The Army insisted on both the forward assist and fences for the M16A1.

There are transitional models of the AR where the fence is only partly present. Originals are rare, custom-made ones expensive (or relatively so) and most don't see the need for their lack, except for retro builders.

SAFETY/SELECTOR

Unless you have an ambidextrous safety, on the right side you'll only see the flat end of the safety/selector shaft. On some models, the flat end will have a notch in it. You can, if you wish, dab a small bit of white or orange paint in there, so it will be easy for the range officer (or whoever is supervising your training/qualification) to see what you have selected.

If you have an ambidextrous safety/selector, then there will be a lever on the right side you can use to change the lever from one position to another.

A rifle built to be ambidextrous may have the selector markings on the right side as well. In rarer instances, the manufacturer may have built in a bolt release lever or button on the right side. On all other instances, that part will be on the left side.

LEFT SIDE: SAFETY/SELECTOR

This is an important part of the lower. If your safety/selector is not properly installed, you may have a rifle that will discharge any time the trigger is pulled. The lower has two bolsters created by the forging process, ridges that limit the rotation of the selector. They do not, in and of themselves, prevent your rifle from being a machine gun, so there is no point in grinding them off.

Also, the lower will be marked as to what setting the selector is at. They may be "Safe" and "Fire." They may be "Safe" and "Semi." Since the markings (again) do not mechanically control what your rifle does, you can, if you custom-order a lower from some manufacturers, have a lower that says pretty much anything.

If you do that, it would be prudent to make them reasonably understandable. Something that makes it clear that the rifle won't fire in one position, and

The original M16 was a pretty compact and angle-free piece of gear.

will in another, will do.

When and how you move the safety/selector is a matter of training and good habits. If you have been trained one way, and you find yourself in a class or training session where another is being taught, use it as an opportunity to learn. Just be safe.

LEFT SIDE: BOLT HOLD-OPEN

This lever, a button, really, rides above and forward of your safety/selector. It can be actuated internally, by the follower of an empty magazine, and thus locks the bolt open when the rifle is out of ammunition. You can also press it with your finger (push in on the smaller, lower part of it, as you hold the bolt to the rear) to lock the bolt open.

To close the bolt, press the larger end of it in toward the receiver.

If you have replaced the empty magazine with a loaded one and you wish to place a round in the chamber, you can press or slap down on the bigger part of the hold-open and it will release the bolt.

As with the safety/selector, use of the bolt hold-open is subject to training and practice. Different instructors teach different methods; use what works.

LEFT SIDE: LOGO/SERIAL NUMBER

On the left side of the magazine well, you will find the manufacturers name, model number and serial number of your rifle. The manufacturers name is often also joined by their logo, another subject of great anguish and controversy in the AR-verse.

You'll notice that only in the case of your rifle

The left side. Selector/safety at the rear, bolt catch up front, and the rear end of the magazine catch bar is visible forward of the hammer and trigger pins.

being an actual Colt will you see the model listed as "AR-15," and sometimes not even then. Colt trademarked AR-15 more than sixty years ago, and has been diligently protecting it ever since. That we all use it in the general sense has to be driving them crazy, but as users we can call the rifles we own anything we want. (You can even call your rifle "Vera" if you want to, and you get the joke.) Other manufacturers, however, cannot use "AR-15" in anything they print or manufacturer.

The serial number has to be unique within a manufacturers production.

Caliber? On some rifles, it will be marked, such as .223, 5.56, 6.5, etc. On others, it will be marked as "Multi." Federal regulations require a caliber be marked. If a maker builds rifles, they know what caliber it is. Making .223/5.56, they can mark their receivers as such. If they sell bare receivers, they would be wise to mark them "multi" just so they

can avoid the headaches of mis-marking. Not that they mis-marked it, but if they mark it "5.56" and you build the rifle as a 6.8, someone, somewhere, is likely to get their panties in a twist, and who will get the blame? The manufacturer. So they just make it easier for themselves, and mark "multi."

However, you are still free to make the receiver any caliber you wish. If you have one marked ".223," you can make it into a 6.8, 9mm, whatever. In that instance, it is like the "do not remove" tag on your pillows. That is there for the manufacturer, not you.

That's our brief tour, and now that you know the names of the various parts, we can get on to keeping yours running.

WHO MADE MY AR?

Before we move on, a quick briefing on a subject that consumes entirely too much bandwidth in arguments, web forums and gun shop debates: who makes ARs? Simple. Lots of people, and not always the one whose name is on the lower.

Let's say you are a guy with a lot of money who wants to be an AR "maker." But, you don't have enough money to invest in CNC machining centers or the trained machinists to run them. You can buy all the parts, assemble them and sell them as rifles. You'll need a location, staff, insurance, papers of incorporation, etc., and you'll need a manufacturers license, listed as 07 in the federal regs, known in the parlance as an "Oh-Seven."

Only Colt makes M4s, and only Colt can call an Armalite-designed, direct-gas impingement rifle an AR-15. Forget that at your legal peril.

"Once a machine gun, always a machine gun" is the working position of the ATF. There's no way around it, so get used to it.

Colt has been making the AR-15, in all its variants, for half a century now. The first ones made will soon be able to claim Curio & Relic status.

An old Colt barrel, back when all twists were 1/12, and all chambers were 5.56.

If you want the rifles to have your name on them, that, too, can be arranged. You simply contract with the company who is doing the actual machining of your lowers and, for a setup fee and a minimum purchase, they'll put your name on them instead of theirs.

As part of the process, the company machining the lowers will send a form in to the ATF (before they do so much as unpack and degrease the first receiver forging of your contract) known as a "marking variance" that informs the Feds that they are making lowers with your name on them, thus the setup charge and the minimum purchase requirement. If it turns out that you cannot, for some reason, accept delivery of the lowers, they can't sell them. How could they, the receivers have your name on them. They can only destroy the

lowers, after informing the ATF of that action. They won't take a bet on you, you have to accept the burden of cost and risk. They'll probably even make you pay 100% up-front, until you establish a track record with them.

As many makers use proprietary tooling and cutting paths, it is possible to get a sense of who made something by looking at the toolmarks left behind. However, it is entirely possible for an end-assembler to have contracts with two or more makers, and marking variances with each, to keep them supplied regardless of contractual conflicts.

This situation leaves people trying to figure out who "really" makes the lowers that so-and-so sells. At this point I throw my hands up and move on to the next chapter.

CHAPTER 2
ESSENTIAL TOOLS

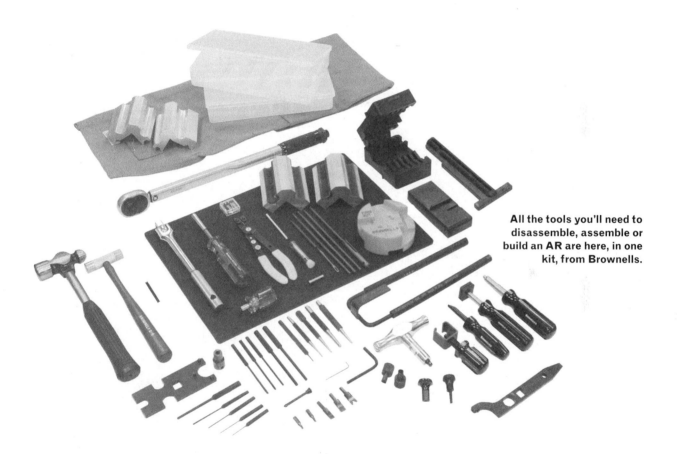

All the tools you'll need to disassemble, assemble or build an AR are here, in one kit, from Brownells.

LET'S ALL AGREE: a fully-equipped machine shop would be nice. But, besides being beyond the needs and budget of most of us, there is the little matter of elbow room. One of the best gun-wranglers I know has all his equipment in what amounts to a one-car garage. But that's the work space, and everything else is stored in the next room, another one-car garage.

How many of us have that much extra space? And a thick concrete floor to hold the machines? Raise your hands. I thought so. You can, in a

moment of weakness, or a day when you are flush with cash, find yourself so geared up, so equipped with extras to make your life and task easier, that you can't find the rifle that was on the workbench a minute ago.

Resist the temptation to get something "because it will make things easier" or "is cool" and get what you need because it will actually help you.

At the other extreme, I've fixed recalcitrant ARs at the range with the one small box of tools I brought to the class (or even borrowed tools) and a portable workbench to work on. A few times even

without the portable workbench, just a bench, and even just my lap. As a "class expedient" work situation, it gets the job done, but at no time was it fun.

So, let's lay out the tools and space and divide them into three categories: the absolutely essential, the "makes life easier" and the "I want to be a pro gun builder."

What you need falls into a few basic categories: a place to clean, a means of holding your rifle or its parts, tools to clean, tools to assemble/disassemble and tools to adjust.

A PLACE TO STAND

If all you have is the option of a fold-up workbench, tucked in the garage, that you have to stand up to do anything, then get one. A solid fixed-in-place bench is better, but only if you keep it clean.

The various portable, worksite benches will do, but they benefit from a little extra TLC. For one,

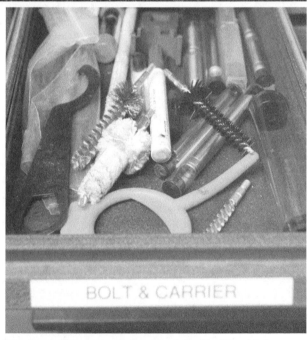

Top: Everything you need can be found in this catalog. Just be careful, you can melt your credit card in an evening of browsing. Above: If you label (and you should) then follow your own labeling system. If it belongs there, it goes there. If it doesn't, it goes someplace else.

Installing pins in a production-line setting, the operator has a fixture to hold everything and align them exactly. This fixture costs more than your rifle, and you won't need it to remove and replace a pin now and then.

they are a little on the light side. Second, they lack a vise of some kind. Oh, the manufacturer says you can clamp lumber in the opening jaws of the bench, but that's just to cut lumber for framing. No way can you clamp an upper receiver in there and then proceed to change barrels.

My temporary bench, the one I schlep to classes and such, is your basic folding workbench. I found it at a garage sale, our dog of the time sniffed it and proclaimed it worthy (and almost "claimed" it) so I bought it for $10 and carried it home. Garage sales can be great.

HOLDERS

Yes, you can hold and clean, even assemble, with nothing but your bare hands, but it gets old fast. And if you want to make any modifications, you'll find the tasks you can do bare-handed to be very limited in number. You'll need a way to hold your rifle. Some of you are thinking, "Hey, I've got a vise, it is bolted to the bench." Wrong.

A vise can hold the firearm holder, but not the firearm itself. At the very least you need some sort of padding, or else leave vise marks on your rifle. (In most instances, the sight of vise marks voids manufacturers warranties.)

A magazine well holder is useful. This slides into the magazine well as if it were a magazine, but is a plastic or aluminum bar. You clamp the bar, not the receiver. Then, you can work on the receiver with both hands. The magazine well block is a holding device that permits you to screw in a buffer tube, or tighten a castle nut. It is simple a third hand to hold the unit while you assemble the internals or fish out that popped primer.

The aluminum barrel-holding plate, the angled one with grooves for two different diameter barrels, is also a useful tool. Not for changing barrels they are marginal at best for that – there are much better tools to be had there. But, if you want to work on the upper receiver with both hands, then clamping the barrel in place (hint; remove the handguards and clamp as close to the

Left: Left: If you plan to remove/install barrels, get this fixture and use it. Use it every time. Right: Barrel blocks. Moderately useful, impossible to break, everyone has a set.

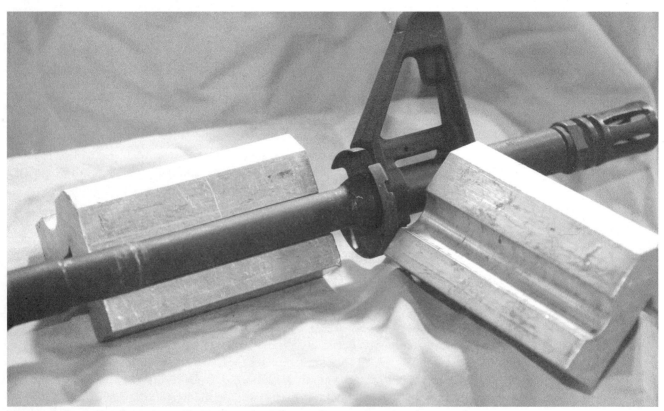

The blocks have two sized slots milled in them, for different-diameter barrels.

This receiver block and holding fixture holds a receiver while the armorer screws on a muzzle brake.

Don't listen to your buddy who says you don't need a receiver-holding fixture.

The lowly **GI** cleaning brush, perhaps the most important tool you can own. With it you can do most of what needs be done to keep your **AR** running.

receiver as you can get it to fit) makes work easier. If you plan to do anything forceful, brace the receiver so you don't bend things.

There are also upper receiver holders, basically polymer blocks that use crosspins and the upper receiver pivot pin holes, to hold the upper into a vise. This is a useful way to do things like bolt on BUIS or optics, paint-in sights, etc.

And last, we have cradles that just hold the entire rifle, assembled. These work to do things like sight adjustments/installations, bore cleaning, etc. But it is hard to work on the interior of the lower with the rifle assembled clamped into a cradle.

CLEANING KITS

You have to have a cleaning kit of some kind, if for no other reason than to be able to scrub off the mud from a hard day's practice. Admittedly, you could clean the exterior off with a hose and a used towel that has been relegated to "dogs and cars" status. For actual cleaning of the interior, you'll be cleaning four things: the chamber and bore, the bolt carrier assembly, the fire control parts, and the interiors of the upper and lower.

BASIC MIL-SPEC

Coming in a flat, rectangular pouch designed to be clipped to web gear or a rucksack, the military cleaning kit contains a joined cleaning rod, a bore brush, a chamber brush, a plastic toothbrush-looking brush and pipe cleaners. (The pipe cleaners are of no use whatsoever, and if in the course of use you lose them, do not regret doing so.) The military kit also comes in a triangular pouch, lacking a lid or closure, that is intended to get stuffed into the buttstock of an A1 or A2 stock.

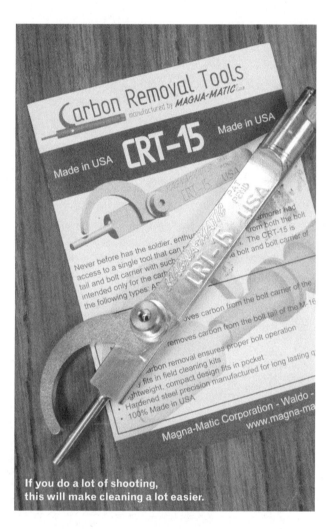

If you do a lot of shooting, this will make cleaning a lot easier.

There may be some patches and an oil bottle. Rifle manufacturers will sometimes toss in a kit with the rifle and other gear, so you will occasionally get these for free. Free is better than nothing, but you can do better, and if you stick with AR use, you probably will.

You'll also need tools besides those.

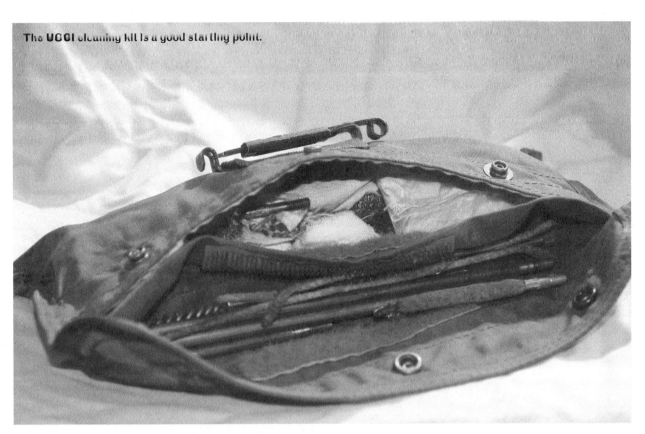

The **UGGI** cleaning kit is a good starting point.

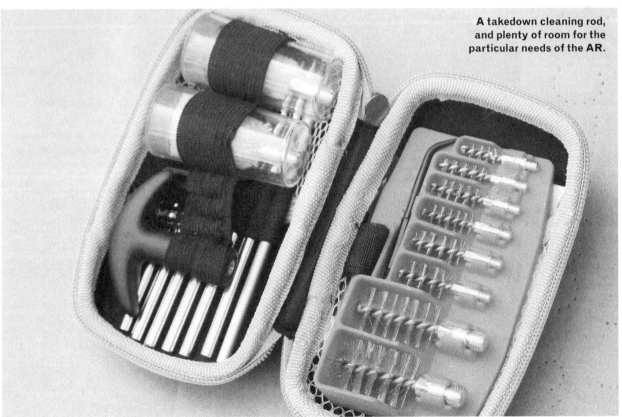

A takedown cleaning rod, and plenty of room for the particular needs of the **AR.**

EXTRA CLEANING GEAR

One approach is the Otis cleaning kit, a cable system that is so compact you can fit it all into a container not much bigger than a pinch can. The Otis will certainly do a lot of cleaning, but it will be work to thoroughly scrub the chamber and locking lug recesses. Since it is based around a cable, you can't use it to punch out a stuck case. However, the utility of the Otis means you can and must have one, and you should keep it in your range bag or rucksack.

The opposite approach is a fixed, one-piece cleaning rod. The one-piece rod will not offer the joints of the mil-spec rod, and thus will be less wearing on your bore when you clean. It has the problem of portability. This is something you either keep at home for cleaning there, or make some special storage accommodations in your vehicle, as these things tend to be more than three feet long. If bent, they are useless.

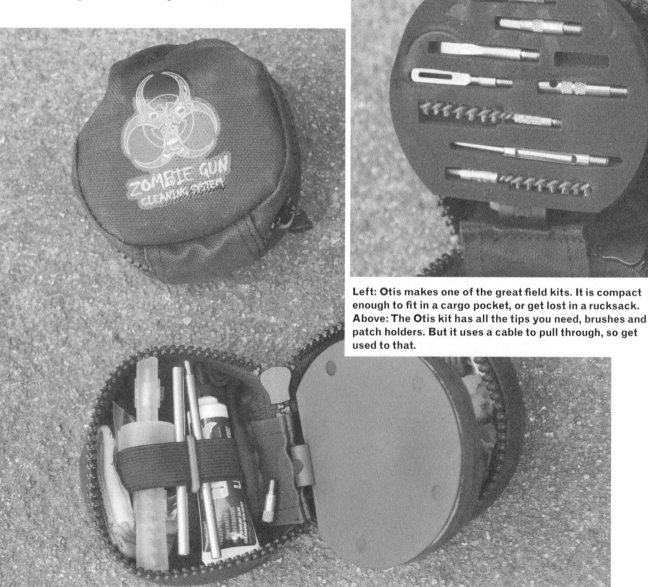

Left: **Otis makes one of the great field kits. It is compact enough to fit in a cargo pocket, or get lost in a rucksack. Above: The Otis kit has all the tips you need, brushes and patch holders. But it uses a cable to pull through, so get used to that.**

REAL AVID

Real Avid makes a cleaning rod-based kit that is more compact than the military kit. The one I have on hand is the Gun Boss universal. It has the brushes to clean everything from .22 up to 12 gauge. The rod segments are 4.75" each in length, so the whole thing is compact enough to cram into a bug-out bag, rucksack or other gear. If you have no use whatsoever for the 12 gauge and other stuff, no problem. Yank it out (leave in the brush for your customary handgun caliber) and replace with a chamber brush for your AR.

BROWNELLS M-PRO 7

A complete cleaning kit, the Brownells M-Pro 7 has all you'll need. This is a bench-based, or workshop kit. It comes in a box that is a bit too big to pack in a bug-out bag or rucksack. If you have a dedicated range truck, then this would fit well there.

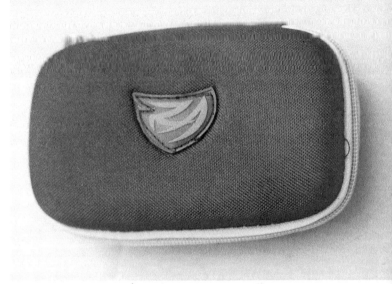

Real Avid makes a compact cleaning kit that you can use, and better yet, rebuild, for your **AR**.

If all you want to do is clean and don't need tools for repair, here you go. Stock up on lots of bore patches, if you are a clean bore fiend.

Iosso makes an all-plastic brush set, except for the gas tube brush, which no-one really needs. (Unless the training sergeant says you do, and then it is vital.)

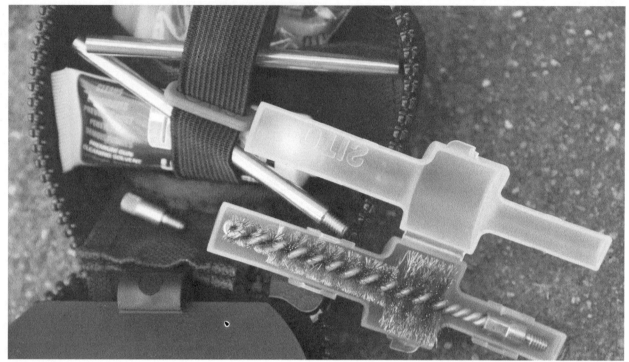

The essential for upper cleaning: A rod guide to protect your leade, a chamber brush to scour it clean, and a plastic chamber brush for cleaning out the scrubbed gunk.

IOSSO

The Iosso kit does not come in a neat toolbox, but you can easily find a box for it. The various brushes can clean chamber and bore, upper and lower, and are all made of a blue synthetic, so as to not be confused with brass or brushes for other applications.

USEFUL EXTRAS

One thing to have on hand is some gizmo by which you can press the takedown pins open. Avoid using a drift punch and a hammer. It is too easy to break the receiver at the rear pin, busting out the channel around the takedown retention pin.

CHAMBER AND BORE

You need a rod, brushes and patches. You also need a special brush, and a rod to go with it, called a chamber brush.

The ideal setup would be a single-piece rod, with a rod guide and a fixture to hold your rifle or upper on your bench, and plenty of elbow room.

All told, with space for the rifle, the rod, and literal elbow room, you need close to eight feet in a line. None of this fits around a corner. If you have that, we all envy you. The next best would be a cleaning kit with a solid rod of sections or pieces, and a rod guide.

A brief aside on rod/bore guides. The guide is a plastic or aluminum tube that fits inside your upper, with a hole down it just big enough to accept the rod and brush or patch. You see, when you encounter resistance in pushing through the brush or patch, the rod will flex. If it flexes against the bore right at the throat, repeated cleanings can rub the rifling and harm accuracy. Long-range shooters worry about this a great deal. If you have spent a large amount of money on a barrel, it is prudent to exercise some caution. To someone whose entire rifle competition experience will be no farther than 300 yards, cleaning rod wear is not so much of a concern.

Now, there is a way to use the jointed rod and mitigate the rod flex problem: pull it through the bore. More on that in the cleaning section.

Next would be a cable cleaning kit, like the Otis.

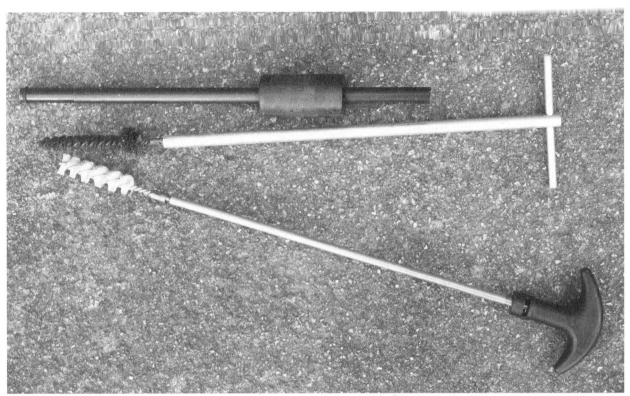

The chamber brush is enclosed in a very clever protective plastic case. It keeps the brush from chewing up the other parts, and keeps the brush from being crushed out of shape.

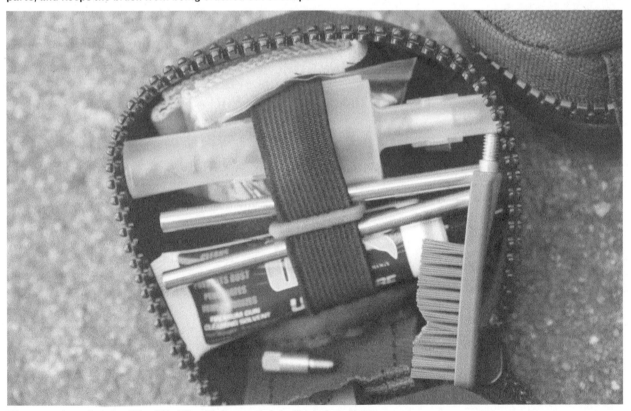

The very clever brush of the Otis kit, which screws into the rod sections.

Here, you use a section of cable, and instead of pushing it through the bore, you pull it through from chamber to muzzle. The big advantage here is that a cable system is so compact you can leave it in your gun box, gear bag, or your web gear, and always have it. The drawback is that you can't use a cable to knock out a stuck case.

The chamber brush is a brass brush that is longer than the chamber, with a collar of stainless steel brush spines around the back end of it. In order to properly use this brush, you need a rod for it. The rod must be one with a fixed "T"

handle. This, alas, will not fit all that easily in your compact web-gear cleaning kit. You can, in a pinch, get by with a rod that does not have a fixed T, but it won't be any fun.

You'll need a bore brush, and cleaning patches of the proper size for your caliber. The size, thickness, composition and design of cleaning patches is a subject that approaches religious levels, exceeded only by the controversy of whether you 'shoot-in' or condition a barrel before you actually use it.

Briefly, all-cotton patches are better, simply because they hold on to cleaning solvent and oil better than the synthetic or synthetic-blend ones do.

The Brownells Field Kit is more than just a cleaning kit, it is an armorers toolkit for the outdoors.

You don't need a compact cleaning kit at home or in the workshop. So make life easier, and take up some room.

BOLT-CARRIER ASSEMBLY

These are parts that will (unless you have a piston-driven AR) get amazingly cruddy with caked-on and even baked-on carbon and powder residue. Once the assembly is out of the upper, you'll need a few tools to get it properly clean. First, some sort of awl, icepick or other tool to lever the firing pin retainer out of the carrier. It is small, set deep in its recess, and if you are cleaning, it will be gunked up and essentially glued into place.

The other tool you'll need is a small pin (a small-diameter Philips screwdriver, like an eyeglass screwdriver, works fine here) to push the extractor pin out.

Your carrier key screws may need to be tightened, and you'll need an allen wrench set if you are building from scratch or replacing a gas key. Get a full set; don't mess with buying "just the size" you need. Also, if you ever need, plan to need, or think you'll need to do anything to an ejector, open up the Brownells catalog and buy the bolt disassembly tool. Brownells, Sinclair, anyone's. Yes, you can jury-rig ways to compress the ejector without this tool, but trust me, they are no fun when something goes wrong.

For the rest, you'll need the plastic brush in the GI kit, and a scraper such as the M4CAT, to scrape the bolt tail and the carrier tunnel.

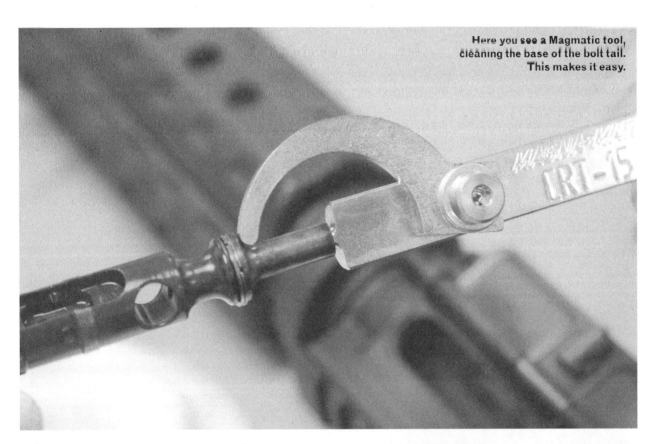

Here you see a Magmatic tool, cleaning the base of the bolt tail. This makes it easy.

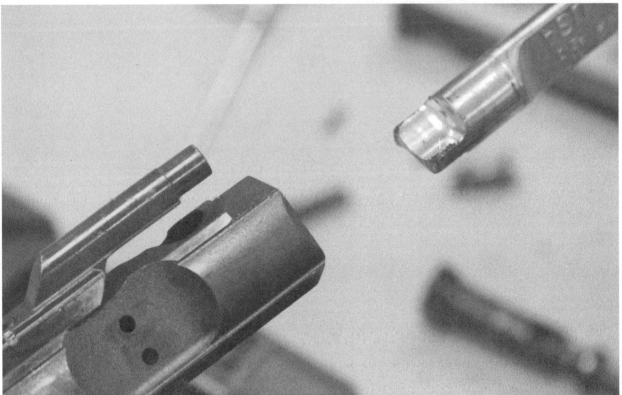

The Magmatic tool also cleans inside the carrier.

UPPER RECEIVER

If you will be working on a lot of uppers with standard handguards, a handguard disassembly tool can be useful. If you have just the one rifle and the handguards are easy to take off, or you plan to never take them off, the tool is an extra in the toolbox you'll never use.

However, if you work on a lot of rifles, one day you will need it.

If you will ever remove or replace a front sight housing, you must have the Brownells front sight block. Even if you aren't planning on swapping out sight housings, get this block. It is not expensive, and you can always find this to be a backing/bench block, and useful in other operations.

There are specialized upper receiver cleaning kits, brushes, swabs and extra gear. If you want them, or will be cleaning a whole rack of rifles, get it.

All the cleaning tools to clean the upper and chamber, before you get to swabbing the bore.

If you plan on removing, replacing or installing barrels, you'll need an upper receiver holding fixture (and not the stupid little aluminum blocks that allegedly clamp onto barrels) or a barrel extension bar. If you will not be doing barrel work, you do not need these.

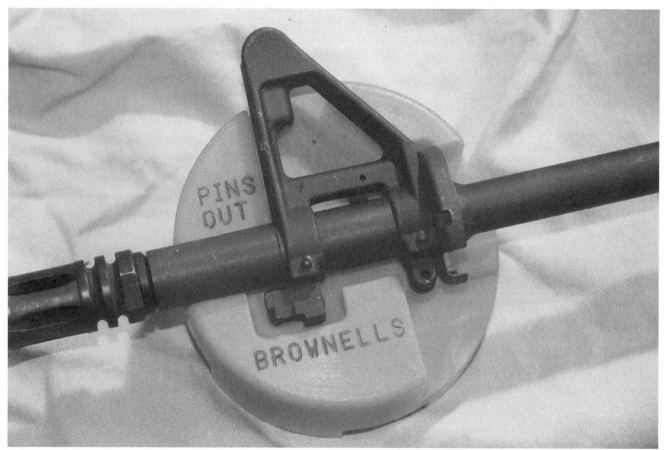

If you do front sight installs, the front sight block is invaluable. If you don't, you don't need it, except to be ready for when you do.

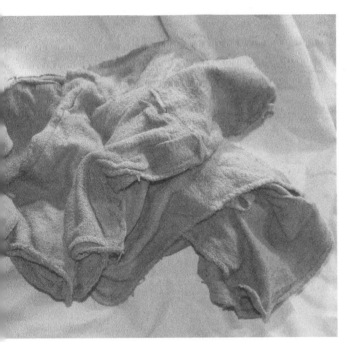

Shop cloths. Buy them, use them, clean them if you are really cheap, otherwise dispose of them.

CLEANING CLOTHS

Not much clothing made these days is suitable as a gun-cleaning "rag." Your typical poly-cotton blend t-shirt sucks as an "oil rag," and the more poly it has in it, the worse it is. It won't absorb enough oil to be useful. And, the "poly" in it may react to cleaning solvents and suddenly or slowly dissolve on you. If you must use an old shirt, use one that is 100% cotton. Go to the local thrift store, find 100% cotton shirts and give them the dollar each they ask for them,.

Or, go down to the big box hardware store, Chinese import store, or other place where men buy tools, and buy a package of shop cloths. These will be the square red or blue cloths with a sewn seam. You could even be a bit OCD about it and buy red for cleaning and blue for oiled-wiping. At the typical cost, and the use most of us give them, you could even consider them disposable. Use a cloth until it is so cruddy you can't stand to touch it, then toss it and grab a fresh one.

But, if you use them a lot, or you are just too cheap to toss them, then you can wash them One bit of advice: DON'T TOSS THEM IN THE

WASHING MACHINE. Putting an oily load of rags into a machine will ruin it for non-oiled clothes. No amount of soap will prevent contamination, and once contaminated/oiled, it will pass on the oil smell to non-oiled clothes for many, many loads of laundry. Once oiled, there is no getting the machine clean again.

So, what to do? Simple. Get a sacrificial five-gallon bucket. On shop cloth cleaning day, take the bucket and the cloths to the range, the gun club, wherever. (You can do this in your laundry room, but exercise great care.) On the way, get one of the industrial-strength stain removers. Spray each cloth and toss it into the bucket. Let them soak. Pour in water, add dish detergent and agitate. Use a piece of lumber, length of shovel handle, that sort of thing, to agitate as much as you can.

Why the range? Because this will take hours. Apply stain remover, soak. Add water and dish detergent (because it cuts grease/oil/crud better) agitate and wait. Agitate some more. Dump (safely, according to club rules and EPA regs) add water, agitate and soak. Agitate more, pour off the water and rinse again. Your final step is to soak until the soak water appears clean, pour the water off, wring the rags dry and let them dry in the sun.

Will they be clean? No. You would never consider using them at the dinner table. But they will be clean enough to use again as gun-cleaning cloths.

The more stubborn/persistent among you will, at this step, consider tossing them into the washing machine "to get them really clean" as a final step. Resist the urge.

See why I suggest that they be considered disposable?

WORKING TOOLS

If you will only ever clean your rifle, and perhaps wrestle some of the more-permanent parts apart to re-fit them, you are probably done with the tools list. Remember, the AR was designed to be cleaned and maintained by soldiers in the field. It is mostly a bare-hands disassembly process, with a few simple tools getting you to almost all you'll need for cleaning and parts swaps. If you are planning on actually taking your rifle apart, building from scratch or re-building, you'll need more. A summary, by the tasks involved:

Lower Receiver Assembly

If you will be putting on stocks or swapping them out, you'll need at the very least a castle nut wrench, a.k.a. stock wrench. Get a heavy-duty one, as the chintzy stamped-steel ones really are worse than no tool at all. The heavier the better, as you'll be putting your weight into this wrench to tighten the castle nut on a tele-stock assembly.

Assembling the tele-stock, you'll need a center punch, either a plain center punch and a hammer or a spring-loaded one. If you can afford the extra few bucks, get the spring loaded one. That way you don't need an assistant. You see, to stake the castle nut with punch and hammer (which staking you must do, don't let anyone tell you otherwise) you have to hold the receiver, the punch and the hammer. That means three or four hands. With the spring-loaded punch, you only need to hold the receiver, and the holding hand can also be the punch guiding hand. Your second hand presses it in to activate it.

A neat tool, one you'll need for installing takedown pins in the lower, is the takedown pin assembly tool. With it, installing the spring, plunger and takedown pin on the front is a no-parts-lost procedure that takes less than a minute. Without it, you risk losing springs and plungers at the rate of one lost for each two installed.

For those interested in installing or inspecting triggers and hammers, Brownells makes a special fixture that installs the hammer and trigger outside of the receiver. That way, you can look directly at the engagement surfaces and see what is going on. If you will be adjusting a target or match trigger, or you just want to know why your mil-spec parts don't work right, this is a boon. But, as much as I love the guys at Brownells, you don't absolutely need this.

You'll need the relevant pin punches, in

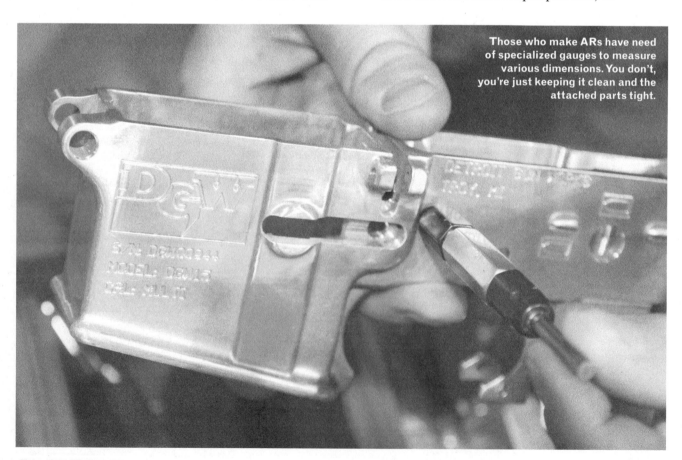

Those who make ARs have need of specialized gauges to measure various dimensions. You don't, you're just keeping it clean and the attached parts tight.

A castle nut wrench is useful only if you have a carbine. It is of no use on a rifle buffer tube.

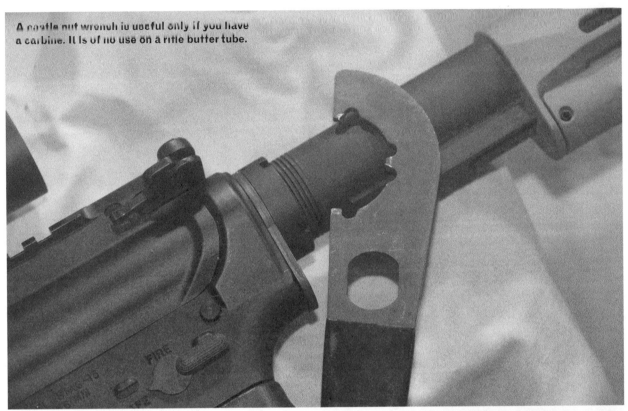

The wrench fits into the slots cut on the back of the castle nut. The big slots, not the staking recesses.

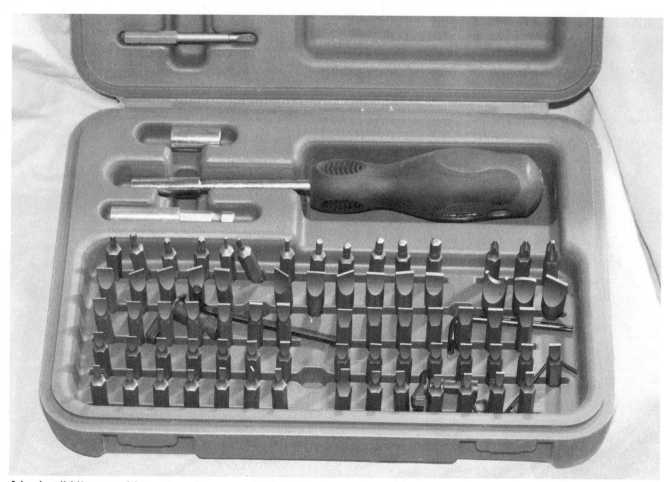

A basic, all-bits screwdriver set can be very useful, in tightening scope mounts, for example, and used as a starter punch to get sticky takedown pins budged.

particular for the bolt hold-open assembly, a long, skinny, flat-on-one-side punch to drive in or out the bolt hold open pin.

And, you'll need the usual assortment of screwdrivers and allen wrenches to tighten whatever is threaded. The screwdriver set need only be a couple, in the correct sizes. Use whatever you have to remove the parts, then take the parts to the local hardware store (not the whole rifle, please) and match the parts to the screwdrivers on the racks. Buy and leave, happy. For allen wrenches, just buy a set. You'll need longer-shafted ones to reach into the pistol grip, but those you get one each, and know that whatever size you need, you'll pick up the wrong one first from the bench. That's life.

Upper Receiver Assembly

The first big tool you'll need will be a barrel nut wrench. This is the one that has teeth for the barrel nut on one end, a screwdriver-like other end, and notches for various wrench-flat openings. It will also have a square opening for the insertion of a torque wrench. You'll hardly ever need either the torque wrench or the opening it fits in.

The barrel nut wrench you will see in many places is the military multi-tool. This should be re-named the military hurt-me tool. It has three small posts, lined up so as to promise the tightening of a barrel nut. It also has the various wrench-flat openings and a torque wrench hole. The little nubs will invariably slip off of the barrel nut, usually when you are at max torque, trying to tighten the

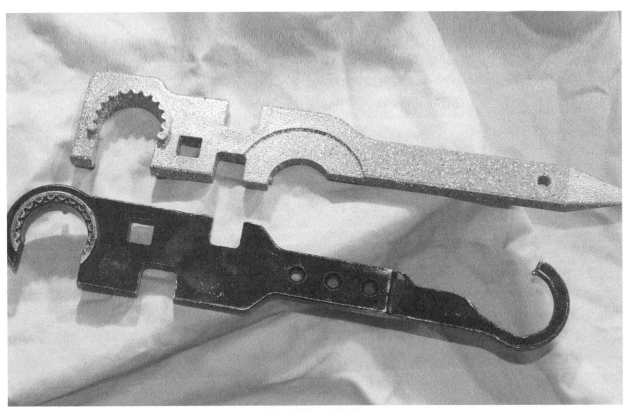

Get the big, solid, useful barrel wrench, not the small, useless, **USGI** one.

The barrel nut wrench slides onto the barrel nut, but you have to push the delta ring back against its spring to use the wrench.

The **USGI** barrel nut wrench is useful only as a paperweight. **Oh,** you can use it as a barrel nut wrench, but your knuckles will pay.

nut that last little bit. You will bang your hands on the bench edge, drop the tool, say very bad words, and contemplate harm to the designer of the tool. The bigger, cast wrenches, available from Brownells, will not slip.

Handguard removal "pliers" are good, if your handguards are really tight.

The flash hider will (probably) fit one of the notches in the barrel nut wrench. That's what they are there for. If you have a non-mil spec flash hider, you may need a narrow open-end wrench to fit the flats. Again, off to the hardware store, flash hider in hand, to get something that fits.

The various pins will require small-diameter punches to fit. In the case of the gas tube pin, you won't find that sized punch at the local hardware store, and you'll be getting it from Brownells.

Bolt & Carrier

To take the ejector out of the bolt, you'll need a bolt disassembly tool. If you aren't going to be doing that, you won't need it. You'll need the various scrapers for bolt and carrier. If you have

to re-tighten your gas key, the use of a MOACKS is essential, but it is a bit expensive to buy for one rifle. If you plan on having more than one, get the MOACKS.

GENERAL TOOLS

Hammers, such as a medium-weight ball peen hammer, screwdrivers, pliers, side-cutters, and so on, all the general toolbox tools that we all have collected over the years, will be useful. Don't forget files (big, clean, new and sharp are the hallmarks here) and the various grades of Loctite.

HEADSPACE GAUGES

Oh god, the inevitable question and discussion of headspace gauges. OK, background: headspace, as a term of art used in the firearms industry, refers to the gap between the bolt face or breechface, and whatever stops the forward progress of the cartridge.

In the case of a revolver cartridge or a rimmed

If you are going to be removing ejectors, you must buy the bolt disassembly tool. No, I'm not kidding. Order it. Right now.

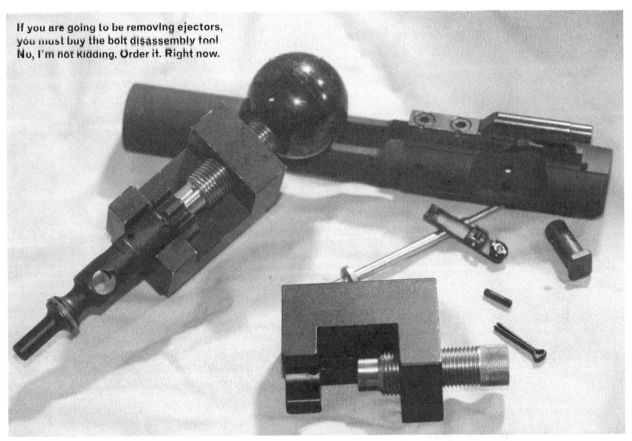

Use the bolt disassembly tool to compress the ejector, then drive out the pin that holds it in place.

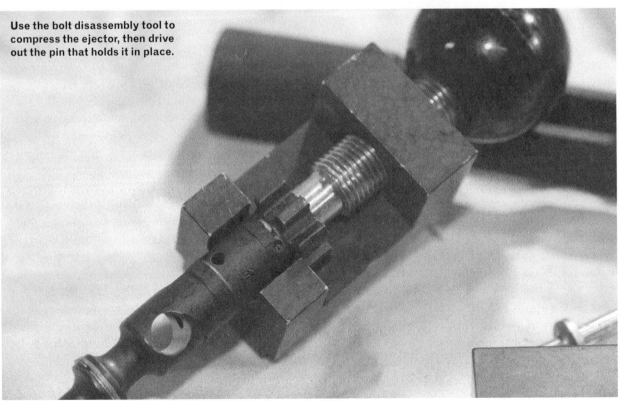

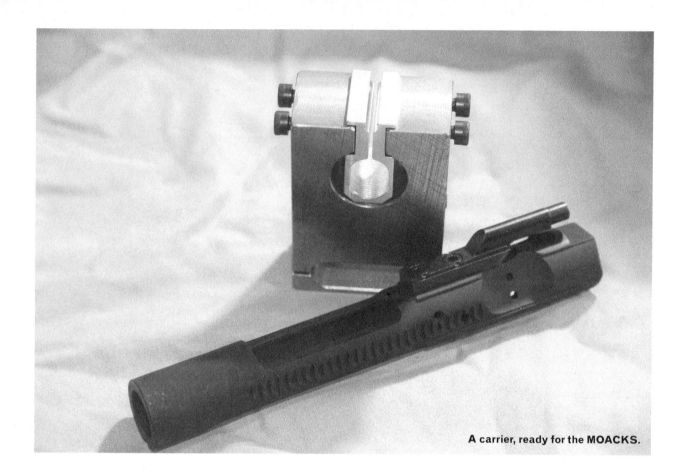

A carrier, ready for the MOACKS.

rifle cartridge, it is the rim, and not the shoulder (in the case of the rifle cartridge, one example being a .30-30). On a belted magnum, it is the belt, again, not the shoulder. On both those rifle examples, a savvy reloader can adjust his/her reloading sizing die to make the shoulder the actual stopping part, using both rim and shoulder to control headspace.

Why? Case life. A belted or rimmed cartridge, with a big gap between the case shoulder and the chamber shoulder, causes stretching. When the round is fired, the case expands to fill the gap. When re-sized, the shoulder gets shoved back. Excessive working weakens and enbrittles the case, and they separate, or break in two, after just a few reloadings. If the headspace is excessive enough, the case can separate into two on the very first firing, no reloading needed.

On a cartridge case such as the .223/5.56, lacking a rim or a belt, the stopping point is the shoulder.

Headspace, in the AR-15, refers only to the gap between the face of the bolt and the shoulder of the chamber. That is all, and nothing more. Do not confuse headspace with the question of .223 vs. 5.56 leade/throat. The two are different.

If someone (or you) asks, "Is my headspace .223 or 5.56?," they/you do not understand the question.

Further background: The manufacturers of ammunition, and of rifles, have gotten together and agreed on a set of dimensions for both ammo and rifles. The idea is simple: to ensure that the largest ever made cartridge will still fit inside of the smallest ever made chamber and work properly. This group is the Sporting Arms and Ammunition Manufacturers Institute. The acronym is SAAMI, and it is pronounced "sammy." That's the easy part. The hard part is/was agreeing on how far those measurements can differ and still have everything still work out well. The answer is about 0.006".

That is, if the smallest cartridge and the largest

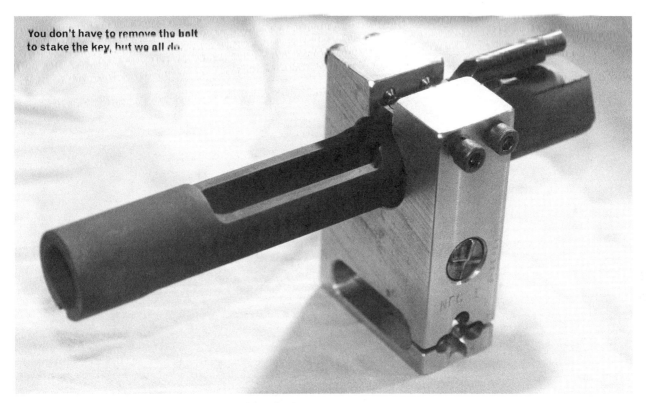

You don't have to remove the bolt to stake the key, but we all do.

Left: You can see how the hardened screws stake metal up against and over the screws holding the key in place. Above: Headspace gauges. Most of us don't need them, but when you do, you do, and nothing else will do.

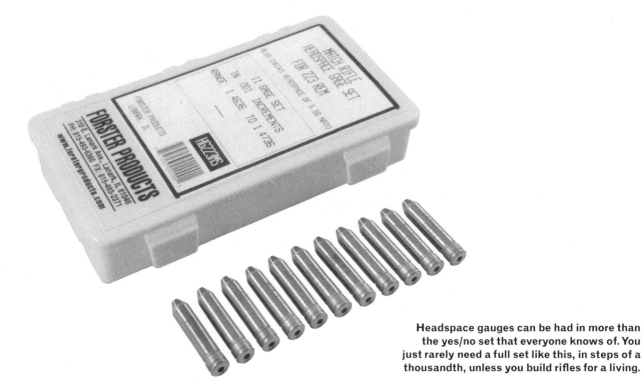

Headspace gauges can be had in more than the yes/no set that everyone knows of. You just rarely need a full set like this, in steps of a thousandth, unless you build rifles for a living.

chamber differ by more than 0.006" (spoken as "six thousandths"), you have excess headspace. That does not mean your rifle is defective or dangerous, just that the brass life will suffer more than is generally accepted.

To check a chamber, SAAMI has determined that certain hardened steel gauges be used, called "Go" and "No-Go" gauges. If a chamber is too small, the bolt will not close and lock on a Go gauge that is placed in the too-small chamber. If the chamber is so overly large that the bolt will close on a No-Go gauge in the chamber, then the chamber is too big. And they tell you nothing else. Is it almost too small? Or just barely too big? Or the opposite? Nope, no way to tell, other than "your chamber is within accepted dimensions."

Also note that a headspace gauge tells you nothing about how wide your chamber is. If the chamber was reamed to the correct depth but the reamer had been sharpened perhaps a few times too many, the chamber may not be large enough in diameter, even though it is long/deep enough. A headspace gauge will tell you things are all right, even though your rifle keeps choking on your ammo.

Here's the part that a lot of people have a tough time wrapping their brains around. The Army does not give squat about what SAAMI thinks. The Army decides what chambers the M16/M4 will have, and the dimensions committee of SAAMI can go pound sand, as far as DoD is concerned. Do not get the two systems confused.

What system does the Army use, then? (And I speak of "the Army" as all of the armed forces under Federal control, not to exclude the Marines, Air force, or Coast Guard.) Simple: a chamber must be over a specified minimum and under a specified maximum. While the Army regs call for measuring with a No-Go gauge, the armorers I've talked to all report the same thing: the Army depends heavily on a gauge known as the Field gauge.

The field gauge is some 0.003" longer than the No-Go gauge, and if a rifle bolt will close on it, the rifle is deemed Unsafe and must be attended to by an armorer.

Why the difference? Why will the Army accept a rifle that gobbles up a No-Go gauge? Are they less concerned about safety? Nope, the reason is simple: the Army doesn't reload ammo. That extra

This is what bad reloading practices or excessive headspace can do to your brass.

Overly-worked brass, or grossly excessive headspace, will do this to your brass.

Manufacturers (this is a Beretta, at the Beretta plant) need to know exact headspace. Here, instead of a simple Go/No-Go/Field set, they have a half-thousandths set to measure the headspace exactly.

0.003" is nowhere near enough to cause cases to separate on a single firing. Anything more detailed than that ("Does it take a Field gauge or not?") is information that is utterly irrelevant to the Army, for rack-grade, issue small arms.

Now, those in the services building rifles for use by Designated Marksmen, or in competition at the National Matches or in Army-wide matches, would look a little closer at headspace. But for an issue "The Chicoms are swarming over the ridgeline, grab this and get to it" rifle or carbine, Field or No-field is all the Army needs to know.

(Apparently the Marines draw the line at a No-Go gauge for everything but emergency issue. Good for them.)

And you will, if you peruse the internet forums long enough, be told, "The only gauge you need is a Field. If your rifle won't close on it, that's all you need." Usually right before or right after you were told "You should have bought mil-spec, and

you wouldn't be having these questions/problems/headaches." You will also be treated to detailed lists of the exact dimensions (down to the ten-thousandths) of whose gauges have what length, and why this or that matches closest to the ones purported to be used by the Army/Marines/SEALs, etc.

So, we finally get to the question: do you need headspace gauges? Yes and no.

If you will be building or troubleshooting rifles, you will , sooner or later, need gauges. You can get by with a simple set, such as one available from Manson Reamers, a Go and a No-Go pair. Now, if you are curious, or are trying to build a rifle to exact specs, then you can invest in a Forster match set, eleven (11!) gauges in stepped dimensions. Starting a thousandth below the minimum, and going up to the Field dimension, you can use this set to determine exactly what length your rifle's headspace. One small detail you may want to be

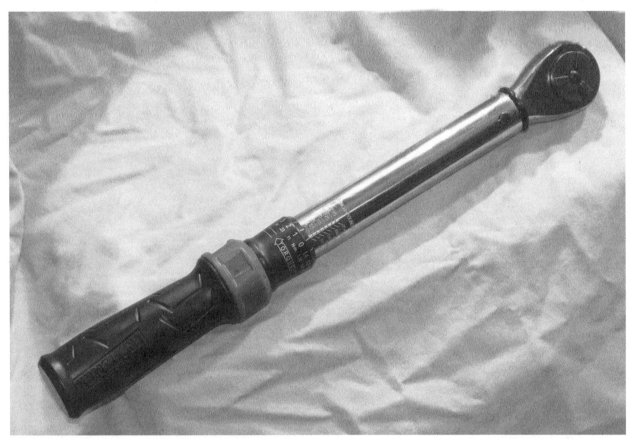

A torque wrench, useful (some say) in getting things properly tight. Most of us simply use our educated arms.

aware of: you should measure, as the final spec, after your rifle has fired a couple of magazines of ammo. The toolmarks and other imperfections on the bolt lugs and barrel extension will burnish against each other, and this can cause a change in readings. I had a customer who was so OCD he used just such a set on his AR before firing a shot. After a hundred rounds or so, he measured again, not knowing about the burnishing. His reading was 0.001" larger than at the start! Ohmygod! At that rate, according to his calculations he was going to have excessive headspace in less than a thousand rounds, and how did he get such an obviously defective barrel/bolt? A different perspective on too much information.

One way to avoid the need for headspace gauges is to simply, when you order a new barrel (or the barrel you will be building a rifle with), buy a matched bolt for it from the same company. The barrel makers know of your worries and have read

all the information, rumors, etc. They know the deal and will be happy to sell you a bolt to match your barrel, made and headspaced by them.

Unless you have a specialized headspace gauge, one made with cutouts to avoid the ejector, you should completely strip your bolt, and scrub both bolt and chamber, before you measure headspace.

TORQUE WRENCHES

A torque wrench is a special socket-wrench gizmo that allows you to tighten a screw or bolt to a specific level of force. You set the torque wrench to a given value (inch-pounds, foot-pounds, dyne-centimeters, grain election radius) and when you have levered the wrench to that point it releases its hold, with a snap, and you have applied that much force.

In the engineering world, fasteners have

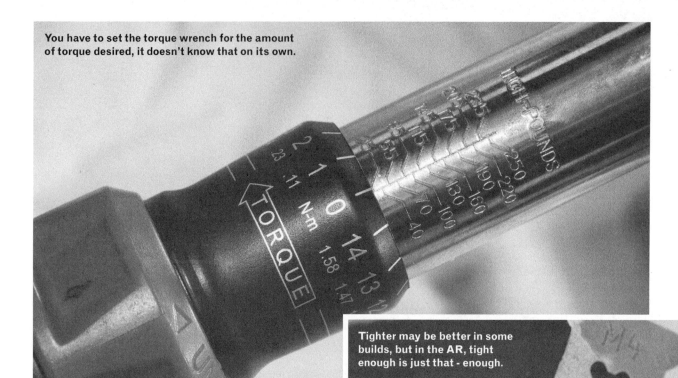

You have to set the torque wrench for the amount of torque desired, it doesn't know that on its own.

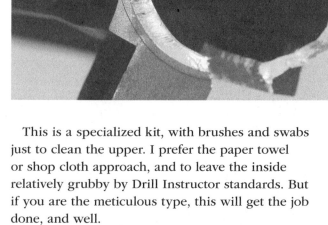

Tighter may be better in some builds, but in the AR, tight enough is just that - enough.

specified torque limits, and good engineers or mechanics use those limits and wrenches to tighten something down. The various screws on your AR have specified torque limits in their assembly, and the manufacturer does as good a job as they can to follow them. Do you need torque wrenches? Probably not. Most of the jobs of screwing things together on the AR can be done by hand, and by feel. But, if you can get them at a discount and will actually use them, go ahead. There is a certain satisfaction in dong things by the book, and torque wrenches can be fun.

SPECIALIZED TOOLKITS

You can get everything you'll ever need in one box. The option is attractive, but I have to warn you, it can get pricey. For information here, we pore through the encyclopedia of gunsmithing tools: Brownells.

This is not just everything you'll need to clean a rifle, it is everything you'll need to clean every AR rifle in your zip code. All the tools, plus multiples of the consumables, in a bench-top toolbox. At $150, the only surprise is that it does not require power.

This is a specialized kit, with brushes and swabs just to clean the upper. I prefer the paper towel or shop cloth approach, and to leave the inside relatively grubby by Drill Instructor standards. But if you are the meticulous type, this will get the job done, and well.

This is a field kit, with just what you'd need to keep rifles running in the field, assuming you can find a suitable surface, and perhaps a vise to hold things in. All in a heavy canvas case, for $260.

Let's be clear about what this kit is. It is every tool you'll ever need if you plan on spending a lifetime of wrenching on ARs. Well, except for the bench and vise, and room in which to do this. The standard kit has a list price of (sit down) $1,229.99. The Premium kit lists for $1,449.99. Yow.

Why?

Simple. This requires you disengage your brain, think like a bureaucrat, and ditch all common sense. What Brownells tells me is simple. When it comes time to buy tool kits, they find that it is easier on all concerned to simply have a single number than a list of tools.

The process goes something like this: the departmental armorer and the head of firearms training sit down with the procurement committee

Lots of tools is a good thing, unless you have to regularly move them.

and cough up one of the above numbers. The committee asks, "Do you need this to make sure your AR rifles are in good working order?" And in all good conscience, the two of them reply, "Yes."

If they, in a good-faith effort to save the department and the city some money, made up a list of just the tools they needed, they'd be putting in a two-page requisition, instead of a one-line requisition. The committee would look down the line, and as sure as the sun rises in the east, someone would ask,

"Do you really need item number seventeen? You list it at $125, can it be had cheaper?" Or, "That looks like something my brother-in-law uses at work, and he says they only cost half this."

And so on.

Rather than get themselves grilled over this and that, simply submitting a one-line, one-price item for everything they need saves the potential ulcers.

Is it something to lust after? You bet. Do you really need it? Mostly not, unless you, too, have to deal with a committee.

WHERE DOES IT END?

That, I can't answer. I've been working on AR-15s now for some twenty-five years. In that time, I have accumulated more tools than you really need to know about. My main toolbox (yes, I have several) is a Kennedy box, an all-steel chest with gliding drawers. With tools in it (and nothing but tools, parts are in separate boxes) it is all I can do to get it off the shelf and into the car to take to a class. Every time I wrestle it out for a class trip, I have visions of losing my balance, falling, and being crushed by my own tool-acquiring excess.

My friend Ned Christiansen arrives at class with a toolkit that would barely hold a complete socket wrench set and a good set of files. But, when something goes seriously wrong and we need to undertake the AR equivalent of open-heart surgery, my box trumps his.

Whatever you do, build a tool set for your needs, not the needs of your buddies, and not to satisfy their idea of status, manliness and perceived need. Unless you want to be the got-to guy at the gun club, when it comes to AR plumbing. In that case, knock yourself out.

NOT A BENCH TOOL

One tool that you won't have on your workbench or in a toolkit is a broken shell extractor. This little gizmo is shaped somewhat like a cartridge case. It has, however, a ratchet-like end to it. When you break a case in two, the front half stays in the chamber.

Sometimes, the round that attempts to chamber behind it will wedge onto (or into) it firmly enough that extracting the second round pulls the front half out. In that case, good, you solved the problem and learned a lesson. But if it doesn't, you have to get the broken half out, or your rifle will not work.

So, you lock the bolt back, drop the broken shell extractor into the chamber, and close the bolt. Then extract the extractor by working the bolt. You have obviously removed the magazine before doing this, or you will be chased off the range by someone beating you with a cleaning rod. The broken case extractor, with case half on it, comes out.

You disassemble the case extractor, remove the broken half, swear never to use brass as much as you're using this batch, and keep practicing.

If you are prone to ham-handed reloading, you'll

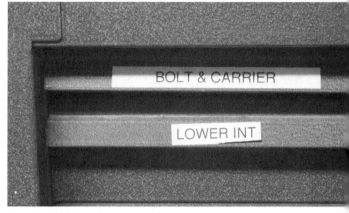

Label everything.

want to keep this in your pocket. If you have it somewhere on your person, or in your gear nearby, you'll be all set. In my Gunsite 223 class, I had brought along a couple of tubs of ammo I had reloaded. It had worked fine up to that point, and hadn't even reloaded it very many times. You guessed it, I had a couple of incidents of broken cases, but since I had the broken case extractor in my pocket, I was able to solve the problem reasonably quickly.

If you reload, or shoot reloaded ammo, you will sooner or later have a broken case. Have one of these handy.

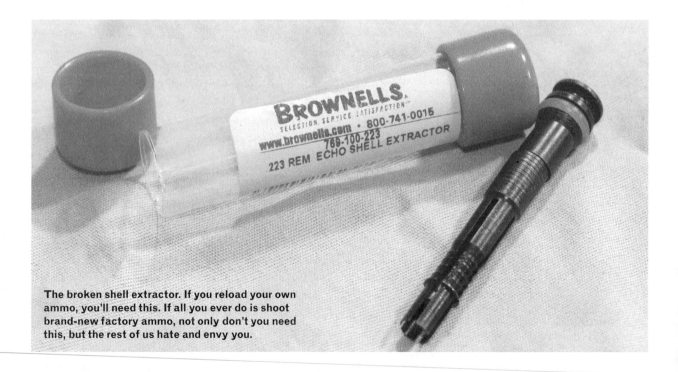

The broken shell extractor. If you reload your own ammo, you'll need this. If all you ever do is shoot brand-new factory ammo, not only don't you need this, but the rest of us hate and envy you.

CHAPTER 3
MIL SPEC

S MIL-SPEC WHAT I NEED?

A word you will hear relentlessly in the AR-verse is "mil-spec." This comes from "military specification" and basically means this is the exact same part/rifle/chocolate chip cookie issued to members of our armed forces.

You will be told, vigorously and repeatedly, that mil-spec is the best, and that if you spend a dime on anything that is not mil-spec, you have wasted not only your hard-earned cash, but time, effort and brain cells. Your choices in rifles, and the options on it, the barrel, stock, optics, handguards, etc. will all be analyzed, criticized and denigrated. If you have the temerity to mention on an internet forum that you own anything but a Colt, you'll be scourged. Or, even more vague, sloppy and amateurish, they will try to cast you out of the tribe for not owning a rifle made by a "Tier One" company. Never mind that they can't agree on who should, and shouldn't be in that tier one category, and they can't explain why. You didn't buy one, and you are to blame for your own misfortune.

You just went there to ask a question and get some info, and now you're the source of all evil in the world?

Here's the truth: the people who tell you that are wrong. Oh, they are earnest, and they may have your best interest at heart, but they are wrong.

First, here's how mil-spec works. The military will specify a part, mechanism, etc. in great detail. Let's take as an example a part as prosaic as the sling swivel on your rifle. It will have, as its specification list, details on the steel used, the vinyl coating used, dimensions and so on. The alloys must conform to the spec sheet, the thickness and type of vinyl coating, etc. The external and internal dimensions of the loop will be specified, along with the radii of the bends.

The specs will also detail what kind of testing must be done, on how many parts of a production run, and what a definition of "passing the test." The specs will also detail packaging, labeling, storage prep and on and on and on.

Once the parts have been spec'd, the contract winner is the one who gets the contract, and that is dependent upon this final detail: they can provide the parts at the lowest cost. Everyone who meets the specs "wins," and the low bidder gets the contract.

In military parlance, this is known as "the minimum becomes the max." If you get no credit for doing more than 20 pushups, you do your 20 and then save your energy for the next phase of the tests, sit-ups, pull ups, etc. On the next phase of the test, you do the minimum, pass, and move on again. There is no extra credit for a higher score or greater performance.

Someone whose parts are "mil-spec" has simply

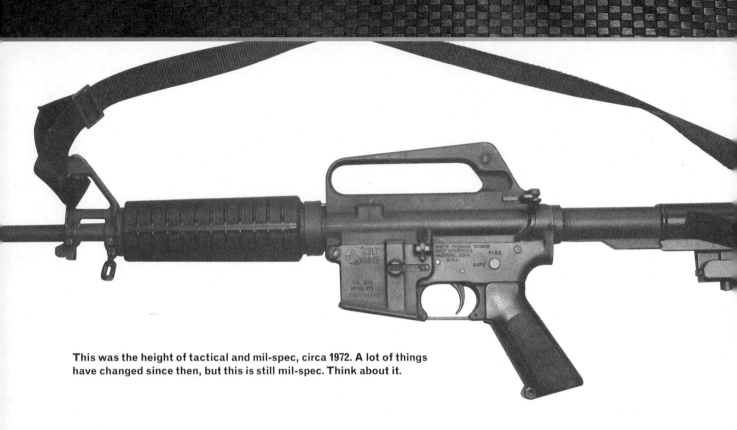

This was the height of tactical and mil-spec, circa 1972. A lot of things have changed since then, but this is still mil-spec. Think about it.

passed the minimum allowable performance. Now, in all fairness, the "minimum allowable" can be a high bar, indeed.

Let's delve into bolts. The bolt of the AR-15 is a small, highly-stressed part, and it dies a quick death under heavy use. The military deems them used up at 7,500 rounds. To be fair, those 7,500 rounds are expected to have a fairly high percentage of burst or select-fire, and be used in extreme conditions, to include heat, cold, dust, snow and mud. And, the Army (and the other services) would rather replace and pitch perfectly good bolts rather than have even a small percentage fail in combat. Your average (OK, not-so-average) shooter, who does not do full-auto mag dumps and maintains his gear properly, can reasonably expect a name-brand bolt to last through two or three barrels. I have a rifle on its third barrel, with the original bolt, and it is working fine. I'll be the first to agree with the engineering adage that "the plural of anecdote is not data," but experience tells me that there is no reason to junk a good bolt at 7,500 rounds just because the army does.

The bolt of the AR-15 was designed in the 1950s, and uses the best possible steel for the use,

machines and heat-treating abilities of the time. The steel is known as Carpenter 158. If you look for it in the SAE manual, you will look in vain. It is not a designation, such as 4140, where the alloying materials are listed. It is steel product number 158 from the Carpenter Steel Company, and they make it. Period. No one else makes Carpenter 158. Oh, it is entirely possible to make a steel every bit as good. You could even match the alloying metals and crystal size, etc. exactly. But it won't be Carpenter 158 unless it comes out of the Carpenter Steel Co mill.

You are, in effect, when you use a mil-spec bolt, installing a bolt in your rifle that is exactly period-correct with a 1957 Chevy Bel Air. Has the field of steel, alloying, heat-treating, metallurgy and design advanced since 1957? Yes. Will you get any of that progress in your mil-spec bolt? No.

However, there is no way to know for certain that a newer alloy, in a particular bolt, from a company other than Colt, is actually superior, and by how much, to a mil-spec bolt made of Carpenter 158. Well, there is, but it would cost you a metric buttload of money to uncover that information. You would have to buy enough of the other brand bolts to be a statistically-

There is nothing wrong with this stock, but it isn't an M4 stock, and someone on an internet forum will "ding" you for it. Tell him to get lost.

valid sample, and then test them to destruction. And, to be a proper engineer in this, and not a government hack, you'd have to do the same to a similar number of Colt bolt, at the same time. Different test, at a different time, under different circumstances, by someone else? The two can't be compared, regardless of what the test committee wants to hear.

So a lot of people, rather than risk getting something lesser, will insist on mil-spec. They will also tell you that you should too, either because they believe you would be well-served, or because they have to sooth their conscience over spending so much more money for a gold-leaf-wrapped bolt.

Now, in all fairness, it used to be that non-mil-spec parts were junk. I was building guns and working as a gunsmith back in the 1980s when the first wave of "assault weapon" bans were floated.

We saw a lot of work-around parts, parts that the company making them couldn't make the real way, so they made them the way they could.

We saw charging handles made of two pieces, welded (and not very well) together. Lower receivers machined from billet, and obviously so. All manner of accessory parts made of what appeared to be recycled gum wrappers and salvaged soft-drink cans. Things got so bad that I was fixing ARs on a regular basis, and got to be very quick with a set of headspace gauges and chambering reamer.

That was then, and this is now. Now, no-one makes really bad stuff and stays in business for long.

So, how do you get good gear, not break the bank, and avoid being savaged by the "mil-spec mafia"? The last part is simple: you can't. If you

By some accounts, everything on this rifle is "wrong" and the owner ought to be ashamed. On the contrary, he is proud of it, and does very well with it.

buy mil-spec, they love you; you are one of the gang. If you don't, they either want to save your soul or berate you for not buying mil-spec. To engage in the discussion is a fool's quest.

Now, why would you not want to buy mil-spec? The answer is simple, and it isn't to save money; it is to buy a better part.

Back to the mil-spec. Once it is graven in stone, it is fixed. No, you don't understand, it is fixed forever. The Carpenter Steel Co. could make a better steel, but they won't, not for government bolts, because the government won't buy it. The spec is C-158, and that's what people buy. If you bought a better steel, you might be able to get a pass on it from the government. As long as it complied with all the tests and specifications detailed in the mil-spec (except, obviously, for the one that says "Carpenter 158") you could probably get them to accept it as a viable substitute.

But they won't pay a dime more for it. So, you're in the position of trying to be the lowest bidder, by using a better steel? And can you make that steel for less than C-158? You see the box the manufacturers are in.

Better alloys, better coatings, better heat-treatments, all have been developed since 1957. And the government, in the form of the Army, will have none of them.

Which leads me to Sweeney's Law of Good Enough Gear: "If your gear is good enough to improve your skills, to let you learn, to serve you in the task you ask of it, then it is good enough. More money spent is wasted."

Two examples: barrel steel and optics. The steel used in mil-spec barrels is an alloy known as 4150. It is an alloy of chromium and molybdenum, with a pinch of manganese, and it contains all of one-half of a percent of carbon. (That's the "5" in the

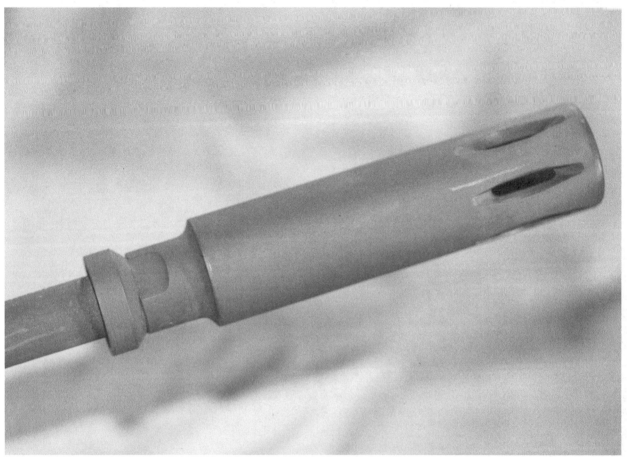

A lot of things used to be mil-spec, and probably haven't been dropped from the rolls. The XM-177 flash hider, for example, is probably still listed with a National Stock Number.

4150.) Ordnance steel is also known as 4140 steel. It has "only" four-tenths of a percent of carbon in it. And worse, the variances can be smaller. You see, 4150 is allowed a "drift" or variance of carbon, from 0.48 to 0.53 percent carbon.

4140 is allowed a drift of 0.38 to 0.43. The highest-carbon batch of 4140 is almost as carboned up as the lowest-allowed batch of 4150 has.

The extra smidge of carbon makes the 4150 a bit tougher, a bit more abrasion and heat-stress resistant. The Army insists on it because they don't care about the cost, and they'd rather that soldier on the ridgeline has another couple of magazines left in his barrels useful life while dealing with human-wave assaults.

Should you care? The mil-spec mavens will cast aspersions on your manhood if you lower yourself to buying a barrel made of 4140. But, if you find

it accurate, reliable and as durable as your ammo-buying ability can withstand, who cares what they think? The barrel passes the "good enough" test.

Optics are worse, because the price difference is greater. A 4150 barrel might only cost you $50 more than a 4140 barrel. But optics can differ by an order of magnitude. It is easy to spend $120 or $1200 on optics. If you buy the $1200 scope, and find it doesn't work for you, you can sell it. Good luck getting much more than $800. So, you took a $400 bite, to learn something.

Had you bought the $120 scope, if you find it doesn't work for you (or doesn't work at all) you're out $120. If it works, you're good to go. If it breaks, you now know you need something more durable. In short, you learned a lot more for your $120 than you would have for the $400 you could have spent.

Good enough.

The engineering and design of rifles have come a long way since the **AR** was designed in the 1950s, but many aspects of the design were frozen in mil-spec in the late 1960s.

God bless 'em, they work hard. But, is a rifle meant for soldiers who will be trained on it for a day a year, the best that you can do? Mil-spec has limits.

Having gone through all that, I'll now apparently contradict myself; you don't have to buy mil-spec, but in many cases you should. If the price between a no-name contractor and an in-the-wrapper Colt is a few bucks, don't be cheap. Ditto springs, pins, etc. The Colt-logo'd M4 stock slider? If you really have to have an as-close-as-you-can-get M4 clone, then get the Colt. Otherwise, there are a lot of stocks that are more comfortable and work just as well.

Buy mil-spec knowingly, and when you will get something for the extra money that is worth it to you.

Oh, and one last problem to buying only mil-spec: you can't. Oh, there are some parts that meet the specification, but the full definition of "mil-spec" is meeting all the specifications, and bought by the government. Yes, your bolt is the same as a USGI bolt, but while it meets mil-spec, it isn't mil-spec, unless you stole it from the government. And, an M4 is a select-fire rifle, so your semi-auto clone is as close as it gets, if from Colt, but isn't completely mil-spec. So the guys who insist you

A mil-spec rifle is meant to be fed mil-spec ammo, and only mil-spec ammo. If that describes your ammunition supply situation, then go for it. The rest of us may be looking for greater versatility.

Do you need a light? Light is good, but it has drawbacks. And you should test and de-bug your rifle before you put a light or anything else on it.

buy mil-spec are actually telling you to buy as close to mil-spec as you can. But they probably don't realize it.

BARRELS AND MIL-SPEC

If you listen to the mil-spec mavens, you will only ever own a rifle with a barrel that has a chrome lining, and has a twist to the rifling of one turn in seven inches. This would be a shame, as there are a lot of barrels out there that would serve you well (and maybe even for less money).

So, what factors should we look at in barrels, and what should you have?

A rifled barrel spins a bullet, and the gyroscopic force created keeps the bullet stable. The spin rate needed depends on the length of the bullet, not its weight, but weight is the measure that all boxes of bullets will have on them, so we have to approach it from that direction. On the assumption that the vast majority of you will have rifles chambered in .223/5.56, let's discuss it from that perspective.

THREE BULLET LENGTHS

The three lengths to consider are in the following groups:
- from fifty grains in weight or less,
- fifty grains to 63-64 grains, and
- those over 64.

The under-fifty crowd are the "varmint" bullets. Used to depopulate open areas of various members of the rodentia family, they are meant to be very accurate, and very fragile. As an example, a 45 grain .224" bullet is intended to be driven at something over 3,500 fps, and while doing so to shoot sub-MOA. After all, prairie dogs are not that big, and have to be shot (generally speaking) out past two hundred yards. So, you want a fast, accurate bullet, that when it strikes a one-pound 'dog, essentially explodes.

Bullets above fifty grains include various equally-accurate varmint bullets, match-accuracy bullets, and – the basis of practice, much competition, and training – the full metal jacket 55 grain boat-tail bullet. At the upper end of this

Nothing, absolutely nothing on this rifle is mil-spec, it all deviates (in most instances for the better) from the specs, and even with a no-magnification red dot sight, I can easily drop the 300 meter pop-ups.

group are stubby (relatively speaking) 63 and 64 grain softpoints.

Above that, the bullets get long. Currently, the darling of the combat-oriented shooting fraternity are 75 and 77 grain bullets – long, pointed, accurate and effective on various members of the felon family.

As an aside, these are all copper or brass jacketed bullets with lead cores. A relatively new type of bullet on the scene is the all-copper bullet, typically with a hollowpoint. They expand reliably and consistently, they shoot accurately, and being all-copper, they are longer than their counterparts of the same weight in lead-core versions.

There is an interesting, in-between bullet, the 68 grain match bullet. It used to be the heavyweight in the .223/5.56 universe, but hasn't been for some years now. It is too long to be stable in a 1/12 barrel. It lacks the ballistic coefficient of the 75-77 grain bullets. The niche it has is for long-range (or as long as you can manage) accuracy in 1/9 barrels. And that leads us to the barrels themselves.

THREE TWIST RATES

The original twist rate for the 5.56, when the AR-15 was new, was one turn in 14 inches. This proved to be a bit too slow a twist rate. The bullet was marginally stable, and when the bores wore, or the air become denser (think Arctic deployments) or ballistically better bullets of 55 grains were used (longer and pointier), the bullets lost stability and accuracy decreased. So, the twist rate was "sped up" to 1/12. For a long time, that was the twist rate.

Then, the A2s came along. The search for a more-effective bullet, one with a heavier weight, had been going on for some time before the mid-1980s when the A2 was adopted. The major effort had used, as a twist rate fast enough to stabilize any bullet tested, barrels with one turn in seven inches. Since the work had already been done, and the rifles so-tested had been accurate, the new NATO twist rate became, almost by default, 1/7. This also allowed for loadings of no use to us non-military shooters, such as the M856 tracer round,

The AR can be built in a number of different calibers. This one is in 5.45X39, a currently inexpensive imported ammo choice. But, the ammo is corrosive, and it takes a lot of shooting to justify the conversion costs (barrel, bolt, magazines).

which in a 1/7 barrel remained stable for the full duration of the tracer burn, 700+ meters.

So we had faster-twist barrels.

Except, not everyone wanted 1/7 barrels. So the AR-verse soon became a two-tier environment, one where the military barrels had twists of 1/7 and the rest had twists of 1/9. For a long time this wasn't a problem, as you really didn't have a lot of choices when it came to .223/5.56 ammunition. If you shot "surplus" ammo, you were shooting 55 grain fmj (full metal jacket) because that was what there was. The new ammo for the A2s, M855, was 62 grains in weight, had a ten-grain steel penetrator inside the jacket, and also had a less than stellar reputation for accuracy.

Plus, it was all being made for the military, and thus hard to find.

The other choice was to pick from various hollow points, mostly varmint bullets.

The Global War on Terror changed that. Long story short, the military suddenly found they had a need for a round that could shoot accurately, farther than the issue M855. The result was basically the NRA High Power loading that match

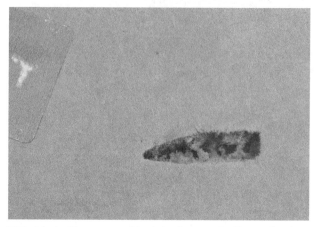

This is what happens, at twenty-five yards, if you shoot an M885 through a rifle with a 1/12 twist. Sideways does not improve accuracy.

shooters had been using for some time: a 75 or 77 grain match bullet, at as full a velocity as could be generated in the 5.56 case. Those bullets needed the 1/7 twist.

If the secret-squirrel groups are using something, then there are a lot of people who have to have it. Suddenly, everyone wanted the new loading,

Piston guns are the coming thing. Or so their advocates say. We'll have to see if they pan out, and what system or systems prevail, but if you can afford a non-standard AR, go ahead and get one.

known as the Mk 262, or Mk 262 MOD 1.

So we have a choice of twist rates, and we have a choice of ammunitions. What happens if we try them all?

1/12 Twist

This will shoot the varmint bullets and the fifties well, in some instances very well. You can get very small groups with a 1/12 barrel and the varmint bullets, fifty and 52 grain match, and fifty-five fmjs. None of these will be long-range loads. The short-for-caliber bullets do not have impressive ballistic coefficients (a measure of the bullets ability to overcome the effects of the air drag on it as it travels downrange) and thus shed speed quickly. But, to 300 yards or so they can still be speedy, and very accurate.

Some 1/12 barrels will shoot the 63-64 grain stubby bullets well. I had a 1/12 military barrel that shot Winchester 63 grain softpoints brilliantly. It shot sub-MOA, until the bore wore out and that was that.

The M855 load, with its ten grain steel penetrator, is longer than the 63-645 grain softpoints, and thus is not stable in a 1/12 barrel. Even at twenty-five yards you'll see "keyholes," the term for bullets that appear to be going sideways through the target. They aren't, really, they are yawing. That is, the bullet is still going point-on (more or less) but the base is circling around the lie of travel, trying to get out in front of the point. No 1/12 barrel will shoot the M855 other than to yaw. The 68 grain match bullet is even worse than the 62 grain M855.

The 75-77 grain bullets that are currently en vogue are utterly hopeless out of a 1/12 barrel. They don't even pretend to yaw, they are inaccurate due to a complete lack of stability.

The all-copper bullets also lose stability, but in their case they become too long if heavier than 52-55 grains.

1/9 Twist

The compromise twist, 1/9 is still slow enough to treat varmint bullets kindly. It will shoot up to the accuracy potential of the bullets from the varmints, up to and including the 63-64 grain softpoints. It will shoot the 68 grain match bullets, and with better ballistic coefficient, shoot them accurately to longer distances than any of the other bullets you can use in a 1/9 barrel. If that matters.

1/9 twist barrels are in many instances also good enough to shoot the 75-77 grain bullets well. I've had some rifles with 1/9 twist shoot them well, and others shoot them with average accuracy. And by "average" I mean 1.5 to 2.0 MOA, which is the average accuracy of most AR rifles and carbines.

If you spend too much time on the internet, you'll come to believe that it is an American birthright to own an AR that delivers sub-MOA (under one-inch groups at 100 yards) with any ammunition pulled off the shelf at random. Not true. Most rifles won't do that, most shooters can't do that, and the government doesn't expect that.

However, the whole point of the Mk 262 load is pinpoint accuracy, Out of the right rifle it will deliver sub-MOA. If the ammo can, and the rifles twist rate is such (1/9, here) that the rifle can't, then why feed that rifle expensive ammo it will shoot below expectations? So, rifles with 1/9 twists, that shoot 75-77 grain bullets accurately, are an interesting curiosity, but not much more.

The faster twist permits the use of all-copper bullets of weights over 55 grains, but not a lot over. Important variables include the length of the medium-weight copper bullet, and how well-made the 1/9 twist barrel is. Again, such ammunition is expensive, so why run expensive ammunition down a barrel in which it will be only average accurate?

1/7 Twist

Here, things can get interesting. The varmint bullets are off the table. The problem is not that the bullets are over-stable, being spun so fast for their short length. The problem is that they are lightly-constructed. A forty-five grain bullet, pushed at the full speed a .223/5.56 case can push it, gets spun so fast it simply breaks apart in flight. If you shoot such through a 1/7 barrel, you'll see a puff of gray dust out past fifty or seventy-five yards. That was your bullet, saying "bu-bye."

The DoD is concerned with reliable function in grubby environments. You can baby your rifle, but the guys on this chopper will have dusty rifles before they fire their first shot.

What Twist, Then?

What twist rate should you use, then? That depends on what you want to do with your AR, and how much you expect to spend. If you will only ever shoot varmints with your AR, you can use a 1/12 barrel. Of course, a 1/9 will be less expensive. All other things being equal, the volume of production of 1/9 barrels, compared to 1/12, will make them less expensive. So a varmint hunter who wants maximum flexibility could rightfully consider a 1/9 twist barrel.

If you will be doing long-range shooting, then you must have the 1/7.

CHROME PLATING

The military wants a chrome-lined chamber and bore. After the experience in Vietnam, that is understandable. However, there is no such thing as a free lunch. To make a barrel chrome-lined, the barrel maker has to undertake all the steps to make a barrel, and then, before it has a chance to be anything other than a brand-new barrel, plate the bore with chrome. This is not the chrome like the bumper on a car; it is a very hard and tough plating. It is also not very thick. Still, the barrel

Once you get up a small amount in weight, or increase jacket thickness even a little bit, the bullets work fine. The chief samples here are the various 52 grain match bullets. Match bullets, not varmint bullets, as the bullet makers make both in that weight. The 555 fmj shoots very well, indeed.

You'll hear from a lot of people that a 1/7 barrel won't shoot light bullets well. The main objection is that the bullets are "over-stabilized." Maybe, on paper. And on paper, bumblebees can't fly. I have yet to see a good-quality 1/7 barrel that would not shoot 55 grain fmjs well.

The heavier weight bullets are all normal for the 1/7 twist. The 68 grain bullets will shoot very well. But since they do not have the ballistic coefficient of the 75-77 grain bullets, why bother? If you wanted to test the limits of stability you'd have to start going up into the 80s, and some High Power shooters do that. However, they can't load the rounds short enough to feed through their magazines. They end up making speciality, single-shot cartridges that have to be fed into the chamber one at a time. Not a problem for them, as they would be using such loads at 600 yards, where it is common and customary to shoot singly.

While this bolt has been magnetic particle inspected, it still isn't mil-spec. It comes as close as you can, but to truly be mil-spec, it has to have been accepted by the government. Since this one is mine, it clearly hasn't ever been in government custody.

maker has to take that thickness into consideration when reaming and rifling the bore. Plus, the chrome plating will not be evenly thick, or applied in perfect smoothness, along the length of the bore.

As a result, a barrel with a chrome-plated bore will not have the accuracy potential of a non-chromed bore. For most applications this does not matter. The High Power crowd does not use chromed bores, but they are after those last few points that equipment will give them. And, they do not have to worry about bores rusting, as they will always have the time to scrub a barrel clean and oil it before the next match.

The rest of us to do not have accuracy requirements so precise that the accuracy loss matters.

Chrome does protect the bore, but since very little of the ammunition you'll get to shoot is corrosive, it doesn't matter much.

If you can get chrome plating without much of an up-charge, do so. If it matters to you, then get it, but stop complaining about the cost. And if you have to have it, you have to get a barrel that has it up front, as un-plated barrels cannot be plated afterwards. They have to be planned to be plated, and then plated at the factory the day they were made, or not at all.

223 OR 5.56?

There are those who will tell you it doesn't matter. They are wrong. There is a difference, and that difference is pretty much 200 feet per second, and the extra chamber pressure it takes to generate the extra velocity. In this instance, the mil-spec guys are correct; mil-spec is good, and you should not settle for something less unless it is precisely what you wanted.

The mechanical difference is not in the headspace, but the leade (pronounced "leed").

Headspace is the room between the face of the bolt, and the chamber shoulder where the cartridge case stops as it bangs forward during feeding. Headspace is a closely controlled dimension, and as long as your chamber is cut within the 0.006" difference between Go and No-Go, your headspace is OK. Too little, and things

can get jammed shut. Too much, and your cases will stretch on firing. If your situation is such that you will never see the brass again, you may not have a problem, at least not until/unless the gap is so large that cases separate on the sole firing.

How does all this happen? Remember, the cartridge case experiences high pressures when fired. A case has to be small enough to fit smoothly into the chamber. That means there is a small gap. When the round is fired, the 50-55-60,000 PSI ignition expands the case tight to the chamber walls. It also blows the shoulder forward. The shoulder going forward means the case stretches, and the stretch has to come from someplace. That place is, depending on the chamber and brass, somewhere along the case body from near the extractor rim up to about halfway.

The natural springiness of the brass then causes it to spring back from the full pressure, and it can then be extracted and ejected.

If you reload the case, you have to resize it to make it a smooth slip-fit. You also have to bump the shoulder back so it won't bottom out on the chamber shoulder before the bolt can close.

Another firing, and another cycle of expansion, shrinkage, and then re-sizing. Excessive headspace simply means each case expands more, stretches more, and is squeezed back more, on each firing.

To the reloader, excess headspace is a bad thing, as it leads to very short case life. An idea of this: if your rifle has proper headspace and you load reasonable pressures, cases can last ten loadings or more. If you have excessive headsdpace, the stretch and then set-back on sizing and loading can cause cases to break in half in two or three loadings.

The leade is the portion of the chamber, forward of the recess cut for the case neck, that acts as a funnel to guide the bullet into the rifling. The rifling does not start immediately after the case neck. How far that gap is, is the basis for .223 or 5.56. The 5.56 is loaded to higher pressures than the .223, and in order to control those pressures, the leade is longer, and the ramp created by the onset of the rifling is shallower, allowing the bullet to travel forward free longer, and jam into the rifling less abruptly.

What happens if we feed .223 ammo to a .223-leade rifle? Nothing untoward. The bullet and powder charge are compatible with the leade, and we see a relatively sedate event, with the bullet leaving the muzzle as expected. Ditto a 5.56 cartridge in a 5.56 chamber. OK, a .223 cartridge in a 5.56 leade? There, we have a slight dimunition of chamber pressure. The bullet leaves the case neck and experiences a longer than expected trip to the origins of the rifling, and that is not something to increase pressure.

That leaves us with a 5.56 cartridge in a .223 chamber. Bad news. The bullet leaves the case neck, and instead of the longer trip, and gentler rifling origins, it abruptly slams into step rifling, sooner than planned. The already higher-than-expected chamber pressure spikes even more.

OK, time for some numbers. A .223 Remington runs at a maximum average pressure of 50,000PSI. The 5.56, a MAP of 55,000. Put a 5.56 in a

.223-leade pressure test barrel and measure the pressure, and what do you get? (This has been done, it's not speculation.) A MAP of 74,000 and a high recording of over 76,000 PSI. Ouch. Each rifle made in America is proof-tested at the factory before it leaves. A Proof Load is generally 130% pressure of the cartridge normal. So, a rifle chambered in.223, a cartridge with a MAP of 50,000 PSI, has a Proof Load fired in it that generates 66,000 PSI. If the rifle does not break, or is otherwise not damaged, it gets shipped. Fire a 5.56 in it, and it experiences more than a Proof Load every time. Double-ouch.

So, what to do? Art this point, the usual response is to ask, "Is my headspace .223 or 5.56?" The problem is, it isn't a matter of headspace. That's a different, albeit related, subject, and one we'll cover in just a bit. No, you need to find out what the leade is on your barrel. For that, you need one of two things: a fistful of Cerrosafe, or a .223/556? Gage. Cerrosafe is a special alloy, a metal that has a low melting point, but one that cools to hard enough to handle lump, and does not stick to other metals when it cools.

To use it, you scrub your barrel clean, stick a cleaning patch on the end of a rood, and insert it from the muzzle end until the patch is a couple of inches in front of the chamber. Pour the melted Cerrosafe into the chamber until the chamber is half-full, then let the Cerrosafe cool. Once cool, you push it backwards out of the chamber with the cleaning rod and patch combo, and inspect. It will be pretty clear if the rifling begins directly in front of the chamber, or it if has a larger freebore.

The advantages are several. You get an accurate record of your chamber, neck and leade. You can measure (within the limits of your measuring tools, eyesight and patience) exactly how much freebore you have, the angle of the rifling onset, neck and throat diameters, and so-on.

However, the Cerrosafe approach is not without its problems. You have to find a way to pour just the right amount of Cerrosafe into the chamber. You have to pour it past the barrel extension locking lugs. And if you slip, you have Cerrosafe cooling all over the locking lugs, inside the upper receiver, and perhaps even the gas tube.

The 223/556? Gage is simple. It is a hardened

You can compare the length of leades, side-by-side here.

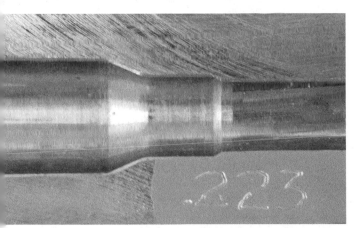

Notice how short the leade is on .223. It barely extends to the front edge of the second "2" in "223"

The leade on the 5.56 chamber extends to the middle of the "N" in Nato.

The modified leade, from the M-guns reamer, extends to the middle of the "E" in NEMRT. This lowers pressure.

steel gauge precision-ground to just under the maximum dimensions of a 5.56 leade. Available from M-guns (www.mguns.com) it is made by a friend of mine, Ned Christiansen. However, it is such a useful tool, and it works so well, I'd recommend it even if I didn't know who Ned was. Using it is simple; you screw the gauge plug onto its rod (or any other rod) and poke it into a clean chamber. If the gauge does not stick, if it turns easily and falls out of its own weight when you turn the receiver back-end down, then the leade is 5.56. If it sticks, if it is hard or impossible to turn, and if it won't fall out of its own weight, you have a .223 leade, and the gauge is wedged in there. Pull it out, and consider your next move.

You have three options if you have a barrel with a .223 leade.

One, you could leave it alone and be careful to only ever shoot .223-rated ammunition through it. The problem with this is, you may find a deal on 5.56-rated ammo. Or, it may be all you can find.

Two, you could leave it alone, and just live with the consequences of shooting occasional 5.56 ammo through your rifle. The problem here is that this is hazardous.

The 5.56 ammo, at the higher pressures, can "pop" primers. That is, it can expand the case enough that the primer falls free. It will, most of the time, fall out of the rifle with the case. This leads to cases that are over-expanded, and thus short service-life candidates for reloading. It also means the occasional primer will stay in the receiver, and will eventually rattle around until it finds some way to cause mischief.

Usually it wedges someplace that causes the rifle to stop working. However, one instance that I had to deal with was at a law enforcement class. The officer had fired a string, and at the end was trying to push his selector to Safe. Luckily for him, one of the instructors happened to be watching him and saw that the officer's finger was off the trigger, because the rifle fired a three-shot burst into the ground and then stopped working entirely.

The popped primer had disassembled itself, and the anvil of the primer had wedged under the trigger, in just the right place to cause the disconnector to mis-time to the hammer, at least for three shots.

The third option is to fix the leade. Sending the barrel back to the manufacturer probably won't get you any satisfaction. Unfortunately, most rifle makers do not make barrels, they buy them. And whoever supplies their barrels is not going to have a secret stash of 5.56 barrels from which they can replace your .223.

No, you're going to have to fix it. Well, along with the 223/556? Gage, Ned also makes a 5.565 reamer. His reamer is specially designed to not cut the shoulder. That way you can't increase the headspace, no matter how much you try. You could, theoretically, use a 5.56 chambering reamer to increase the leade, but it takes a delicate touch to cut the leade, stop when the reamer makes contact with the chamber shoulder, and not increase headspace.

Ned's reamer is made of a special tool-steel and given an extra heat-treat process, so it will cut through the hard chrome in your bore. Yep, that's right, it cuts the hard chrome in the leade. There's no way around it, if you want to go from .223 to 5.56, you have to cut, and that means the chrome. Now, before you recoil in horror, guess where the

chrome wears off first, just from shooting. Yes again, the leade. If you have put a few hundred rounds through your bore in the process of discovering that you have a .223 chamber, you've probably already shot some of the hard chrome off anyway.

"But, my bore will rust." Perhaps. If you clean it, it won't, and if you shoot it on a regular basis, it won't either. And, if you have shot it and the hard chrome has any wear on it, it will rust even if you don't ream the leade. Hard chrome slows down rust, it doesn't prevent it entirely.

Now, there are limits for the 5.56 reamer. Despite its special heat-treat (titanium nitro-carbide, in case you were curious), the 5.56 reamer is not going to cut a Melonite-treated barrel. In fact, that's pretty much the one thing that will dull the reamer, short of doing an entire police department's inventory of barrels. How can you tell if a barrel has been melonite-treated? Read the manufacturers specs. If they did it, they'll be proud to tell you.

Reaming is easy. Scrub the chamber and bore. Lube the reamer and insert, turning once it makes contact. Continue turning clockwise (do not

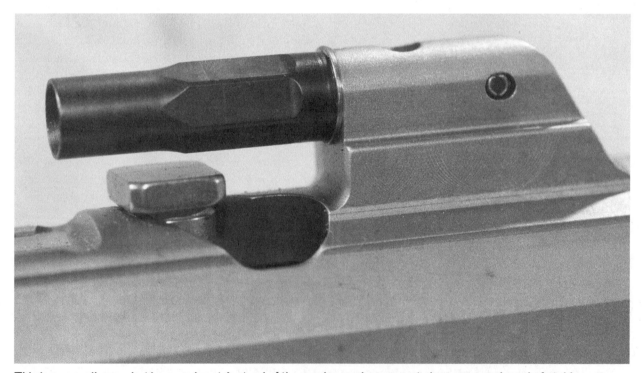

This is a non mil-spec, but improved part. Instead of the regular gas key, prone to looseness and need of staking, we have an integral key. And the wear part can be easily swapped, and never come loose. Thank you, LWRCI.

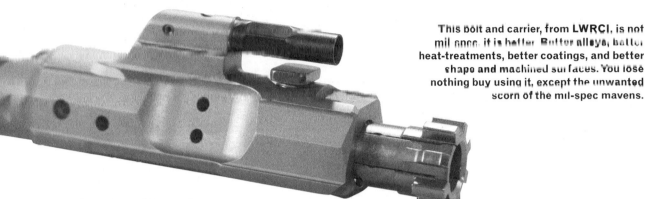

This bolt and carrier, from LWRCI, is not mil-spec, it is better. Better alloys, better heat-treatments, better coatings, and better shape and machined surfaces. You lose nothing buy using it, except the unwanted scorn of the mil-spec mavens.

reverse, there is nothing to be gained by reversing except dulling the reamer), until you can feel the reamer has stopped cutting and is simply riding on the surface. Lift out as you turn. Clean the reamer. Clean the chamber and bore. Enjoy your new 5.56 leade.

Do you have to do this? No, not really. There are lots of shooters who are blasting ammo through ARs with .223-leade barrels, and they generally don't have problems. They also don't shoot much, and they probably shrug off the occasional malfunction that they experience. Now, the mil-spec mavens will tell you that there is an easier solution to this problem: buy a rifle that only has a 5.56 leade. As in, Colt, and one of those on a short list of real-deal, honest-to-god, I'll tell you who's on the list, rifle makers who make 5.56 leade barrels. Or, replace that "tomato stake" of a barrel with a good one. Well, the problem with either is simple: expense. Yes, you can make sure you have a 556 leade barrel, but you'll pay more than the cost of the 556 reamer for it.

So, if you occasionally find your brass has lost a primer, or you otherwise suspect you have a 223 leade, find a gunsmith who can check, and ream if need be, to 556. Or buy the 223/556? Gage, the 556 reamer, and be the guy at the gun club who can check and ream.

MIL-SPEC AND PROGRESS

Let's take a step to the side for a moment and look at this from another angle. Consider the 1911. (Oh, stop whining. You knew this was going to happen, too.) The zenith of the 1911, the 1911A1, came about in 1926. As a WWII sample, the serious martial 1911 collector wants to have an "unmolested" specimen of the 1911A1, as made in one of the arsenals in the period 1941 to 1945. If you follow the mil-spec model exactly, as many would have you do, then the "perfect" 1911A1 would be a WWI rack-grade pistol. Not an Ed Brown, a Bill Wilson, a Les Baer, or a custom-built by a one-man-shop master.

All the progress we have made since then, in IPSC competition, in learning how to build 1911s that are both accurate and reliable (not to mention exquisite in appearance) is for naught, because they aren't mil-spec. Nope, the 1911A1 residing in a rack, in 1946, in its parkerized glory is better, because it is mil-spec.

The comparison is not right on the AR situation, but it does illustrate something: mil-specs don't account for progress.

Oh, some of the marksmanship teams would take advantage of progress, such as the USMC adopting Bar-sto barrels for competition. But as an "improve the pistol" process, well, there wasn't one. And so it is with the AR-15, in all its iterations. The Army and DoD have floated program after program to "improve" and to "replace" the M16/M4, but all have foundered. This is, in part, because no-one can agree on just what its replacement should be. (And that, in part, is due to the people in charge not knowing squat about small arms.)

Such changes that have been made – rails, free-floated barrels, improved ammunition – have all come from civilian competition.

You'd think someone in charge would have the good grace to thank us.

CHAPTER 4
FIELD STRIP

THIS IS HOW you get your rifle apart enough to inspect it or do some cleaning. You'll need your rifle, some basic cleaning equipment and materials as outlined previously, and a couple of tools.

You'll need a chamber brush, on a T-handle, lubricant, cleaning cloths or paper towels, and if your rifle is a tight fit, something to press the first pivot pin with. Useful additions would be a small knife or sharp-pointed awl, and a cleaning brush such as the one that comes in every USGI kit and many commercial kits.

UNLOAD

Yes, I know it is obvious, and you are told this over and over, but every year enough people have accidents that we should reinforce proper habits every chance we get.

In some circles, such "accidents" are classified as ND, negligent discharges. In those circles, the punishment can be as small as a fine/cost of repairs and a period of social ostracism. Or it can be more. When Gunsite began operations, safety was stressed. Still, tired students would go back to their hotel rooms and every few years have an AD/ND in quarters. That is, the student would have

fired fire off a round, not intending it to be fired, in the hotel room. This happened to one of the guys in my class at Gunsite. (Jeff Cooper was still teaching then, and Bart had to find "the Colonel" when we arrived that morning at Gunsite, and 'fess up. Of course the Colonel already knew about it, and would have tossed him if Bart hadn't said something. Times were different then.) I'm sure it happened (and happens) in other schools, too. Gunsite finally got so tired of it that they instituted a simple policy, an AD in quarters meant your class was over. You would be sent packing, no refund, no excuses. That is, in effect, a $2,000+ fine (class, travel, etc.) for an "oops." To the amazement of no-one, the incidence of AD/NDs went down to nothing.

In extreme circumstances it could mean regulatory or criminal punishments. And this doesn't begin to account for the consequences of where that bullet lands. Don't take this lightly. Unload and double-check.

Push the safety/selector to "Safe." Press the magazine button and remove the magazine, if any. Set it aside. Grasp the charging handle and pull it fully to the rear. Look to see if a cartridge comes out. With your other hand, press the bottom of the bolt hold-open, to lever it up into the path of the bolt. Ease the bolt forward until it stops, and then turn the rifle so you can look into the chamber.

Here you can see the differences between the standard takedown, and the Colt two-screw front takedown pin.

(Still keep it pointed in a safe and socially-acceptable direction, however.)

Once you have looked into the chamber, and perhaps even poked something in there to make sure it is empty (a dark steel case can pass a quick visual inspection as an "empty" chamber), ease the bolt forward.

Press the rear pivot pin out to the right. If it is very tight, or sticks, resist the urge to hammer it with something. I've seen lower receivers with the pin detent wall busted out from over-enthusiastic pin-whacking.

Grasp the charging handle and pull it to the rear enough to unlock the bolt, and move the carrier far enough back that you can grab hold of it. About two inches should do.

Now grab the carrier and pull it to the rear and out of the upper receiver. Set it down.

Pull the charging handle to the rear until it stops, then move it downward, toward the lower receiver. This will remove it from the "T" slot it

rides in, and you can now set it aside also.

Put the rifle down on its right side, and press the front pivot pin. When it stops, flip the rifle over and pull the front pin up until it stops. You can now separate the two receivers, upper and lower.

If you have a sling on it, and it can be readily removed, do so. There is not much more of a hassle than trying to clean a rifle with the sling attached, especially if it is also still attached to the other half of the rifle.

At this point, you have a decision to make. You can proceed to disassemble the bolt/carrier, you can yank the buffer weight and spring out of the receiver extension, or you can just leave the parts as they are, for the next step.

If you are disassembling for cleaning, more stripping would be warranted. If you are going to install or remove some extra gear or make a modification, you may or may not need to do more disassembly, depending on just what you're going to do.

LEVELS OF "CLEAN"

Let's work on the lower first, in part because there is less crud in there (or at least, a lower potential for crud) and also it gives us a chance to talk about the three levels of clean: clean enough to work, clean enough to be clean, clean enough to pass inspection.

Clean enough to work is simple: is there so much crud, gunk, carbon and debris inside your rifle that it won't work? Then it isn't clean enough to work. You'll have to clean it enough to get it working again, and lube it too. If you are in a class, or in a "hot" situation, and you need your rifle up and working again, this could be as simple as a chamber brush to scrub the chamber, some more lube, and a fresh supply of loaded magazines.

Clean enough to be clean is more involved. It is a basic level of not-dirty, such that you can pick up your rifle with clean hands, look it over, inspect it, and not have to wash your hands afterwards. A rifle that isn't clean enough to be clean could fail this from being caked with carbon, caked with mud, or otherwise clean but oozing oil from every gap. The carbon and mud is obvious, but a rifle that was racked with an extra dollop of 10W40 added before getting stowed isn't really "clean."

However, clean enough to pass inspection is going too far the other way. In order to pass a white glove inspection, a rifle has to not only have every trace of carbon scrubbed off, it also has to be degreased. Otherwise, it will soil a glove. That's too clean.

In the field, in action, overlooking a prairie dog town, you need clean enough to work. Once home, you need it clean enough to be clean. The only time you need it clean enough to pass inspection is when there's an inspection. And that is also when the bosses doing the inspecting don't know what "clean enough to be clean" is all about.

LOWER RECEIVER: BUFFER AND SPRING

If you have to/want to remove the buffer and spring, take the tip of your small knife or a screwdriver (blade, not Philips) and, while holding the buffer in place in the tube with your thumb,

Carbine buffer weights come in varying masses now, with the standard (not shown) unmarked, and increasingly heavier ones marked "H" "H2" and "H3".

A weak extractor spring, or one lacking its internal buffer, is an invitation to extraction difficulties.

The safety plunger is unlike the others, it has a small head, like a nail, and is larger in diameter.

use the tool to depress the plunger that retains the buffer. Ease the buffer out, and then grab hold of the buffer and spring and pull them out as one. The ratcheting noise is the spring clanging over the plunger. Don't cringe, it doesn't do any harm.

You do not need your Rambo survival knife to disassemble this. While you have the parts out, wipe the spring and buffer weight clean. If this is the first time you've had the spring out, count the coils on your spring. Carbine-stocked lowers should have a spring with 37 to 39 coils. Rifle-stocked lowers should have springs with 41 to 43 coils. Close enough is close enough, as long as your rifle has been working properly. If it hasn't, this may warrant further inquiry, so count. The worst case I've ever seen was a rifle that was short-stroking, and when all other possibilities turned up nothing, I looked at the spring. It has 50 coils on int. I kid you not, 50. I'd still have it, but the owner was going to take it back to where he bought the rifle, and do something physically improbable to the seller with it.

Take the buffer weight and give it a good look-over. The front face of it will no-doubt have some circular scoring on it, from where the carrier has been rubbing. No problem. The rear part, the synthetic buffer, should be in good shape. If it is gouged, torn, crushed or breaking, then you need to tend to it. The basic means of "tending" to it is to replace the whole thing. You could, if you wanted, find someone who had just the synthetic part, but why bother? Besides, there was a reason the back end started busting up, usually having to do with the roll pin being loose and drifting out. If that is the cause (in the half-dozen or so busted buffers I've seen, it was), putting a new synthetic back end into a buffer assembly with a loose roll pin is simply asking for trouble.

Despite a loose roll pin being the likely cause, you need to figure out why it is breaking. If it was just a crappy, low-bid part, then a better replacement is the solution. If it is getting shredded due to some other cause, you'll need to find it. In years of doing this, I have run into half a dozen bad buffers, and replacing them was the solution.

While you have it out, lift the buffer up near your head and give it a good shake. You should

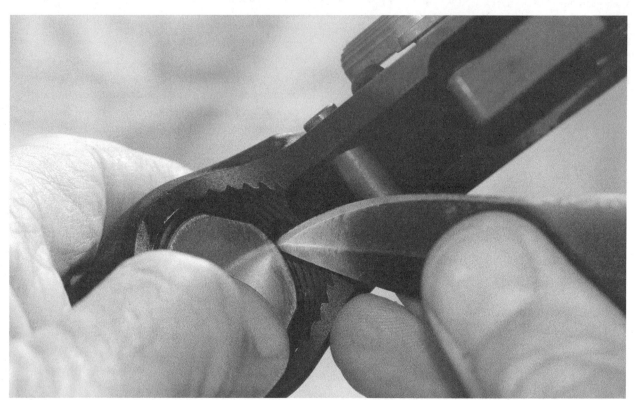

To remove the buffer and spring, push the buffer back with your thumb while you press down the retainer with a knifepoint or screwdriver tip.

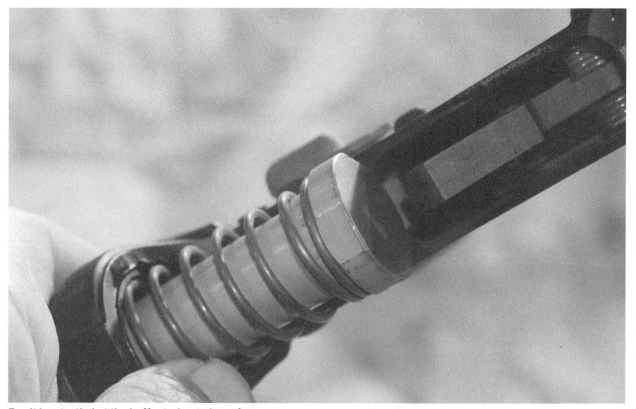

Don't be startled at the buffer trying to jump free.

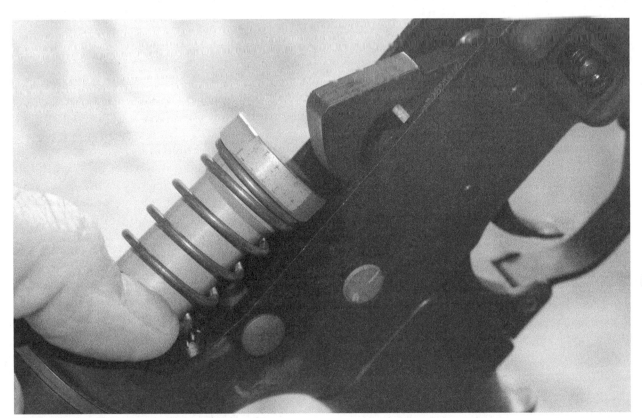

The buffer usually stops when it hits the hammer.

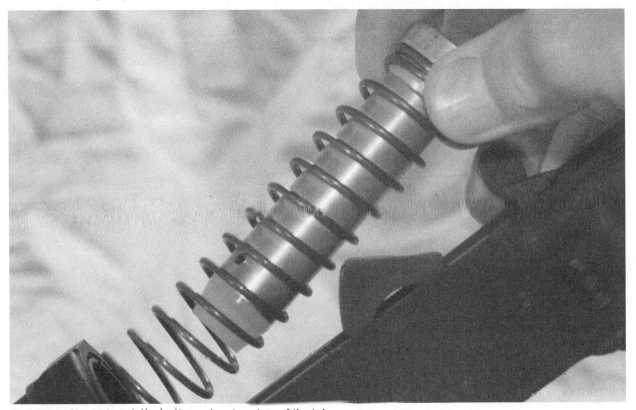

Grab the buffer and yank the buffer and spring clear of the tube.

hear the clank of metallic weights slapping back and forth inside of it. If you hear something else, like nothing moving, or pellets, then you need to change. In a previous chapter I told you not to worry too much about mil-spec, but in this case it matters. The buffer weight acts as a dead-blow hammer, and the weights are there to diminish carrier bounce. This can be a problem in full-auto guns, not so much in a semi, but right is right. And in this instance, it matters.

I have never had anything but miserable luck with the buffers filled with lead shot. So, if yours is one such, I'd suggest strongly that you replace it with a proper, mil-spec buffer.

While you've got the spring and buffer out, look inside the buffer tube. It should be clean and clear of debris. If there is stuff in there, get it out.

Let's take a moment to talk about noise. The spring and buffer – the spring flexing and the buffer cycling – make noise. Some shooters find that "boing-boing" of the spring distracting. Others, not so much. If the noise really bothers you, you can do what the NRA High Power shooters (and some others) do, grease the spring. A good application of grease dampens the noise. It also does a few other things, things that may not be so beneficial. First, grease attracts grit. A greased-up buffer tube in the Southwest with wind-driven dust and grit may not be so much fun after a few days of shooting or practice.

Conversely, grease will keep water droplets trapped in the buffer tube, and if you have too much grease and water, you may get hydraulic locking, where the incompressible goop in the tube can't be shoved around by the buffer.

Nope, keep the inside of the tube clean and lightly oiled, if oiled at all.

On top, a carbine buffer. In the middle, a JP Enterprises competition-only lightweight buffer. And on the bottom, a rarity: one of the original M16 (pre-M16A1) buffers, which proved to be too light.

Reassembly

Reassembling the buffer and spring is easy. Push the buffer into the spring (either end, they are the same) until the first coil up snaps over the shoulder on the buffer meant to retain it. Then stuff the open end of the spring down into the buffer tube, followed by the rest of it. You should not have to push down the retaining pin to get the buffer in; the buffer should cam that out of the way. Once it is in, this part is done.

LOWER RECEIVER INTERNALS

These are the fire control parts, also known as the LPK (Lower Parts Kit). They are the hammer, disconnector, trigger and safety, and the springs that run them. For the lower, there are two ways to do a field strip and clean. One is to leave things in, and the other is to take them out. Let's do the "leave in" first.

The process is simple, look inside. Do you see any bits of grass, expelled primers, egregious chunks of carbon, or other debris that rises above the level of greasy carbon? Fine, use an aerosol degreaser/cleaner to hose the interior.

With your left thumb (right-handed shooters) on the hammer, rotate the safety to Fire and then press the trigger. Ease the hammer forward. Look inside, and make sure all the parts you need/want/should have are in there. Specifically, hammer and hammer spring. Trigger and trigger spring. Disconnector and disconnector spring. Nothing broken, missing or mis-assembled? Good.

With a suitable disposal site, hose the interior with the aerosol cleaner and sluice out the gunk. If you see built-up or moraine-like deposits of carbon or gunk, scrape with a brass or aluminum scraper.

To start disassembly, push the safety to fire and get your thumb in front of the hammer.

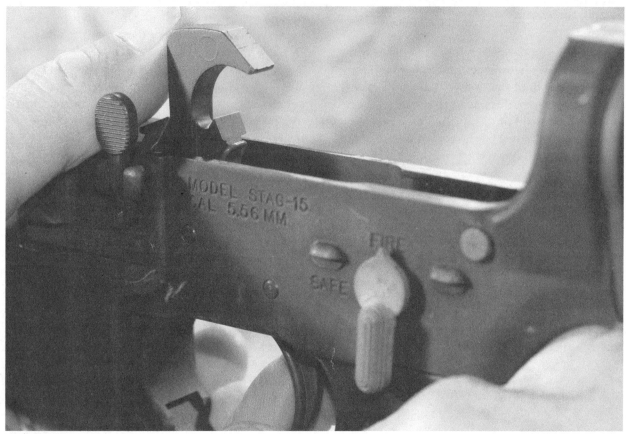

Ease the hammer forward.

(Avoid steel.) If you have an aerosol lubricant, give the interior a light over-spray, just to get a light layer on everything. If not, you'll just have to drop in droplets of lube, and let them wick over the dry surfaces to cover.

Now, put a drop of lube on each of the following locations:
- hammer springs and the pivot points of the hammer
- interior sides of the receiver
- hammer sear surface
- trigger pivot pin
- sides of the disconnector
- pivot points of the trigger with the interior of the receiver
- disconnector spring
- safety/selector, at each end, where it goes into the receiver wall

If you want to take the internals out, start at the point where you'd have hosed the interior, with the hammer forward. Use a drift pin to push the hammer pin out. Right-to-left or left-to-right, it doesn't matter. Push the pin out and maintain some control over the hammer, or its spring will cause it to jump on you.

At this point you may run into a slight problem. The next step is to push the trigger pin out. It will move easily, as it will not have the legs of the hammer spring retaining it. The problem you may run into is that even with the pin out, you can't remove the trigger. This problem arises from the location and size of the trigger hole in the bottom of the receiver. It is not precisely located and sized on a lot of receivers (it doesn't have to be, to do its job) and if it is a bit small or not in just the right spot, you can't wrestle the trigger out. The trigger will bind under the safety, against the opening, and won't come out.

If you have a rifle with this dimensional situation, the only way you can get the trigger out

This is how both legs of the hammer spring should look, on top of the trigger pin, outside of all the trigger spring coils.

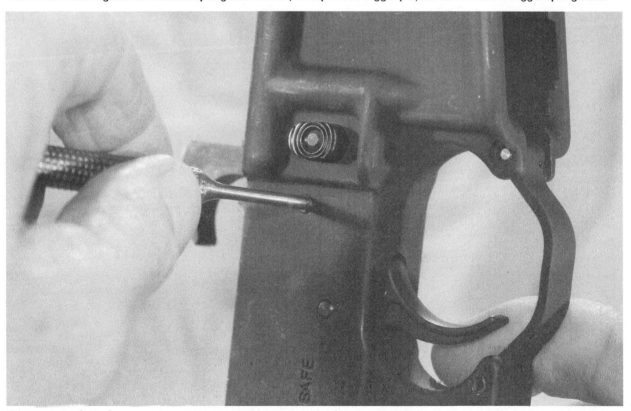

When you push the hammer pin out, it may need just a tiny bit of encouragement.

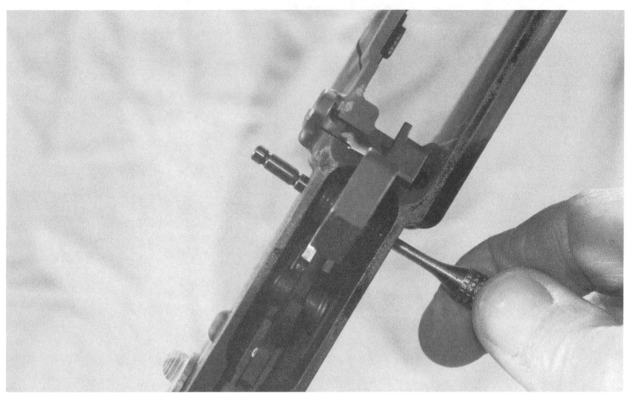

The hammer has a retaining spring inside (the "J" spring), and you have to press the hammer pin off that spring before things come free.

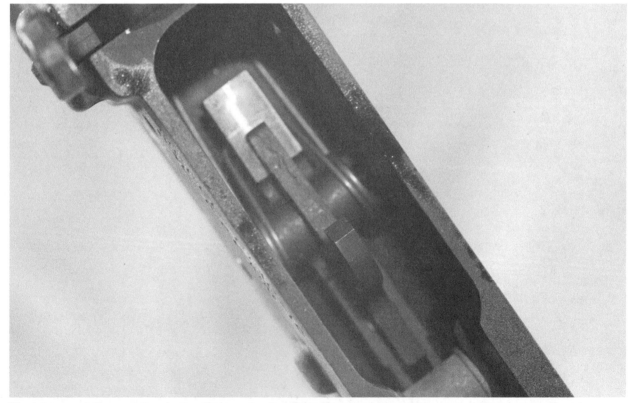

The trigger and disconnector pivot on their own spring, Once the hammer is out, the second pin moves easily.

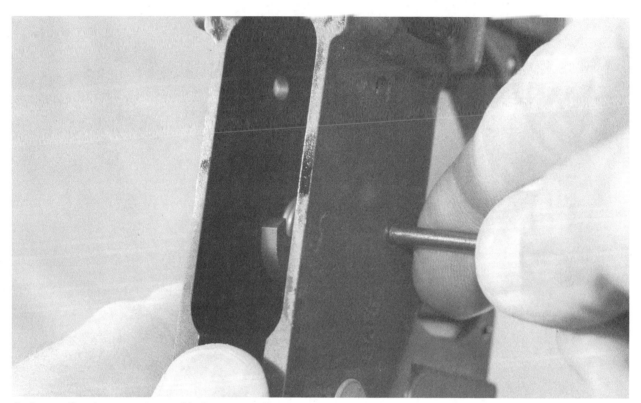

Just press the pin across, no need to hammer on it.

is to remove the safety. That's a different chapter. So for now we'll just assume you can get the trigger out. (If you can't get the trigger out, and you don't want to remove the safety, then simply proceed from here as if you hadn't taken anything out of the lower.)

With the hammer, trigger and disconnector out, scrub and scrape them clean. Scrub the interior of the lower.

To reassemble, start with the trigger alone. Slip it into the lower, tuck the tail back under the safety, and insert the trigger pin part-way into the trigger. (The trigger pin and hammer pin are interchangeable and identical.) Only press it across far enough to catch one side of the trigger, and not across the gap for the disconnector. Then, press the disconnector down into the slot in the trigger for it, and press down against the disconnector spring, and slightly backwards.

You can, at this point, if you have arranged your workspace properly, look through the trigger pin hole in the lower, and see the alignment of the disconnector hole with the lower pin hole and

the pin. This does not require force. If you try to tap or hammer it across, you will mar the pin in a particularly egregious way.

The trigger has several sharp edges on the pivot hole, and if you try to tap the pin across you will cut a gouge on the pin face, and that kicked-up gouge will foil all attempts at assembly. If you've so-marred the pin, the solutions are simple: stone it clean or replace it.

Once the disconnector lines up, the pin will slide right across.

Now the hammer. The hammer springs act to retain the trigger pin. That's what the grooves on the pins are for. The legs of the hammer spring ride in the grooves and keep the pin in place. The hammer has its own retention spring, but it is on the inside of the hammer. Called the "J" spring, you can see it through the small hole in the hammer.

Pick up the hammer, and make sure the hammer spring "box," the part of the spring that passes across the hammer, is resting against the back side of the hammer, not the front. There are two

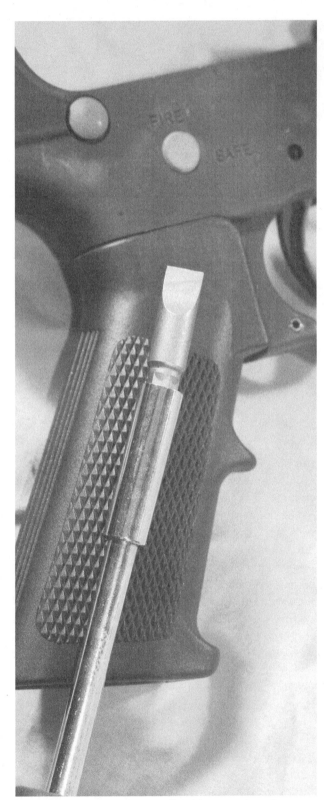

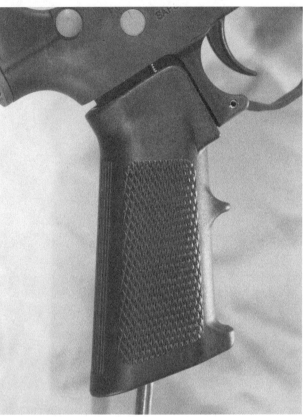

As the bolt threads out, the safety plunger spring will push the pistol grip away from the receiver. If it is a tight fit, then the pistol grip won't move at all.

To remove the pistol grip and the safety, you have to unscrew the bolt that holds on the pistol grip. You need a tool that is long enough to reach, and with a wide blade (unless it is one of the blankety-blank allen-head bolts).

A small wrapping of tape on the bottom end of the safety spring will keep it from falling out of the pistol grip when you take that part off.

This is an M16 trigger. The back of the disconnector slot is open, and you really should close this if you plan on using it in an AR-15 build.

ways to install the hammer, and they both start with making sure the legs of the hammer spring are correctly resting on the trigger pin: outboard, directly against the interior wall of the receiver.

One hammer installation method is to simply shove the hammer down into the receiver, and while doing so press it back toward its cocked position. Once the hammer sear hook catches on the trigger sear face, the spring will lock it into a more-or-less correctly assembled position. At least, close enough to let you then wrestle the hammer pin and receiver, while inserting the pin.

Me, I'm not a fan of that. A different method is to hold the lower receiver by the pistol grip, in a firing grip. Hold the hammer in your left hand, with your forefinger down the face of the striking surface, and your thumb against the back, at the pivot point.

Catch the hammer spring legs on the trigger pivot pin, and press the hammer down into the receiver. As your forefinger comes to the receiver, slide your finger into the magazine well. You'll be pinching the hammer into the receiver, with your thumb on the hammer, and your forefinger in the magazine well. If you have even a little hand strength, you can hold the hammer in place, and hold the lower receiver, with your left hand. You can also look through the hammer pivot pin hole to check alignment. Insert the hammer pin and press it in.

This is the one time you may need (and can actually use) a hammer. The "J" spring in the hammer will resist your pressing the pin through, and you may need a tap to get it across.

Now, once the pin goes through the hammer, it will not be aligned with the hole on the far side of the receiver. Stop hitting it with your hammer. Hold the receiver, and use your other hand to move the hammer as a lever, to move the hammer pivot hole into alignment with the receiver hole.

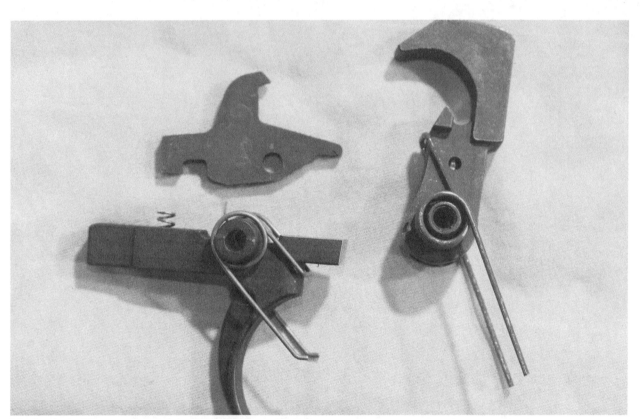

The hammer, trigger and disconnector, out of the receiver.

To install the hammer, pinch the hammer between thumb and forefinger, and catch the hammer spring legs over the trigger pin.

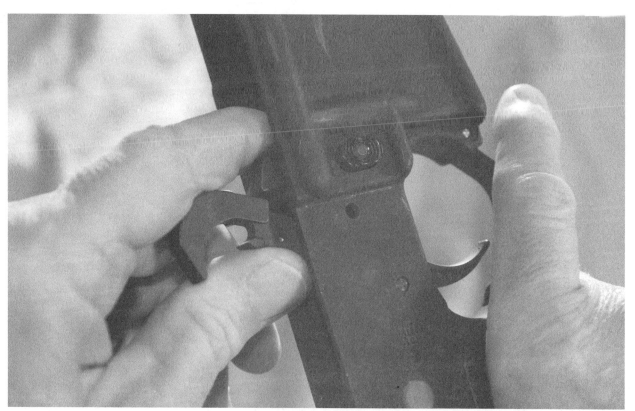

Lever the hammer forward, compressing the spring and sliding it down into the receiver.

Then slide your forefinger into the magazine well and clamp it all into place.

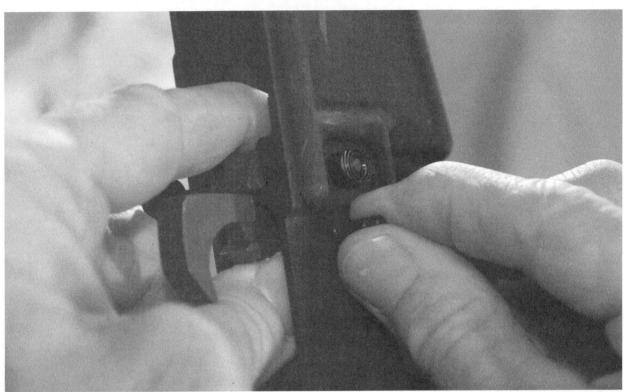

While holding the hammer in place, get the hammer pin started. Once it stops on the "J" spring, then get the hammer to tap it past the spring. But just past the spring, not all the way through.

When reassembling the hammer, you can't just pound the pin through, you have to use the hammer as a lever to align the pivot pin with the receiver hole before pressing it through.

Then press the pin through. What, you don't have a third hand? Sure you do. Use the edge of the table or bench to press the pin from the other side, toward you, as you line up the hammer and receiver pivot holes.

I like as you would had you not taken things apart.

UPPER RECEIVER

With the upper internals out, use paper towels to wipe the incredible amounts of gunk out of the upper receiver. Use the aerosol cleaner to hose out even more, and brush thoroughly. Unless you use an ultrasonic cleaner, even when you think your upper is clean, there is more that can be scrubbed/hosed out.

Unless you took a dunk in mud or water, there isn't any reason to take the handguards off. Also, chamber and bore cleaning are covered elsewhere. If you feel the need to scrub them in a field-strip and clean, then we've got that elsewhere. But, removing the original-style handguards is both a learning experience, and can in extreme cases be a good reminder of one's place in the universe.

Original handguards (we aren't going to cover free-float handguards here) come in the A1 style and the A2 style. The A1s are triangular, have a smooth surface, and taper toward the front sight, and come in rights and lefts. The A2s are ribbed, taper only slightly, and are identical, being assembled as top and bottom.

Look at the rear of the handguards. They should pass under a ring, called the delta ring. On most A1s the ring will be tapered, and all A2s it will be tapered. On very early A1s, or retro builds, the ring will not be tapered, but will be a ridged cylinder, and was called back then the "slip" ring. (Probably not because it slipped over the rear of the handguards, but because it readily slipped out of the grasp of those working on it.)

This ring is spring-loaded, and the spring pushes the ring forward. You have to compress the ring back in order to pivot the rear end of the handguards out of the way and off the rifle. You'll do this one at a time. The "interesting" detail here is that loose handguards rattle, and tight ones, well, are tight and near-impossible to remove.

This is the spring, inside the delta ring assembly, that resists your attempts to take the handguards off.

The Army manual that shows how to take off the handguards is a drawing with four hands in it. Yep, the Army assumes you and your buddy will collaborate on this. I have some rifles where I can take the handguards out myself. I also have rifles where I can't do it and need help. A tool that helps is the handguard tuning fork. This gizmo hooks into the magazine well, and the two arms clamp down on the delta ring. Hook, clamp, pivot, and the delta ring is pushed out of the way. Of course, you still have to balance the rifle and remove the handguards, while keeping the tool clamped and pressed.

Once the rear is free, pivot the front edge out of the cup that is right behind the front sight housing. The A2 handguards, as I said, are identical, and are assembled as a top and a bottom. They are also designed at the front to fit both the triangular cap of the A1 and the circular cap of the A2, behind the front sight housing.

Damaged A2 handguards can be replaced with any matching handguard. (Believe it or not, they can be found with minor variations in color, surface gloss, ridge sizes, etc. So much for "absolutely identical" military parts.) The A1 handguards are rights and lefts, and you have to replace them that way. You can't make a right fit as a left.

With the interior and exterior cleaned, check the movement of the dust cover. It should move briskly and firmly when you pick it up and let it go. If it moves in a desultory fashion, the spring has probably unwound a coil. Not a problem, as long as it does move, and it's a hassle to correct.

Once clean, re-lube. Again, cover the interior and exterior with enough of a mist of aerosol oil to make it un-dry. It doesn't have to be dripping. And then, put a drop of lube on the shaft of the forward assist, if you have one. On the rear sights, the A1 gets a drop on the adjustment dial, at the plunger, and on the windage screw cross shaft threads, next to the aperture. On A2 sights, into the shaft of the vertical adjustment wheel, and on the threads of the windage cross shaft.

The coil spring of the dust cover gets a drop. Also, the front sight post shaft, on the retainer, gets a drop.

If you have been heavy-handed with the aerosol scrubber, turn the receiver over and put a drop into each of the assembly pin lug holes. Also, put a drop into the slot of the charging handle.

BOLT AND CARRIER

If you have to take the bolt and carrier apart, make sure you have a small cardboard box or cloth to lay the parts on, so you can put the parts down without losing them. It is a real bite to be diligent in cleaning your rifle, and then to lose a part for which you don't have a replacement. (Murphy's law, paragraph seven: If you had a replacement for it, you wouldn't lose it.)

Use the awl or small knife to lever the cotter pin out of the side of the carrier. Pull the cotter pin out, and put it in the box/on the cloth.

Push the bolt to the rear (into the carrier) and then tap the carrier into your other hand or onto the workbench. The firing pin will drop out the back. Again, box it.

Rotate the cam pin one-quarter of a turn, and lift it out of the carrier. Depending on how tightly it fits, or how much carbon has built up, it may take some work, even some prying with the screwdriver. Once the cam pin is out, you can pull the bolt forward out of the carrier.

You are probably done, unless you really feel compelled to remove the extractor. So, let's assume you want to remove the extractor.

The extractor is held in by the small pin you see just ahead of the rotating band machined into the body of the bolt. The extractor, if it is properly sprung, will be under a goodly amount of tension. On some bolts, you'll have to press firmly to push the pin out of the way. Resist the temptation to use the firing pin for this. It is not good for the firing pin, and besides, the firing pin is not the right diameter. You'll only get the extractor pin part of the way out and will have to go looking for the proper tool anyway.

Once the pin is out, set it aside, pull the extractor off the bolt (if you hear a petroleum-based sucking sound, perhaps you have not cleaned the extractor for some time, eh?) and set it aside.

You are ready to clean.

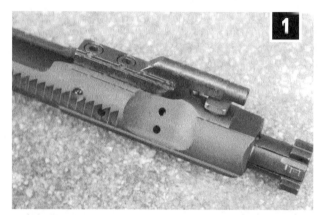

The bolt and carrier, ready to be taken apart for cleaning.

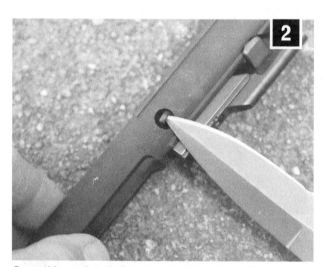

Something pointy helps a lot in getting the cotter pin started.

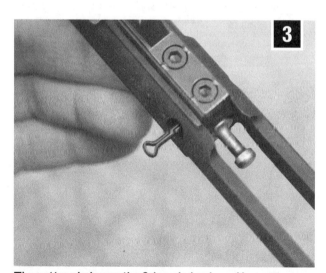

The cotter pin keeps the firing pin in place. Here you see that the firing pin has already started to slide out, backwards, from the carrier.

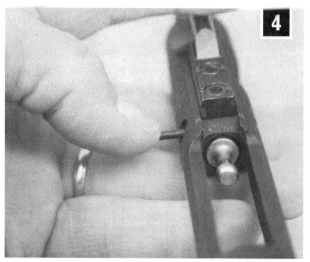

On reassembly, to get the cotter pin to co-operate, turn it sideways and press down as you press in.

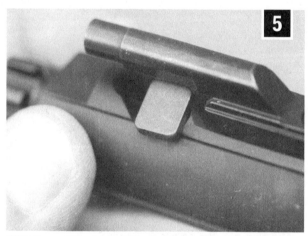

With the cotter pin and firing pin out, push the bolt back, camming the cam pin.

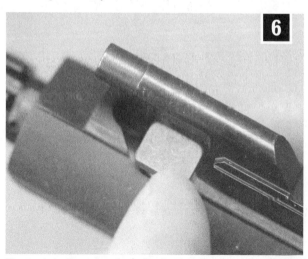

Now rotate the cam pin so the longer side is parallel to the gas tube.

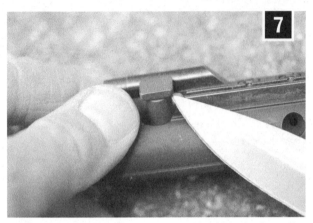

Lift the cam pin out. If it is really grubby (this one is really clean) you may need to use some kind of prying tool to convince it to move.

With the cam pin out, you can pull the bolt forward out of the carrier.

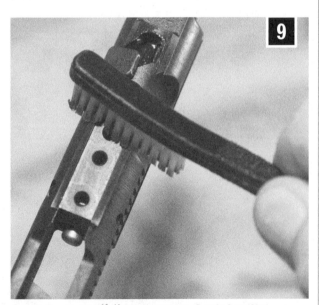

Scrub the gunk off, then de-grease. Apply Loctite.

The extractor should have a slight inward tilt, indicating that the spring is strong enough.

On the upper side of the bolt is the extractor pin. That can be pushed out. Below and forward is the ejector pin, that you'll need a disassembly tool to remove.

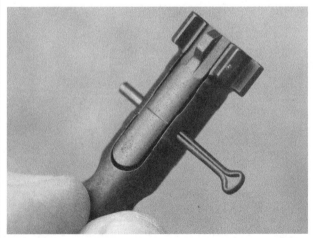

You can use the cotter pin to push the extractor pin out of the bolt.

CARRIER CLEANING

Wipe the wet, goopy carbon off the exterior. What, it isn't wet and goopy? It is hard, baked-on, and tough as all get-out? You didn't listen to your buddy, the operator/SEAL/ninja, who told you to run your AR dry, did you? You did? Oh darn. OK, everybody who has been paying attention, and has a properly-lubed rifle, wipe off the carrier and take a break. Those who didn't listen, here goes.

Break out a bottle of penetrating lubricant. CLP works, but something like Kroil, or a super-penetrant, to loosen loose screws and bolts, will also do. Spread a liberal application of this on the carrier, all over it and into the bolt bore. Or better yet, set the carrier in a stainless pan or dish, and pour the lube on.

Let it soak, and then do the same to your bolt, extractor and cam pin. After all, if you didn't lube, they will all be caked with baked-on carbon.

Once the lube has had a chance to soak in, wipe the loosened carbon off and re-apply lube. If you have the parts soaking in a pan, use the plastic bristle brush to scrub them. This will take quite some effort, and we can only hope it is a learning experience. Don't shoot your rifle dry again.

For those who paid attention and lubed their rifle, wipe the carbon off. Keep using CLP/lube/whatever to soak and wipe, until the carrier is clean. The outside, anyway. To clean the inside, you'll need some degreaser. All that lubed-up, gooey carbon on the inside? You need it dry. First, use a Cat M4 tool to wipe out as much as you can. You can also use an old bore brush with an over-sized cleaning patch wrapped around it, to mop out as much of the gooey carbon as possible. Then, spray the inside with a degreaser to remove the lube. With the bore now dry, use the Cat M4 tool to scrape the dry carbon. Scrape, pull the tool out, bang the open end of the carrier on the benchtop, repeat.

Do this until nothing falls out when you tap the

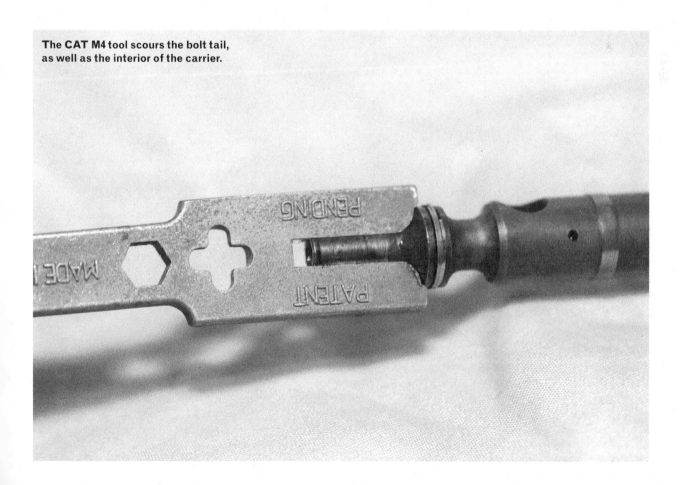

The CAT M4 tool scours the bolt tail, as well as the interior of the carrier.

The Otis Bone tool cleans both the bolt and the carrier.

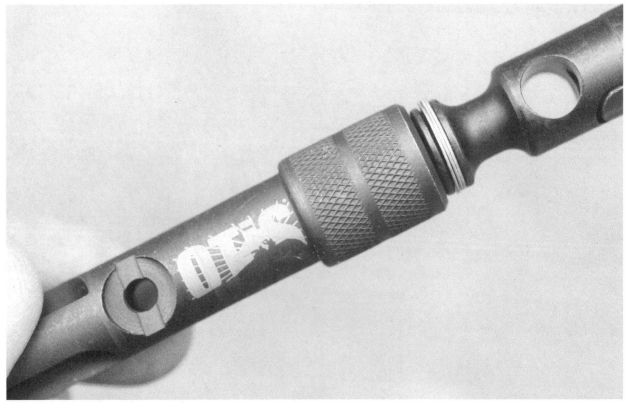

With the Bone tool you can scrape the bolt tail clean.

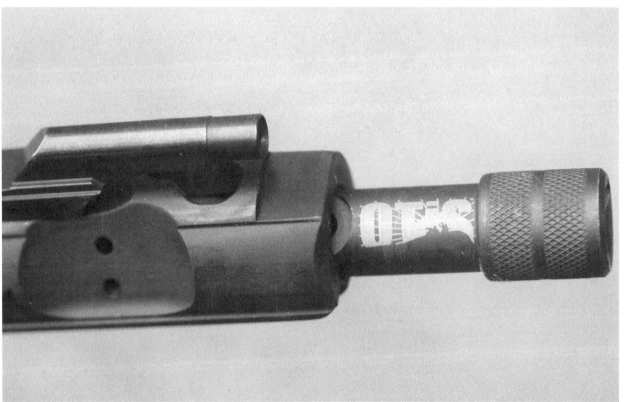

The other end of the Bone tool cleans the inside of the carrier.

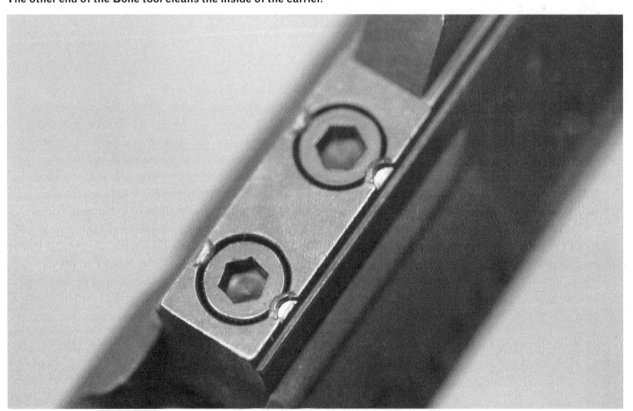

While you have it in hand, check the gas key screws for proper staking, This one is proper.

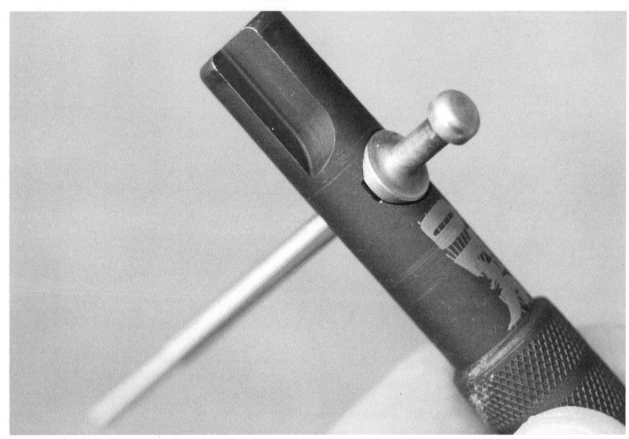

And as a bonus, the Bone tool also cleans the firing pin.

bolt end of the carrier onto a hard surface. (Not too hard, wood is fine, concrete and steel are too much.)

At this point, you have a clean and degreased carrier. Time to do some inspecting.

Look at the rear of the carrier. As unlikely as it seems, you want to check for cracks, rust, etc. Not that shooting it will crack it, but if your buddy took your rifle apart when you were in the men's room, and dropped the carrier, he of course would not say anything. (He'll self-deduct points from his man-card for dropping, but he won't take the hit for admitting he dropped it. If he is the kind of guy who does, you should consider marrying him. Kidding.)

Look at the front. Any dings, cracks, rust, etc? If it is all clear on the ends, look at the carrier key.

The carrier key is the spigot up on top, and it mates with the gas tube to channel gas back into the carrier, to cycle the rifle. Is the end of

it even and circular, or has it worn oval? Is it smooth along its circumference, or is it dinged, cracked, bent or otherwise not whole? A worn, cracked, dented or otherwise not-perfect key, if it is in a rifle that works properly, is not necessarily something that must be replaced. But, it will need to be sooner rather than later, so you might as well sit down with the Brownells catalog and order a replacement, now. And a pair of carrier key screws, too.

If it is perfect, then you next need to check tightness. Hold the carrier in one hand, and grab the key with your other. Try to wrestle the key around. Don't be gentle, there is not a one of you reading this (and probably no-one, anywhere) who has hand strength enough to harm a carrier key. If it is the slightest bit loose, you need to correct that.

If tight, set it aside so you can clean the rest. If it needs fixing, then fix it. And yes, you should do this every time you clean your rifle. Sure, if it is tight it probably won't ever come loose, but it is a good habit to have, if you are going to spend quality time with the AR-15 system.

LOOSE CARRIER KEY

Before you can tighten it, you have to remove it. Use an allen wrench, one of the two sizes the screws come in. (And keep both wrench sizes on hand. Murphy's law, again.) Unscrew the screws and remove the key. Scrub clean the bottom of the key and the channel for it in the carrier, and even go so far as to scrape off any smut still left after you scrub.

Ideally, if the key itself is in good shape, you'll use it again. Sometimes when they get too loose, they also get damaged in the rattling around (banging into the gas tube and all) and have to be replaced. You also will want to replace the screws, even if you use the same key again.

You can re-use the original screws, but that isn't ideal. Still, I've tightened lots of loose carrier keys using the original screws, and have not heard of any breaking. However, the screw is small, highly-stressed, and sooner or later one of them will break when re-tightened. Use new if you can.

Once the parts are clean, degrease them and put a line of Loctite around the base of the carrier key. You don't need it on the screw threads, but some guys put it there, too. I avoid it simply to keep Loctite from getting down into the bolt channel.

Place the key on the clean and dry carrier channel, push the screws in and tighten them. If you do not have a torque wrench, then hand-tighten, as tight as you can, with a normal-length allen wrench. If you have a torque wrench, set it for 50 or 55 in-lbs. Tighten to click, and leave alone.

Wipe the excess Loctite, then get out your MOACKS. What, you don't have one? Then you need to use a centerpunch and hammer, or a spring-loaded centerpunch, to stake the key down over the screwheads. And then counter-stake the screws themselves so nothing can ever move. The MOACKS, in all its variants, was designed to properly, securely and permanently stake the key and screws so nothing could move.

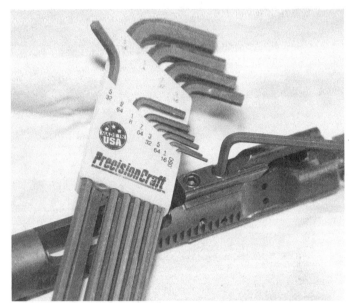

Before you can stake the screws, you have to remove them.

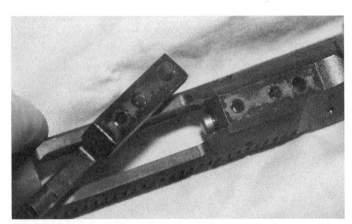

Once off, clean the carrier and the key. Wipe clean.

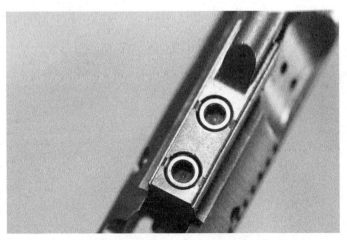

This is what they key looks like before you stake the screws.

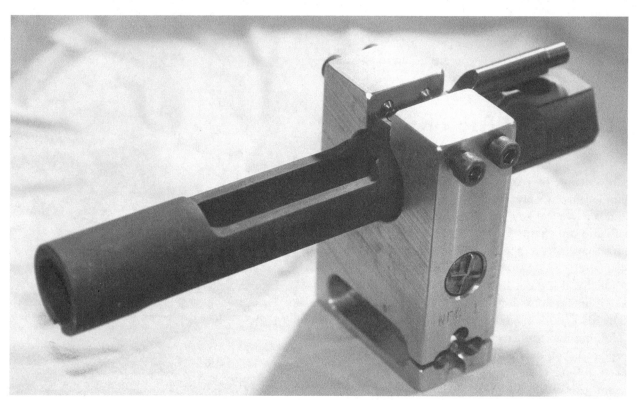

The gas key on the carrier must be tight, or function will suffer. The **MOACKS** solves the problem of looseness, but only if you do it right.

Once the carrier is located properly, tighten the screws until they bottom out.

This is what the screws look like after they have been **MOACKS**'d.

Clean the burrs with a file.

Why are we doing all this?

The operating system of the AR uses a jet of gas, back through the gas tube and into the key, to blow the carrier back off the bolt, turn the bolt and cycle the action. If the gas key is loose, it leaks. Leaking gas, just as piston blow-by in your gas, is bad. At a high enough loss level, the rifle will not fully cycle. So, tightening the screws is not enough. They clearly came loose from when they were tightened before. So, you use Loctite to seal the gap (not just to keep the screws tight) and then you tighten them down. Once tightened, you peen the metal of the key over onto the screw so it can't come loose.

As a last step, take a fine-tooth file and file down the edges kicked up by the staking. Yes, this removes parkerized surface metal, but the staking already did that. And considering how much lube you're going to keep this area flooded with, it isn't going to rust any time soon.

BOLT CLEANING

The bolt is going to be as dirty, and in the same way, as the carrier you just cleaned. So treat it accordingly. Soak the hard carbon, or wipe off the soft carbon. Use your green GI brush to scrub it clean, and then dry it.

The tail of the bolt, the curved section that the firing pin passes through, will be caked with carbon. Resist the temptation to grab your tactical folder, Swiss army knife or Leatherman tool and "scrape that stuff off." Sooner or later (usually sooner) you'll slip and cut yourself. Don't use a steel or copper bristle brush, as you will, sooner or later, hook a gas ring (more on those little devils in a bit) and sling them off the bolt, never to be seen again. Back in the old days we'd take fired .50 BMG cases, and variously mangle/modify the case mouth to make a bolt tail scraper. Now there is no need, as we have tools for that.

The back end of a Cat M4 tool scrapes the inside of the carrier. The front, the "tuning fork" end of it, scrapes the bolt tail. So, with your as-clean-as-it-is and dry bolt, insert the tail in the Cat and rotate. Once you have a disgusting amount of carbon scraped off, pull it off, and wipe things clean. Repeat. After two or three applications, you'll have as much off as you can get off. The Cat tool and the bolt tail are radiused, and there is no way to make them match exactly. There will be some carbon left, but it is little enough that you can deal with it.

Another bolt tail cleaning tool comes from Magna-matic. Their CRT-015 uses a guide pin that fits into the firing pin tunnel. There is a hinged arm, ending in a curved scraping surface. Insert the guide into the bolt, press the scraper against the bolt tail, and rotate. Again, you'll get most, but

The bolt face should be clean, unmarred and not have pitting around the firing pin hole.

Gas rings, three and undamaged, correct. Don't waste
a moment's time getting the gaps un-aligned.

Gas rings come in sets of three. Make sure yours pass the test. If they don't, replace all three.

not all, but that's OK.

Check the front of the bolt. You'll find a lot of carbon packed into the corners and edges of recesses, in the bolt face and in the extractor groove. Brush them out. You may also find that there is a whole lot of brassing on the face of your bolt, as well as evidence of primer leakage around the firing pin hole. A certain amount of brassing is expected and normal. The case base receives its fair share of the pressure generate by firing, and some brass will rub off. Also, the cases, in chambering and extraction, will have small amounts of brass rubbed off simply due to the harsh environment it passes through.

In the years of work on ARs, I've only ever seen one that brassed so badly it actually caused problems. Despite fussing over many different details, the problem never got solved in the life of the barrel. A new barrel stopped the problem, but that is hardly a cost-effective solution. ("Brassing? No problem, let's just swap your barrel out for another one, they are only $600 this week.")

With the bolt clean fore and aft, it is time to inspect and test. First, the ejector. That's the cylindrical thingie poking out of the face of the bolt. Clamp it in a holder of some kind, vertically (a padded vise will do) and put a drop of oil on it. Let the oil run down into the bolt, and then take a drift punch and pump the ejector down into the bolt, and let it ride up as you release. If nothing comes out except some carbon-laced oil, you're good to go.

If pieces of brass come out, or the ejector stays down, you need to jump to Chapter 5, and the complete disassembly of the bolt.

Take the bolt out of the vise and look closely at each locking lug. Is each one clean, straight, and have clean edges? Or are there dings and dents, or peened parts? Is there evidence of cracks? Peening is bad, the bolt is made of steel that is very hard, and peening means something very wrong is happening. Cracks are a reason to immediately (as in, right now, do not see if you can get "a few more rounds" out of it) replace the bolt with a new one. Bolt replacement also requires a headspace check, again, Chapter Eight, bolt or barrel replacements.

Now inspect the gas rings. Are there three? Are

they intact? You'll test them later, no need to take them out now. Also, don't even bother trying to mis-align the gaps. First, they move on their own each time the bolt cycles. Second, they close up and are much smaller when they are compressed to fit into the carrier. And last, the gaps aren't big enough to matter. If someone tells you that allowing the gaps to line up will cause your rifle to malfunction, they are spreading an urban myth. Avoid future advice from them, or at least take any other advice with a great big grain of salt.

Wipe/scrub the firing pin and the cam pin, and remove the carbon that has been caked in the corners. Wipe the cotter pin clean.

EXTRACTOR

Wipe the extractor clean, and scrub the carbon and gunk out of the hook. Check the hook by rubbing it against the heel of your hand. You should have the impressions of "kitten teeth" from the corners of the extractor. If you do not get that feeling, and this is a high-mileage extractor, you may want to swap it out for a new one. Then again, extractors pretty much work until they break, so you can leave it alone if the bolt it goes into is still serviceable.

Look at the extractor spring. It should be un-bent, and have a little plastic insert in it. Ideally, the insert is black. Earlier colors of inserts were lighter in color (white, tan, red, blue) and offer less extractor tensioning than the black does. The earliest ARs (and M16A1s) lacked the insert altogether.

The current vogue is a gold-colored spring, the stiffest one the army authorizes. If your rifle has an un-mangled spring and a black insert and works fine the way it is, there is no need to go tearing it apart to put in a "better" spring.

But if you've been having extraction/ejection issues, replacing them is prudent.

Also, you should have an external extractor booster. The best is the D-Fender, wedge/axe shaped, and designed specifically for the job. (Match the curve of the D-Fender to the curve of the extractor.) When it came time to pony up, the government did not want to spend the money to buy a designed, trademarked part, so they simply

The extractor cannot have too much oomph to call on. You want a good spring, an internal buffer, and an external **O** ring or **D**-Fender.

Make sure your spring is actually attached to the extractor. I've seen them not pressed in place, and prone to falling out when disassembled.

bought a gazillion rubber "O" rings from an industrial supplier. Those donuts go around the extractor spring and greatly increase the extractor tension. (The AR system has been historically under-tensioned in the extractor.)

Check the spring for being upright, the insert for being present, and the D or O ring for being un-scarred. Replace if they are not to spec.

LUBRICATION

As a general principle, if it wears bright, put lube on it. With the bolt and carrier, make sure all the parts have a light film of oil on all surfaces, especially if you have used a degreaser to clean and scrape the parts as clean as possible.

A quick summary: all the parts get a light and even coating of oil or lubricant. The gas rings get an extra drop, as does the ejector. Once the cam pin is in, it too gets a drop. No oil inside the carrier key, and no grease anywhere on the bolt-carrier assembly.

REASSEMBLY

Bolt

If you took the extractor out, you need to put it back. Press it into the seat in the bolt, and start the pin across. If you have a proper set of spring, internal booster and D or O ring, you'll have to have strong hands to compress all that and get the pin across. But, you can. Once it gets started, press it until it is below flush on both sides.

Bolt and Carrier

If you've taken them apart, they have to go back together. Take the bolt and shove it into the carrier. There will be some resistance, as the gas rings have to be compressed in order to fit. Shove it in, and turn it so the extractor is on the right side, the side with the forward assist notches cut into the side of the carrier.

Look down in the cam pin slot, and line up the bolt cam pin hole with the slot, at the back end. Take the cam pin and push it down into the carrier and bolt. You'll need to turn the rectangular head of the cam pin so the long side is parallel to the bore to do this. Once it is in all the way, turn the cam pin a quarter-turn.

Push the firing pin into the rear of the carrier, into the tail of the bolt, and press it all the way forward. You want the large flange of the firing pin to be forward of the hole for the cotter pin. (This is also known as the firing pin retainer.)

With the firing pin in place, press the cotter pin across. It probably won't cooperate, so here's a trick.

Insert the cotter pin into the carrier and press it over until it stops. If it is not recessed into the depression milled for it, turn the cotter pin so the length of the head is parallel to the length of the carrier. Now, push down on the head of the cotter pin, as you push in to press it across. This should

Carrier design can be almost anything these days. This is a shrouded-pin, cut autosear AR-15 carrier, kosher just about anyplace.

not take a painful amount of force. The legs of the pin will now co-operate, line up with the hole on the far side, and go through.

In the classes, this is one of the times we start to hear "tap-tap-tap" of small hammers, loose tools, etc. There is nothing in the disassembly or assembly of an AR that requires hammer force. If you have to hit it, something is wrong. Find out what that "wrong" is.

That's it. The bolt and carrier are reassembled. Now you test.

ASSEMBLY TESTS

First test: is the firing pin in correctly? You laugh, but it is a common enough slip-up, we see it in classes fairly regularly. Hold the carrier assembly in one hand, open end down. Slap the open end into the palm of your other hand. Did the firing pin stay in? Good, it passes. If the firing pin came out and whacked the palm of your hand,

then the cotter pin did not capture it. Worse yet, in that state, it would not fire. How does this happen? Simple. In pushing the firing pin into the bolt-carrier assembly, something catches (there are more than enough edges in the path) and the large flange doesn't go fully into the carrier. The cotter pin will go across regardless of where the firing pin is, provided the flange isn't directly in the path. So, pin in, but not all the way, cotter pin across, and firing pin not held. Not good.

Second test: push the bolt all the way down into the carrier. Push a finger up against the back end of the firing pin (the part the hammer this) and press the pin forward, while keeping the bolt pushed back. You should see the firing pin protrude through the face of the bolt. If it does not, something is wrong, Take the cotter pin out, remove the firing pin, and make sure the tip is there. Reassemble and try again.

Third test: pull the bolt out as far as it will go, and stand the carrier assembly on the bolt, on a

When you inspect, expect to see bad things. This rifle stopped working, and it is easy to see why. What is curious is that it is mil-spec marked, "MPI" and it should not have broken so early.

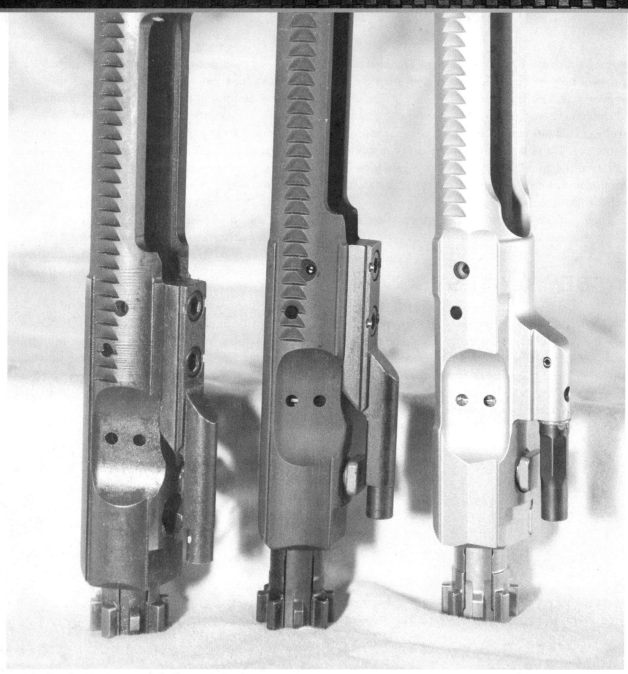

The first bolt gas ring test. Stand it up, if it collapses, it fails. The one on the left fails. New rings for it.

table or bench. Balance problems aside, it should stand upright. If the weight of the carrier causes the assembly to collapse down onto the bolt, the gas rings are worn and must be replaced.

Actually, if the rifle has been working properly, the rings are probably not worn out, but there is no way to know how much longer they will last. And since they are as cheap as dirt, replace them. Replace all of them at the same time.

This test is actually one of a series, as people have been obsessing over gas rings since the first day someone took apart the AR and one of the group lost a ring or two. The variants are, in the increasing need to replace the rings: disassemble the bolt and carrier, and then re-insert the bolt into the carrier, without the cam pin or firing pin. Pull the bolt forward, but not out, and stand it on its head. Next, with the bolt forward but not out, stand the carrier on its back end. And finally, invert the carrier and bolt, and see if the bolt falls out.

Really, though, if a bolt fails the first one, the stand-assembled, you needn't bother with the rest of them.

Now, you may discover that the bolt fails the test, but you don't have worn rings. You have too-few of them. If, despite your best efforts, your cleaning has pitched one of the rings into the weeds, then by all means, replace the missing one or two. Reassemble, and do the test again.

What Wears Rings?

The rings expand to fill the gap between the bolt tail gas shoulder and the bore of the carrier. That seal is necessary to drive the system. As with the carrier key, gas pressure lost can mean reduced function. The constant rubbing of the rings in the bore (exactly as a piston in a cylinder, and rings for the piston) wears on the rings. Even when everything is perfect, there will be wear. If the bore of the carrier is a bit undersized or the surface of it is rougher than called for, the rings will wear faster. I've seen rifles where the owner reported less than a couple of thousand rounds before the bolt fails the "stand-up" test.

I have bolts with rings in them that have lasted as long, or longer, than the barrel.

It all depends on variables beyond your control. A bolt may chew through gas rings like they were breath mints (actually, the carrier does the chewing) or the gas rings might last until you lose them. You can't know ahead of time, and you can only test and replace as-needed.

One Ring To Rule Them All

You didn't think I was going to let you get away without the obvious joke, did you? And answer the obvious question: do you need all three? The answer is an unequivocal maybe. I have a rifle in the rack that will function 100% with no gas rings at all. With some softer ammo it won't always lock open when the magazine is empty, but it feeds and functions just fine right up to that point. Clearly, add a ring to that rifle and it will perk along just

fine. (That's an observation, not a suggestion.)

Other rifles I have will work with one or two rings. However, the bolt is being worked harder when the gas rings are lacking, and it is not a good idea to depend on sub-marginal setups. So, replace missing rings, replace broken rings, and replace them all if a bolt/carrier combo fails the test.

But what about non-ring rings? Specifically, the McFarland gas ring, which is actually a coil of flat spring steel, replacing the three rings? In an interesting switch, I, generally being fond of improvements, don't like them. Those that do, love them, and advocate their use for all other shooters. Me, I figure the original design, when properly assembled, works well enough to wear out barrels from malfunction-free shooting, so why change?

If you want one, or want to try one, go ahead.

CHARGING HANDLE

Inspect the handle to make sure it is still straight. It is made of aluminum, and lots of practice at malfunction clearances can bend it. Also, make sure the front end is still square, and not bending or cracked. Inspect the charging handle retainer to make sure the pin is flush and the latch pivots. Wipe clean, then put a drop of oil into the rear of the latch where the spring and plunger reside.

UPPER REASSEMBLY

Take the charging handle and poke it into the receiver. Push toward the slot, and run the charging handle back and forth until the front, riding tabs drop into the retaining slots, and it rests in the slot made for it.

Leave it sticking out of the receiver by a couple of inches.

Take your assembled bolt/carrier group, and snap the bolt forward. Put the gas key into the interior of the charging handle and press it all forward, bolt/carrier and charging handle. It should move all the way forward until the bolt rotates and locks into the barrel extension and the charging handle latches on the upper.

RIFLE REASSEMBLY

Take the complete upper and place it on the lower. Press the forward takedown pin across to capture the upper receiver. Here's a hint: don't keep the two (upper and lower) clamped together. Pivot the upper so just the front pin is lined up, and wiggle it around as you press on the takedown pin. Once it lines up, it will slide through without a problem. Again, you do not need a hammer at this point. Using a hammer on the front pin is a social faux pas, like eating with your hands at a formal dinner.

Once the front pin is in place, pivot the upper down to the lower, and press the rear pin across. This you might need a bit of persuasion. The fit of upper to lower is a subject of much discussion, angst and struggle. Ideally, the rear pin should slide over with firm finger pressure, and once home there should be no wobble between the upper and lower.

However, wobble is not a functional problem, and lots of rifles exist that have wobble in the fit. The problem arises when the fit is so tight that you have to hammer the rear pin in and out just to work on the rifle. This will lead to damage sometime down the line, so if you need to use force, be careful.

ASSEMBLY CHECKS

Once back together, you have to perform basic checks to make sure you did it all correctly. The first one, and one that may seem just a bit simple (or embarrassing) is to look at the workbench. Is there anything still there, besides the sling?

We all know people who are amused or pleased at assembling something (bookshelves, appliances, internal combustion engines) and having "parts left over." This is not a time to be amused. Look, and if something is still there, get it into the rifle, properly.

Next, open up the action, remove the bolt/carrier group (yes, I know you just put it all back together) and look down the bore. A fellow gunsmith I know had a customer bring in a rifle with a destroyed barrel. The customer had cleaned his rifle, and in cleaning the bore, hadn't noticed that the cleaning rod jag had unscrewed, and was left being, held by the patch, in the bore. When he fired it, the bullet could not escape, and wedged in the bore. The resulting pressure blew the case (the extractor was toast, but the bolt and carrier survived) and the barrel was finished.

So, look down the bore and make sure you haven't left anything behind.

Close it back up. Work the charging handle several times. Does the bolt and carrier move smoothly, and when you run it forward, does the action spring forcefully move the parts back into battery? Good. Close the action.

Rotate the safety. Does it click briskly from one position to the other? If it is a bit stiff, you may have to work in the oil you applied, after degreasing it in cleaning.

One more time, make sure it is unloaded. Point in a safe direction, press the trigger. There should be a loud click. That is the hammer striking the firing pin. Hold the trigger fully back and work the charging handle. Ease the trigger forward, and there should be a less-loud click. That is the disconnector handing the hammer off to the trigger. Press the trigger again, and there should be another loud click. Now, take your finger off the trigger and work the charging handle as briskly as possible. Pull it back and let go. Now, turn the safety to Safe. It should go. If it does not, press the trigger. If there is no click, the hammer has followed the bolt down, and you need to find out why.

In 99.99% of cases, your rifle will pass these tests. If it did before you stripped and cleaned it but it doesn't now, then it is something you did. Dig in, find out what you did, and correct it.

CHAPTER 5

COMPLETE DISASSEMBLY

YOU HAVE THE field-stripped parts lying there on the bench. You need or want to completely disassemble your rifle. How to? First, resign yourself to a couple of probabilities. One, if you insist on taking everything off that can be taken off, you will lose one or more small parts. Tiny retaining plungers, springs and such have a way of disappearing themselves, even on a bare concrete floor.

Second, taking everything apart risks damaging some parts and cosmetically marring others. But, if you are going to be the complete AR owner you need to know what you can and can't do, and how to do it. That said, I will, in each area, give you a head's up. That is, in some instances you can take the parts completely apart, but there is no good reason unless you are upgrading or changing configurations. As an example, if you really want to, you can take the buffer tube off of your lower receiver when it is a tele-stock setup. However, there is no reason to do so, provided the current rig is tight and straight, unless you are switching it to a different tube. "Just because" is a poor reason, and there is no maintenance need to remove it.

But, I'll tell you how anyway.

Also, the disassembly and assembly instructions in this chapter go hand-in-hand with those of the previous chapter. I'm not going to repeat the disassembly part that got us here or the assembly part that we just did. I'll assume you remember what we just did, a few pages ago, and only cover the parts specific to our actions here.

So let's jump in.

BOLT AND CARRIER

The carrier is a non-disassemble-able part. It is a solid chunk of hardened steel, and the only part of it that comes off is the key. You need remove the key only to re-set it, when it is found to be loose, or to replace it if it is damaged or worn. If it is tight and undamaged, leave it alone. Let me repeat that, leave it alone. However, if you do have to remove it, you'll need an allen wrench. The bolts that hold the key in place come in two sizes. Invariably, whichever of the wrenches you pick up, your bolts will be the other size. That's life. So, you just pick up your allen wrench set and check for fit.

Look, I've told you, it isn't worth using. Buy the correct tool, or give up the idea of barrel changes.

To remove, unscrew the bolts and lift the key off. If it was properly tight, you'll feel and hear a snap as the bolt breaks loose. This was your clue that you need not have removed it, and should have left well enough alone. If, however, it loosens without that snap, it was going to come loose some day. And we all know that day would have been when you would not have liked or been helped by it coming loose.

If the key is damaged, replace it with a new one, using new screws. There is no amount of filing, peening, stoning or other hand-tool work you can do to salvage a worn or damaged gas key. Pitch it in the trash and install a new one. If not damaged, but found to be loose, clean and degrease the key and carrier, apply Loctite to the base of the key (one of the very few places you'll legitimately not just need to use, but are required to use, Loctite on the AR) and tighten the new screws down. Then stake the screws in, using a MOACKS, file/stone the burrs down and wipe clean. Can you re-use the old screws? Yes, but they are a highly-stressed

part at their torque setting and they are cheap. Buy and install new if you have the option.

Quick technical point: the torque limit on the gas key screws is 55 inch-pounds. That's right, 4.5 foot-pounds. If you do not have a torque wrench, simply use a regular-length allen wrench and reef the screw down tight. Do not use a longer one, or use pliers or a breaker bar. If you do, you will break, as the bar is so-named. You see, the failure point of the screws is under 100 in-lbs. You can shear the screwheads off, if you enthusiastically over-tighten them. Don't do that.

The bolt at this point (we've done a field strip) will still have the ejector in place. Clamp the bolt in the bolt disassembly tool and, using a small drift punch (1/16 inch), tap out the ejector retainer pin. Unscrew the ejector compressor bolt, and you now can remove the ejector and its spring.

While you have them out, drop some oil in there and let it soak while you do other things. You can't fill the hole, as there is an observation port in the bolt on the side, and the oil will run out.

The ejector must be removed by using the correct fixture. To do otherwise is to risk injury and loss of parts. Trust me, I did it enough the wrong way, you want to do it the right way.

Here is the bolt, ejector, spring and pin, out of the fixture.

If you need to remove the extractor spring, use a small screwdriver to pry it out, as close to the extractor seat as possible.

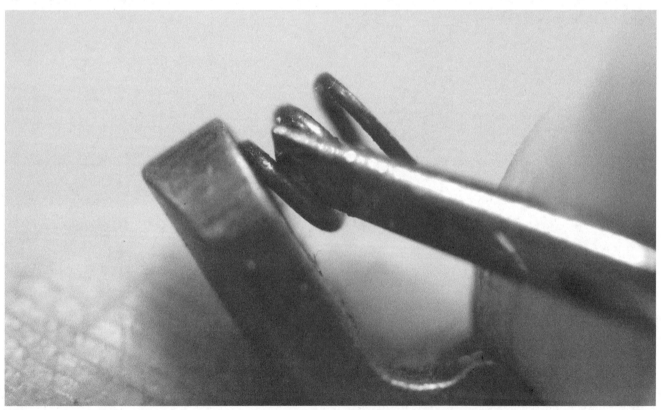

When pressing the new one in, hook one edge in the lip and then press with the screwdriver. (Internal buffer left out for clarity.)

When it comes time to reassemble, first clamp the bolt in a padded vise, face up, and put just the spring in. Take a close-fitting punch and pump the spring up and down, to cycle the oil through the hole. Then take the bolt, spring and ejector, and reassemble in the Brownells tool. Hint: the ejector has a clearance cut on it, where the retaining pin will capture it. Line up the cut with the location of the pin hole before you compress the ejector and spring. Once compressed, there is no way to re-align the ejector, so get it correct from the start.

The extractor, despite being disassemble-able, is something you should leave alone. If the extractor spring is the correct, stout, one, and it has a black buffer inside of it, don't take it apart. However, if it is an incorrect spring, or lacking the internal buffer, here's how to do it. Take a small, thin-bladed screwdriver (an eyeglass one will work well) and run the edge of the screwdriver blade into the coils, as close to the body of the extractor as possible. Push the blade of the screwdriver sideways, rotating it into the coils of the spring as much as possible. Once it is in tight, use it exactly like a bottle opener, and lever the spring out of its seat.

The extractor, if it has been properly made, has a recess, or lip, in the seat of the spring location, and the bottom-most coil of the spring locks into that recess. In any and all instances, removing the spring stresses the spring and incurs the risk of damaging it. So, do not remove the spring unless it has to be replaced or the proper internal buffer needs to be installed. Taking the spring off "to clean the extractor" is not needed and not wise.

To install the new/replacement/old-with-new-buffer spring, first take a close look at it. The coils taper out toward the bottom. That is, the bottom coil is larger in diameter than the top coil. That is so the bottom coil will seat in the recess. Put the extractor on the bench top, flat on its back. Take the spring and tip it so the coil-end of the bottom is slightly down more than the rest. Push the coil-end tip into the recess. Take your small screwdriver and place it on the top side of the bottom-most coil. Not the whole spring, but just the bottom coil. Push the bottom coil down, seating it in the recess.

Trying to press the whole spring with a screwdriver blade risks damaging the spring. Or, the spring will flex sideways, jump out from under the blade and disappear under the workbench, not to be seen until after the Brownells package with

Now this is incorrect headspace. Here, a rifle in .30-06 had a round of .308 fired in it. Note the shoulder has been blown forward, and the escaping gas from the primer blew off the extractor.

new springs arrives.

An alternative way to install it incurs other risks. If you use the tip of a loaded round, one with a relatively blunt tip, and push straight down on the spring (using the cartridge straight down) you can compress the spring into the seat without it squirming and jumping out. But, this means having a loaded round on your workbench, a hazardous situation. A suitable replacement is a dulled centerpunch. Use the tip of the centerpunch to press the coils straight down. Even with the dulled centerpunch, one slip and your extractor spring and its internal buffer have been launched across the room.

Extractors wear, but not like people expect. One test is to run the clean and dry extractor, hook down, across the palm of your hand. If you feel a grabby, "kitten teeth"-like edge on the corners, the extractor is in good shape. If not, it is a bit worn but will probably still work just fine for a long time. The thing to really check for is cracks. A crack, or anything that looks like a crack, is cause for a new extractor. The extractor is a small, highly-stressed part, and once cracked it won't last long.

When reassembling, make sure you have the D-Fender or O ring around the extractor spring, and compress the extractor into the bolt, at the pivot pin, as you press the pivot pin through.

UPPER RECEIVER

There is really nothing you have to take off of the upper receiver in the normal process of cleaning or inspecting., Of the things you might need to take off, you will need to do so only if you are replacing them. However, here's how.

The front sight, if zeroed, need not be removed, In fact, you probably, if you sight it in properly, will leave the front sight un-touched until you remove the barrel from the upper due to wear, and contemplate salvaging the front sight parts before you turn the shot-out barrel into a tomato stake. But, you still need to know how, and you might need to swap it out.

The front sight is spring-loaded, and the spring and plunger fit upwards into the notches around the base of the sight post. To press the plunger, use a small pin punch. To rotate the sight to unscrew it, use a sight adjustment tool. Or, if your sight is an A2, use the head end of a Philips-head screw.

Excessive headspace can be bad. This was an extreme example, and it blew out the primer, trashing the extractor.

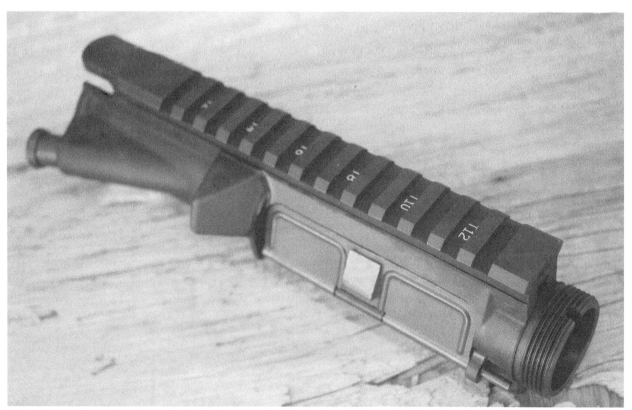

A flat-top upper receiver. Some will have the rail slots numbered, some won't.

The front sight is best adjusted with two small punches, one to press down the plunger, the other to turn the sight. Don't believe the "use a bullet tip" approach.

OK, a slight back-up in this process, and background on sights. The A1 front sight post is a tapered round post, and the adjustment skirt of it has five notches. This works fine for people-shooting. The Marines, however, wanted something better for the A2, and thus the A2 sight is a four-sided vertical post. (They wanted all the advantages they could get, limited to iron sights. Remember, this was back in the early 1980s, when only bolt-action sniper rifles had optics on them.) It has four notches in the skirt, so that when you turn the sight to screw it up or down, you always have a flat facing you and square edges on the sides. You see, a round post reflects light differentially, and in long-range shooting you would be aiming very slightly off-center due to the light reflecting off of one side of the post cylinder differently than the other. Actually, you'd be aiming off at all distances, but it doesn'; really show up until you're out past "plinking" distances. An inch or two at 100 yards is no big deal in people-whacking, but when you get to five or six hundred, that can mean a miss.

Despite the protective wings, light from the side has the effect of making that side of the cylinder brighter, optically thinning the post, and creating an effect where the shooter "shoots toward the light." A square post does not do that.

Thus a four-sided post, and four adjustment notches per turn. This increased the distance each click of a sight change makes at 100 yards (or any distance, for that matter) but being off half-a-click is a minor, almost inconsequential, offset.

So, the square-sided post of the A2 fits into the head slot of a Philips screw, and you can use one of them to turn the post easily.

Inside, the front sight assembly consists of the front sight post, the adjustment plunger and the adjustment spring. If you do remove them, take the time to scrub the threads on the sight post, and aerosol-clean and brush the threads in the sight base. Then hose it with oil and screw the sight back in. If you have it, screwing a tap of the correct thread pitch down into the front sight housing (8X36, a bottoming tap works well, but you probably won't need to clean up the threads all the way down) and cleaning up the threads will make reassembling the sight easier.

Once you have your front sight properly adjusted, you might never need to touch it again. But it can be adjusted if you need to.

While we're up here, should you remove the front sight housing? As in, take it off of the barrel? In my opinion, no you should not. If you are replacing it with a low-profile gas block or a folding front sight assembly, fine. But there's nothing to be gained by removing it just to put it back. However, if you must, then you should start by not doing anything more, picking up the parts catalog and waiting for your front sight bench block to arrive. The block not only holds the front sight housing in place for you to remove the pins, it indicates which side is which, so you don't spend time fruitlessly trying to pound out the tapered pins in the wrong direction.

Before you remove it, inspect the front sight assembly and see just how far the pins protrude from the "hoop" on the base. The pins, when you put the front sight housing back together, have to

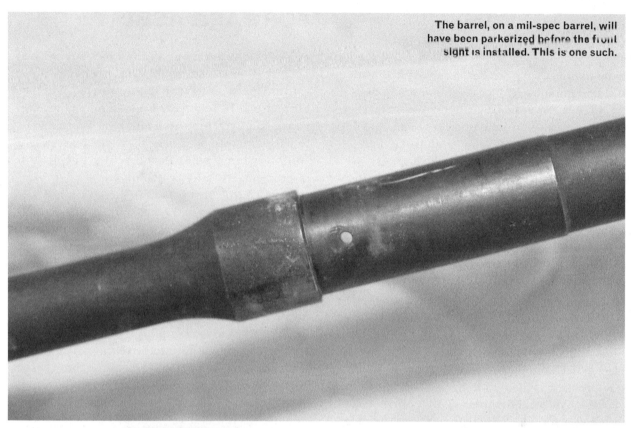

The barrel, on a mil-spec barrel, will have been parkerized before the front sight is installed. This is one such.

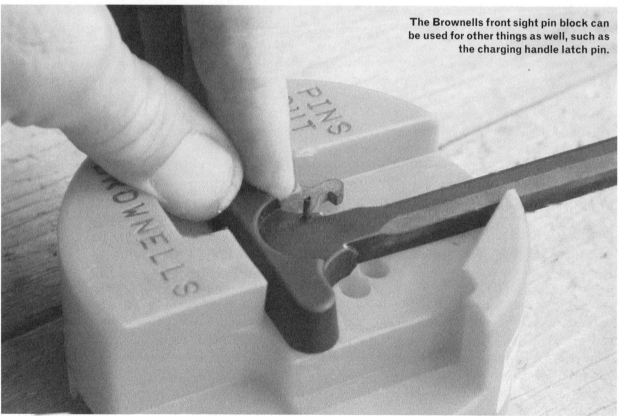

The Brownells front sight pin block can be used for other things as well, such as the charging handle latch pin.

go back to the level you see them at now.

If you must do this, strip the bolt, carrier and charging handle out of the upper. Remove the handguards. Clamp the barrel in your vise with the aluminum barrel blocks, and unscrew the flash hider. Place the barrel in the block, on the "remove" side, on a sturdy bench or concrete floor. With a large ball-peen hammer and a tapered (but not pointed) punch, strike the ends of the retaining pins a sharp rap. You aren't trying to drive them out with this hit, only to loosen them in their seat.

Once they are loose, take a close-fitting punch and tap the pins out. Once the pins are out, take a rawhide mallet or rubber hammer and tap the front sight housing off the front of the barrel. Leave the gas tube attached to the front sight.

While you have the front sight housing off, you can take a look to see if the mil-spec mavens have cause to mock you for your choice in barrels. They place great store in the barrel, before the front sight housing is fitted to it, having been parkerized or black oxided. If the front sight housing was installed before the Parkerizing or black oxiding instead of after, the part of the barrel that is underneath the front sight "hoops" will be bare steel, not parkerized.

Does it matter? To the government it does, they are paying extra to make sure the parkerizing comes first, followed by sight installation. The rest of us? No big deal.

To re-install turn the bench block over to the install side. Press the front sight housing back down on the barrel to line it up with the cross pin holes. When you do that, make sure you thread the gas tube through the gaps in the barrel nut, spring and delta ring, into the receiver. Line up the pin holes for the front sight housing with the pin holes in the barrel. Do not count on forcing the front sight housing and barrel to line up by forcing the pins. Line them up as best you can.

Press the pins in as far as you can by hand. Then select the largest-diameter pin punch you have, and your heavy ball-peen hammer. Give each of the pins a solid rap, and drive them in as far as they were before you removed them.

Screw the flash hider back on, and replace the handguards.

FORWARD ASSIST

On the upper receiver, if it is a modern one and not a retro or pre-1970s-era Colt, you'll have a forward assist along with the dust cover. Will these ever have to be removed? No, not unless they are damaged or you are detail stripping the receiver to have it refinished. These parts just don't break. Well, very rarely will a dust cover have some sort of problem. Forward assists, never.

The forward assist is held in place by a roll pin through the angled housing that sticks out of the receiver. To remove it, select a fitting roll-pin punch. Remove the upper receiver from the lower (if you haven't already) and place it on the bench, on its assembly lugs. Place an edge of the bench block under the edge of the receiver, at the rear lug. You can then tap the roll pin down until the forward assist assembly pops free, driven by its spring. You do not have to drive the pin all the way out, and leaving it sticking out of the receiver will make reassembly easier.

The forward assist is a two-part assembly. The cam itself is a round bar, and it has a hinged forward section with a spring inside and a camming hook. This never comes apart. It may be shown in an exploded parts diagram, but the individual parts are not parts you can order. If, for some reason the forward assist needs service, you replace this assembly.

The forward assist is pushed back (after doing its job) by the bigger spring that surrounded it when you pulled the assembly out of the receiver. The spring probably won't need replacing unless, in all this, you drop it and step on it while trying to pick it up. It just doesn't receive that much stress in its normal workday, and almost never needs replacing.

To reassemble, turn the upper receiver over and rest it on the carry handle or, if you have a flat top, on the top rail. (Take the sights off.) Press the forward assist assembly into the receiver, clearance flat oriented to make room for the roll pin. Press the forward assist forward, and hold it there. Brace the receiver with your hand, and use the ball peen hammer to tap the pin back into place. (Now you see why you left it still in the receiver.) Once the pin is in far enough to hold in the forward assist,

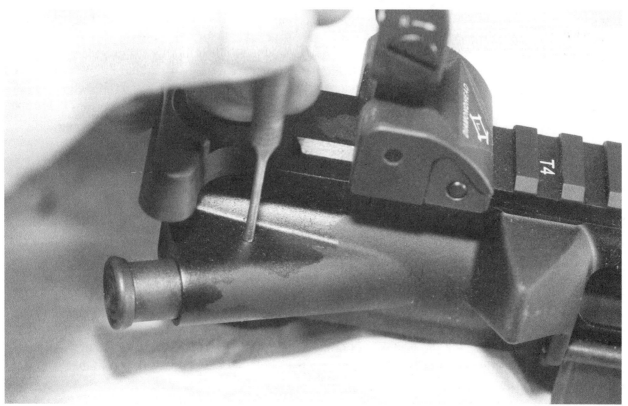

Removing the forward assist assembly is simple. Stand the upper on its lugs, and tap out the roll pin.

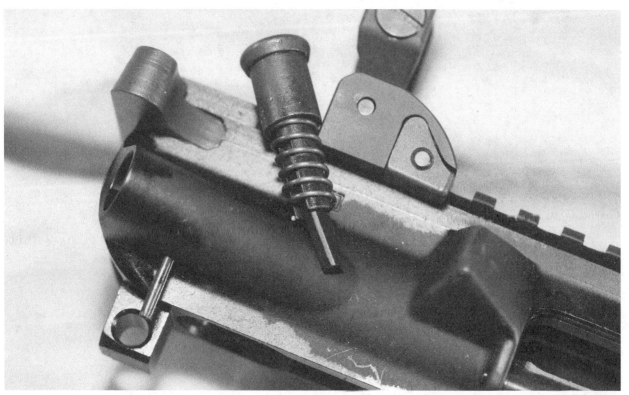

Leave the roll pin partially in the upper, it saves work later. Notice that the forward assist is an assembly, and you won't ever have to take this apart.

you can let go of the pressure on it. Tap the pin flush, and then use a roll-pin punch to tap it just below flush. Check both sides to make sure you don't drive it in too far causing it to protrude from the other side. That's wrong. Get it flush or under-flush on both sides.

DUST COVER

The dust cover is an entirely different matter. Where the forward assist is almost a trivial exercise in removal and replacement, the dust cover is an incredible hassle. Why?

The dust cover is powered by a spiral spring that wraps around the pivot pin. It has two legs, one pushing against the cover to open it, and the other pushing against the upper receiver. It works exactly like a mousetrap. Look closely at the pivot pin, at the front. You'll see a tiny little "E" clip on the shaft. That clip, forward of the dust cover boss, keeps the pin from sliding out the back. And what

keeps it from sliding out the front? The delta ring.

Your options for removing the dust cover are limited to two, and both are a great hassle. To remove it from the rear you have to first find a pair of pliers small enough to grasp the E clip and yank it off the shaft. Then, pulling the pivot pin out the rear, you run the end of it into the forward assist housing. That's as far as you get, and you have to then tip it and wriggle the door off, replace it, get the spring on in the process, and wind the spring. Then, the real hassle begins. You have to find a way to hold the E clip while you press it back on to the dust cover door hinge pin.

To remove it from the front, you don't have to remove the E clip. No, you have to remove the barrel. And having tried many times to make "remove it from the rear" work, I'm here to tell you, leave it alone. If you absolutely must replace it (damage would perhaps be the only good reason), take the barrel off. No, I'm not kidding, take the barrel off. We'll get to that in good time.

A correctly-assembled dustcover hinge pin spring.

The front of the AR receiver, and the threads onto which the barrel nut will screw. Also note the dust cover hinge pin and its retaining clip. The hinge pin has to come out of the receiver to the front, which means taking off the barrel.

A close-up of the dust cover hinge pin and its retainer.

REAR SIGHTS

Rear sights are the only thing left.

The A1 is simple, durable and, in a lot of circles, out of fashion. But it certainly is a viable iron-sight option for shooting people. Not so much for full-on target competition, but more than enough for defense, duty and combat, and certainly more rugged than the A2.

To disassemble the A1 you need a drift pin, preferably a roll-pin punch, of the right size, and a screwdriver that fits the sight adjustment screw slot. You will also have to re-zero your rifle after you are done.

Turn the rear sight windage wheel until the roll pin is in the most upward orientation possible. Clamp it in your fixture, or hold the barrel in a vise, and support the receiver firmly. Line the roll pin punch up with the roll pin and tap it out. You can try to leave the roll pin still attached to the wheel, but you'll fail most of the time and it will fall off when you go to reassemble. The wheel comes off, and the spring and plunger underneath, the one you have to depress to rotate the wheel, can then be pulled from the handle.

At this point, you are left with two options. One, congratulate yourself for not losing anything, and put it back. Or two, remove the rest of the sight and have to re-zero your rifle at the next range trip. You want to continue? OK. Use the best-fitting screwdriver in your collection and screw the adjustment screw counter-clockwise. You are screwing the rear sight aperture to the right, until it rests against the right-hand wall of the inside of the carry handle. Then keep turning, and unscrew the screw from the handle and aperture.

Once it comes apart, you'll have the screw, the aperture and the flat spring that rests under the aperture and keeps it in whichever setting you place it. OK, it isn't really a flat spring, it is a curved little bit of flat steel with small "feet" on the ends.

To reassemble, place the flat spring in the recess, hump up and feet down. Press the aperture down against it, and press the adjustment screw in from the side. Turn the screw to capture the aperture, and keep turning it until you get the threads of the screw caught on the threads of the aperture.

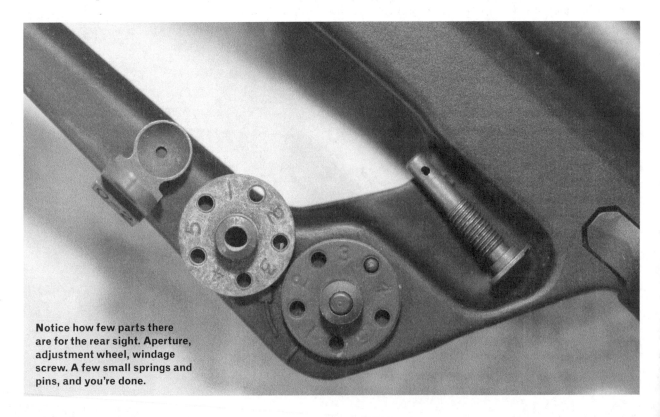

Notice how few parts there are for the rear sight. Aperture, adjustment wheel, windage screw. A few small springs and pins, and you're done.

Keep turning the screw until you can line it up with the hole on the right-hand side, and press the aperture down to let the screw tip pass through the hole. Keep turning the adjustment screw until the aperture is more or less in the middle. This will save you work later.

Once the aperture is reasonably centered, turn the adjustment screw until the hole for the roll pin is in its previous upright orientation. Install the spring and plunger in the hole in the handle, and press the plate down onto them. Now, use another pin punch as a slave pin to hold it all in place. Use a small-tipped pliers to hold the roll pin, and tap it into the hole and plate, using it to displace the slave pin/pin punch.

On your next range trip, do your zero process all over again.

The A2 sight? Really? First, take a good, long look at it. The A2 sight has both a windage wheel (the knob on the right side) and an elevation wheel for range (the one enclosed by the handle, underneath), and they work separately.

You can remove/disassemble each without having to take a single piece off of the other. The windage is dead simple, it is the same process as the A1 sight, just with a bigger knob to hold on to. So, see above.

Elevation, not so simple. To do this right and get it back together again, you need a special tool: the elevation adjustment spring compression tool. This will cost you eleven dollars from Brownells. You could make one, but by the time you do, you'll wish you had just added one to the previous Brownells order.

Before you start, note the position of the wheel. At the lowest, or zero, setting, you should have two or three clicks of additional downwards movement. If so, good. If not, then it has been assembled incorrectly, and you'll have to correct that when you re-assemble.

On the upper receiver, below the A2 sight, you'll see a cross pin. Take a correctly-fitting pin punch and drift this pin out. Take some care, as it contains the elevation spring, and when the pin is out (and you pull the punch out) the spring will attempt to launch itself.

Here, minus the springs and plungers, are the main parts of the A2 sight assembly. The knob adjusts windage. The wheel, trapped in the upper receiver, lifts or lowers the housing when it is turned. Clever, complicated, and useful mostly on the target range.

Before you go any further, take some notes. Start with the zero setting. Two or three clicks down, still? Good. If not, then you'll be building from scratch. When you get to the point in the following process that the elevation shaft, the threaded portion, comes free from the elevation wheel, note the exact orientation of the wheel. With a bit of luck you can re-assemble it exactly as it was and not have to re-set things. Of course, if it is wrong now, you'll have to re-set, so we'll go over that when we get there.

With the pin and spring out, turn the elevation wheel to lift the sight, and keep turning it until the sight comes free. Again, take some care here, as there is a little spring and plunger in the upper edge of the front of the A2 assembly. That spring and plunger act to keep the A2 sight housing tensioned and running up and down smoothly. It, too, lives to jump free when uncovered.

With the assembly out, the wheel will come out as well. More cautions: the clicks you have been experiencing are brought to you courtesy of the spring and plunger that are in the upper receiver,

in the elevation wheel window, and they too will squirrel out. They are also a royal pain to get back in, and hold in place, when it comes time to re-install the wheel. Notice that the wheel is actually two wheels; one is the threaded portion, and the other is the distance setting wheel. You will probably have to re-set this, unless you were very careful in removing them.

This is the disassembled A2 elevation assembly.

If the original assembly was wrong (i.e., not 2-3 clicks down to bottom) then take a tiny allen wrench and loosen and remove the screw that holds the two halves of the elevation wheel together.

Hold the two halves together as you screw the wheel onto the elevation shaft. Get the tensioning spring and plunger into their hole, and a screw the assembly all the way down. Once all the way down (one of the two knurled rims of the assembly will do all the work, the other will simply spin, loose on the shaft) you are almost there.

Take the actual adjustment wheel and give it two

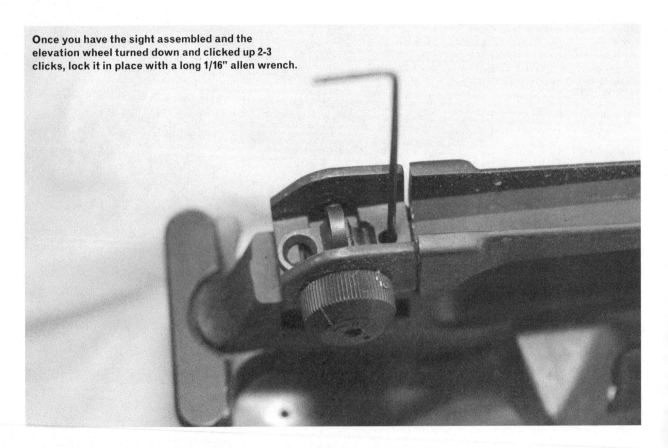

Once you have the sight assembled and the elevation wheel turned down and clicked up 2-3 clicks, lock it in place with a long 1/16" allen wrench.

or three clicks up from bottomed-out. Then take the tiny allen screw you removed, and the allen wrench you used to remove it. Look at the front of the A2 assembly. See the little hole there? That's the access hole for the elevation wheel lock screw, the tiny allen screw in your hand. Adjust the free-spinning part of the elevation wheel until the 3/6 or the 3/8 markings are on the direct left side of the handle. Insert the locking screw into the hole, and tighten it down, locking the two wheels together. Your sight is now set at the proper mechanical zero for the A2 rear elevation.

You will in all likelihood have to do a re-zero process at the range, especially if the wheel had been improperly assembled before.

But wait, you aren't done yet. Put the upper receiver on its side. Insert the elevation spring in from the interior of the upper receiver. Compress it with the tool from Brownells, and drive the roll pin back in place.

The only times you will ever do this again is in assembling an A2 upper from scratch. If you have to re-set an incorrectly assembled elevation assembly, the process is a lot easier. To do that, turn the wheel until you can see the locking screw, down at the bottom of the access hole. Unscrew it. Then turn the wheel down to bottom, and then back up 2 or 3 clicks. Rotate the elevation indicator to the 3/6 or 3/8 setting, and lock them together again. Then re-zero.

Technical notes: the "3/6" and "3/8" are the range markings in meters, for the sight setting. The 3/6 is meant for carbines, and the 3/8 is meant for full-sized rifles.

BARRELS

The subject of barrels is one that gets more over-thinking, and less preparation, than any other in the AR-verse. To start, you'll need the proper tools: an upper receiver clamp or barrel extension bar; a barrel nut wrench; a big, solid vise to clamp things; and that vise on a solid bench. Useful, but not always needed, would be a barrel nut alignment gauge, and gas tube clamp.

Field strip the upper receiver. Remove the handguards. Use the bench block and remove the gas tube roll pin, and wrestle the gas tube out.

Clamp the upper receiver in the holding fixture, or clamp the barrel extension bar in the vise and slide the upper receiver over it.

If you are taking the barrel off to learn how, and will be putting the same barrel, with the same nut, back on, take a moment. With a paint pencil or grease pencil, mark the notch on the barrel nut that is in line with the gas tube clearance hole. That's the notch you'll want back on top when you re-assemble.

The back of the barrel, with the barrel extension unscrewed and removed.

Put the barrel wrench over the barrel nut. If your rifle has the delta ring or slip ring, you'll have to press back against the waffle spring to make sure the wrench gets a solid bite on the barrel nut.

Unscrew.

Ok, stop laughing, those of you who have done it. The torque limits for the AR-15 barrel nut are impossibly wide. Where the bolts on the carrier key have a torque limit of 55 in-lbs, +/- 2 in-lbs, the barrel nut is 30 to 80 foot pounds. Stop blinking, those are the numbers. What this means is simple, if a barrel nut had been torqued on to the upper limit and has since then been shot a lot, or painted to camouflage it, the barrel nut could easily require more than 80 ft-lbs to remove it. You may have to struggle to get it loose.

Once you have it loose, spin the nut off. Remove

the barrel by simply pulling it straight out of the receiver. That's it.

To re-install, first take a moment to wipe off all the excess carbon and gunk that you find. You might as well start out clean, after all.

Press the barrel back into the receiver. (If you used holding blocks, it is still there. If you use a barrel extension bar, it is riding on the bar.) Line up the alignment pin with the notch on the receiver, and press until it stops. Hand-screw the barrel nut back on as far as you can, and then get the wrench. Tighten the nut until you can't. Look at the notches. Does the original one line up? Then you're done.

If it does not, you have to keep re-tightening. That's the reason you have such a wide range. 30 ft-lbs (which a strong man can almost do bare-handed) is the threshold. Once you reach that, you go as tight as you need to get the notch to line up. Once you reach 80, something is wrong and you should stop. Most AR assemblers have learned how much is enough, and how much is "too much" and don't use a torque wrench.

If you are re-installing the barrel, just keep at it until you get the original notch to line up.

If you are installing a new barrel, you have a few extra steps. Loosen the barrel nut and re-tighten. Repeat. The third time, torque to line the notch up. This is to burnish the threads of the nut and receiver, and iron down any irregularities that might be there.

A question that comes up repeatedly is, "what do I put on the threads?" Some advocate anti-seize compounds. Some, Loctite. (Stay away from advocates of the latter.) Me, I just wipe the threads with a bit of oil to keep them from galling. Once tight, it won't come loose, and Loctite just makes it impossible to take apart when you need to replace a barrel. Anti-seize might have some applications if you spend all your time in the surf zone and worry about galvanic corrosion. If you don't, then don't.

Here is where the alignment gauge might come in handy. Strip the bolt and carrier, and plug the gauge into the gas key of the carrier. Then hand-insert the carrier into the upper receiver (clearly you'll have to remove the receiver from the holding fixture to do this) and see if the gauge clears the notch in the nut. If it does, you're done. If not, you

have to either tighten or loosen until it does.

Once the nut is lined up, re-install the gas tube and put the parts back on.

BARREL NUT ASSEMBLY

While you have the barrel off, let's look at the barrel nut assembly. The assembly is comprised of the delta ring, a multi-section spring called the waffle spring or weld spring, and the retaining clip, known in the industry as a "C" clip. (In the official manuals, it is the "barrel snap ring.") To strip this assembly, you need reverse pliers. Stick the tips of the pliers into the little holes in the C clip and spread the clip. This removes it from the groove on the barrel extension. The waffle spring and delta ring then come off the back of the barrel. You'll notice that there is no way to disassemble this unit, or even remove it from the rifle, without having the barrel out of the upper receiver.

Its design explains a lot of dremel action in AR gunsmithing circles. If you want to install a free-float forearm, one that clamps onto the barrel nut, but don't want to remove the barrel, the only way to do this is to cut them off.

Of course, most users who want to install a free-float handguard also want to replace the standard front sight housing, so they are taking that off, and might as well remove the barrel, too.

To re-assemble, clamp the barrel in a padded vise. Push the delta ring on the barrel, then the waffle spring. Put the C clip in your reverse pliers and use it to press the waffle spring forward enough to get some part of the C clip into the groove. Once you have it secured enough that it won't come off, press the rest of the C clip forward until it all snaps down into the groove.

GAS TUBE

Oh, that is a hassle? Notice the bend, the dogleg in the tube? Use that to your advantage. Turn it so the dogleg lets you clear the front sight tower, and thread it into the receiver. In all the barrel nut screwing and un-screwing, the gaps in the delta ring, snap ring and waffle spring have gotten out of alignment. So use a small screwdriver to push

The gas tube has a hole in it for gas flow. When assembling, make sure that hole is down, towards the barrel. Otherwise the rifle won't work, and you know how I know that.

The gas port, hidden under the front sight assembly.

Here you see the correct alignment of the gas port, tube and front sight housing.

them around until they line up.

Thread the tube into the upper, then back to the front sight housing. Make sure you have the open end of the gas tube down and press it into the front sight housing or gas block. Watch through the gas pin hole as you press it forward, and line up the gas tube pin hole in the front sight block pin hole. Put it in your block, and drive the gas pin in.

Last check. Once the barrel is on and the gas tube installed, grab your stripped carrier and take the barrel nut alignment gauge out of the gas key. Slide the carrier in, and feel it slide over the end of the gas tube. Or rather, feel that there is no feeling of it sliding over. If it binds, resists, catches or rubs, you need to align the gas tube.

Your alignment tool is a big-blade screwdriver to adjust side-to-side, and a narrow-blade long screwdriver to adjust up and down. If it binds and you have to adjust, turn the receiver over and watch the gas tube as the key slides over it.

You'll probably be able to see which way it moves. Grab a screwdriver and bend the tube to relieve the binding. Do this until the two slide together smoothly.

LOWER RECEIVER

We're starting on the lower with the buffer and spring out, and the internals of the lower out (the hammer, trigger and disconnector). Your safety may or may not be out, depending on the state of the groove it uses to fit with the spring and plunger. Turn the lower over and peer up into the handle. In a mil-spec, or even a properly-built lower, the screw that holds the pistol grip ion will be a big-slot regular screw, nickel-plated. Some love the allen screws that have snuck into use, I hate them. There are two sizes, and you never have the proper one in hand (or on the bench) when you need it. A big screw just needs a big screwdriver, and finding one that fits and is long

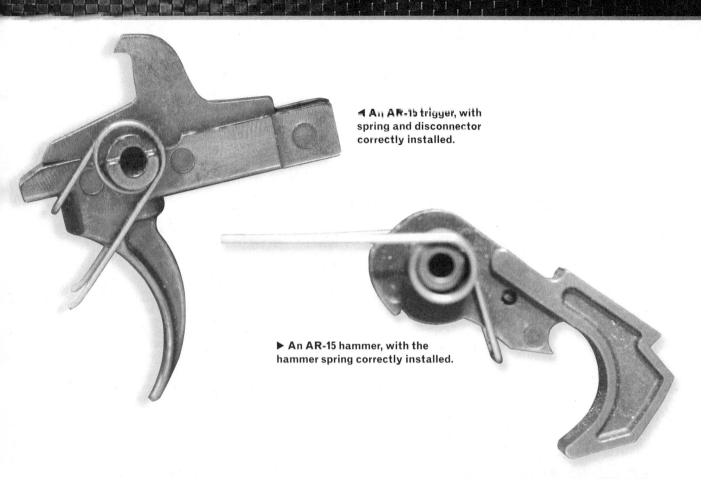

◀ An AR-15 trigger, with spring and disconnector correctly installed.

▶ An AR-15 hammer, with the hammer spring correctly installed.

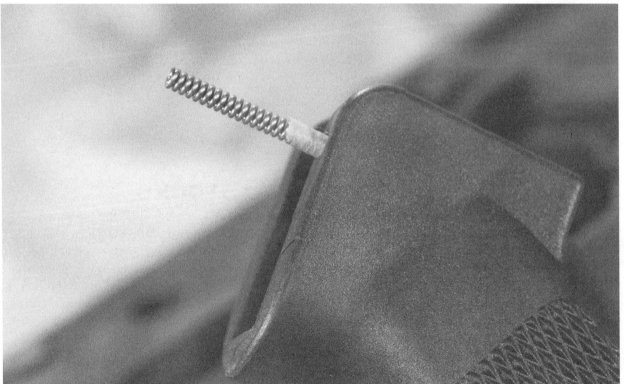

Save yourself some hassle and use a bit of tape. Wrap it around the bottom end of the spring and stuff it back into the pistol grip. Now it won't fall out.

enough is easier than finding the correct-size allen wrench, and is also long enough. Your standard hardware store allen wrenches, sold practically by the pound, will be too short. (That's the other reason I hate them.)

Unscrew the screw, whatever type it is. The pistol grip holds in the spring and plunger that bear on the safety lever.

When you pull the pistol grip off, the spring will try to leave, but the plunger will often stay put, held in by grease, oxidized oil or sheer willfulness. Don't trust it to stay. Turn the safety lever, which pushes the plunger down a bit. Remove the safety lever. Then poke a stiff spring down into the plunger hole from the top (the leg of the hammer or trigger spring will do nicely) and catch the plunger before it has a chance to scurry for the shag rug.

The trigger guard is held by two pins. One is spring-loaded, and depressing it allows you to pivot the guard down and use the rifle with mittens on, humorously referred to as a "winter trigger' adaptation. The other end is held in with a roll pin. Do not remove this. No, I'm not kidding, don't remove it. The only reason to screw around here is that you are replacing the standard trigger guard with something else, or building from scratch.

The danger comes from the small, delicate ears that the trigger guard pin goes through. Break one off, and you've effectively trashed a lower.

If you must, here's how. Find a backing block that allows you to put the lower down flat and supported without wobble. Take a closely-fitting roll pin punch, or flat-end drift punch, and drift the pin almost out. Leave it as much in the opposite ear as possible, to make life easier when you put in the new trigger guard.

Check the new one for fit and alignment. If you're sure it fits, then turn the lower over and tap the pin just hard enough to capture the new guard. Once you know the new guard is lined up and caught, then (and only then) drive it flush. If you just hammer down on it, assuming the pin will find the hole, you'll break things.

On to the back end.

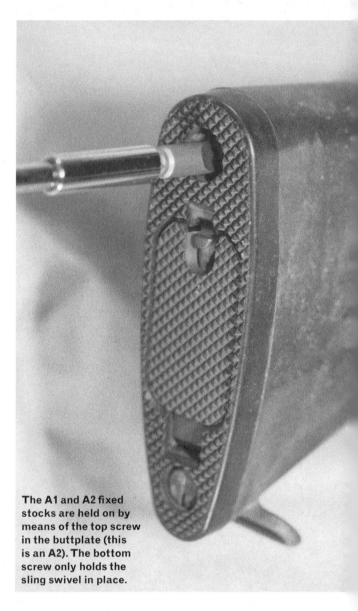

The A1 and A2 fixed stocks are held on by means of the top screw in the buttplate (this is an A2). The bottom screw only holds the sling swivel in place.

A1/A2 STOCKS

The fixed stock is held on by the big screw you see on the top end of the buttplate. With a big screwdriver, unscrew it. Before you get too far, take a look at the rear of the lower receiver. See the raised ridge, running back from the rear takedown pin? That covers the plunger and spring that keep the takedown pin in the receiver. That spring is held in by the stock. If you remove the stock, the spring can fall out.

Don't let it.

Once the screw is out, pull the stock back off the buffer tube. Grab the takedown retainer spring

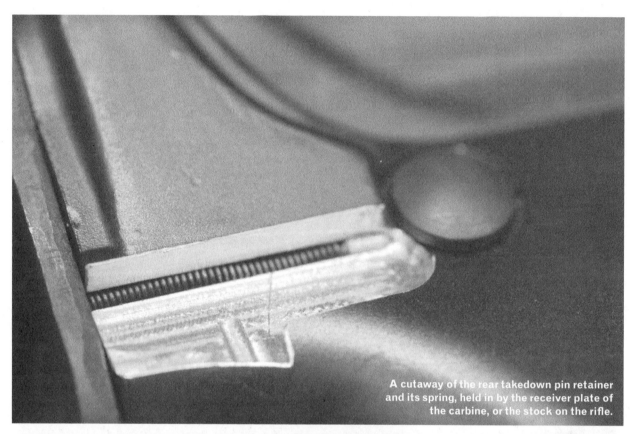

A cutaway of the rear takedown pin retainer and its spring, held in by the receiver plate of the carbine, or the stock on the rifle.

The fence at the top of the magazine well holds the front takedown pin's retainer and spring.

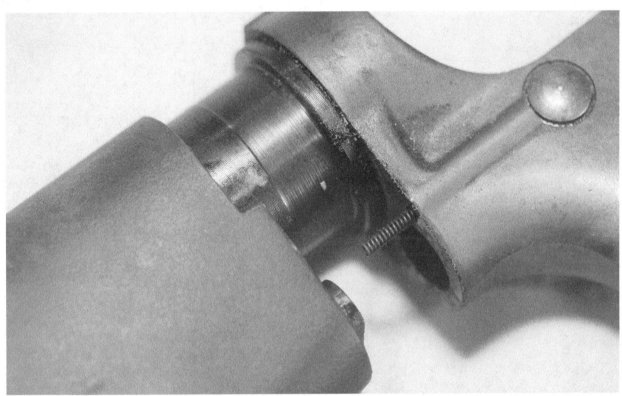

The A1/A2 fixed stock buffer tube simply screws into the receiver, and stops on the machined ring. The stock then traps the rear takedown spring inside its tunnel.

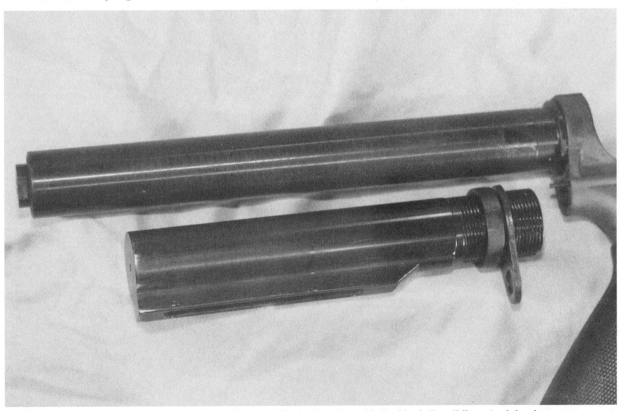

The carbine buffer tube is shorter, and has a rib along the bottom to guide and lock the sliding stock in place.

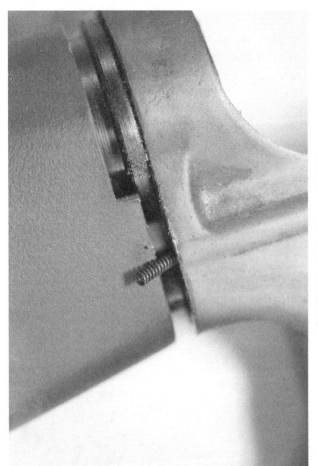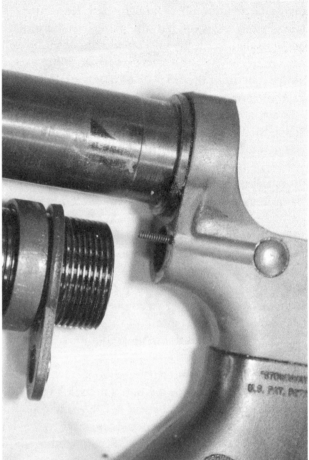

Left: When re-assembling, take care to not pinch the takedown spring in the gap, or else it won't work. Right: The carbine stock needs extra parts to do what the fixed stock does. It needs the retaining plate to hold in the takedown spring, and the castle nut to lock the retaining plate in place.

and pull it free. The plunger in there is even more obstinate than the one in the safety, but don't let it have its way. You can use a tool you're going to have to make, that will come in handy for the front takedown pin. Take a small allen wrench (an extra, and these things practically breed on your bench top, so don't worry about practicing, or using one up) and file the short leg at an angle. You want to make it so when you plop the short end into the groove on the takedown pin, the angled tip acts to pivot the plunger back out of the way. Pry the plunger back, remove the pin, and use your hammer spring leg to push the plunger all of the way out the back.

The buffer tube on the fixed-stock rifles is simply screwed into the receiver. Yes, there's a torque setting/requirement for it, but no one

bothers. It is probably only on there hand-tight. Hold the receiver firmly in one hand and use the other to wring the tube off. If it won't budge, then you need to clamp the lower. Use a heavily-padded vise. (Do not use a magazine well block and clamp the vise on the block. You have been warned.) Clamp down at the bottom, so the bottom of the receiver acts as a lateral support to the clamping. You won't need much. Use a crescent wrench, or the curved opening in a stock wrench, and get the tube free. Only break it free, don't spin it off just yet.

Remember when you took the buffer and spring out? The plunger and its spring are held in by a lip of the buffer tube. Unscrew the buffer tube, and you let loose the retainer plunger and spring. So, put your thumb over the plunger, and then unscrew the tube. Once the tube clears the plunger you can stop, pull the plunger and spring out, and then continue unscrewing the tube.

To re-install is simple. Start screwing in the buffer tube until the front lip of it gets to the hole for the retainer and spring. Insert the spring, then retainer, and hold them down with your thumb. Screw the buffer tube back on. When it stops, you're done. Torque it up however you wish; either grab hold of the tube and receiver and wring it on as tightly as you can with your bare hands, or clamp it as before and use the wrench to give it a tweak. You do not need a breaker bar to get it "tight enough."

Slide the takedown pin back in. Push the plunger back in (it is double-ended, so don't worry about which is which) and then push in the spring. Slide the stock on, and as you push it to the back of the receiver, make sure it pushes the retaining spring in evenly and doesn't just fold it over and crush it.

Tighten the stock screw. You're done.

The bottom screw on the buttplate holds in the sling loop. (We can't really call it a sling swivel, since it doesn't swivel, but people do anyway. Don't worry too much about it.) If you need to take the buttplate off of the stock, remove both screws.

Tube off and back on, that leaves only a few other things.

LOWER RECEIVER, LEFT SIDE

The bolt hold-open lever? Leave it alone. Seriously, and even more-so than previous times I've told you to leave it alone, don't touch it. Unless you are building from scratch, all you can do, practicing here, is scratch your lower receiver, even with the proper tools. So leave it.

The magazine catch is another matter. This is easy. If you have another magazine button, place it over the button on the right side and press in. Bottom out the assembly, and the leg of the magazine catch will stick out past the sidewall of the lower, on the left. Unscrew the leg. Continue until it comes free. To assemble, place the spring

in the mag well button shaft, and compress it with the two-button stack. Insert the leg from the left, and screw it until it catches.

Now it is a simple matter of screwing it in far enough, but not too far. Screw and check until the tip of the magazine catch leg is flush with the surface of the button top, on the right side. Less, and you might not be able to press the button enough to release a magazine. Too much, and you leave the shaft protruding, gain no extra latch surface, and give critics a chance to "dis" your rifle-building skills.

That leaves the miserable little s.o.b., the front takedown pin.

The fence, the rounded ridge that runs along the top edge of the receiver on the right side, holds the spring and plunger for the front takedown pin. To work here you'll need your modified allen

The bolt hold-open lever is held in by means of a roll pin. You need a special, flat-sided punch, fixture and patience to install it. You do not take it out just for practice. If it is in and works, leave it alone. All you can do is gouge your receiver "practicing."

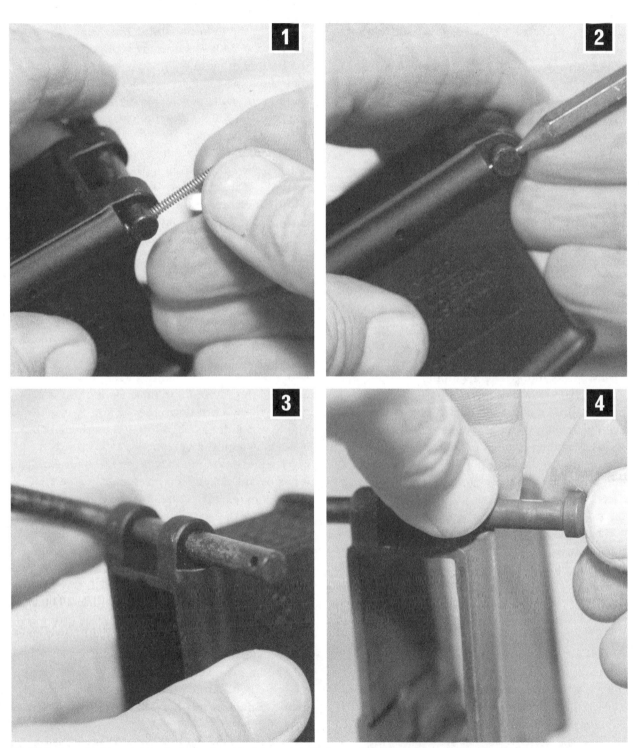

(1) Slide the takedown tool in from the far side. Line up the holes and press in the spring. (2) Drop in the plunger and press it down with the drift punch. Once level, rotate the assembly tool, trapping the plunger and spring. (3) With the plunger and spring trapped, you can grab the takedown pin to install it. (4) Tent your fingertips over the tunnel, to keep things in place under spring pressure. Then use the takedown pin to push the assembly tool out of the receiver.

wrench, to reach into the groove, and a front takedown pin assembly tool. You can get the parts back together without the tool, but having it makes the job so much easier, and avoids parts loss, that you should buy it. No, you must buy it if you are going to work on the front takedown pin.

Open the takedown pin. Insert your special tool. Lever the retaining plunger down until you can pull off the takedown pin. Keep your third hand over the end of the receiver so the plunger doesn't get launched free by its spring. To remove the spring, use the gently bent end of a paperclip to fish down and hook it, and then pull it out. Unless, of course, it decides to fall free on its own.

To get the parts back in, use your assembly tool. Notice one end has a hole through it? OK, insert the end with the hole into the loops of the receiver front, from the left side. Line up the hole in the tool with the hole in the receiver. Press the spring, and then the plunger. Press the plunger flush with a pin punch or allen wrench of the right size, and then turn the tool to capture the plunger and spring in the receiver channel.

Now, press in the takedown pin from the right side. Do not pull the tool out. Instead, push the tool with the takedown pin, as you keep your thumb and forefinger tented over to keep everything pressed in place. If you do this correctly, the takedown pin will push the tool out, replacing it, and capturing the plunger. If you don't, the plunger will push the takedown pin to the side, get launched, and you'll lose it.

When I began working on ARs, I didn't know this tool existed, and I assembled a slew of them with just my bare hands. This is a good way to have a 50% loss rate on plungers, at least until the next time you use a vacuum to clean the shop.

TELE-STOCK ASSEMBLY

I leave this for last, and do not include it with the A1/A2 stock instructions for a simple reason: it uses different parts and is much more involved. First, let's take a look. The stock slides back and forth on the buffer tube. The tube has a ridge, spine or dorsal fin on the bottom that keeps the stock aligned.

Up front, the tube has a locking ring, called a castle nut, and a retaining plate. Some may have retaining plates with wings, loops or ovals on them, places to attach a sling.

Look at the buffer retaining pin. Notice that the buffer tube lip keeps it in the receiver. On some, the bottom of the tube lip actually protrudes more than the top. This is to provide a secure hold on the pin, while not interfering with the upper receiver as it hinges down to close.

Take a close look at the joint between the castle nut and the retaining plate. Are the smaller notches toward the front of the rifle? Is the retaining plate staked, that is, metal pounded, into the notches on the castle nut? If so, it is done correctly, and you should leave it alone.

If not staked, it was not done properly, and you should at the very least stake it. This is an opportunity to see how it goes together, and to make it right.

Leave the stock on the tube. Place the receiver flat on your bench, right side down, top away from you. Take your stock wrench and slide the three pegs in it into three notches on the castle nut, with the wrench oriented in such a way that you can turn the castle nut to unscrew it. (You will be pulling the wrench down toward you to unscrew.) You may find it has been torqued on tightly. Or, if done by a moron or someone who spends too much time looking for advice on the internet, that it has been Loctited. If it has (you can sometimes tell by looking at the threads where you'll see the gloss of the goo in the threads), you'll have to do more work. If it is tight, straight and glued together, you might just stake it, call it done, and look to learn more on a different lower.

Loctite needs heat to break it down. Don't go overboard, as you can hurt the aluminum heat-treat if you get too heavy-handed. Heat with a propane torch just until you see smoke whisping out of the joint. Lay off the heat, let the smoke stop and repeat. Let it cool, then try again. The broken-down Loctite becomes a powder and still gums up the threads, but you can at least unscrew the castle nut.

Once the castle nut is loose, unscrew it as far as you can. You'll notice a problem here: you're unscrewing, but it is retreating further up the buffer tube. No problem.

This is a correctly-assembled, correctly-staked castle nut and retaining plate combo.

With the castle nut unscrewed, slide the retaining plate away from the receiver. Notice several things. It allows the takedown pin spring (remember that, from the A1/A2 work?) to expand out of the tunnel. The retaining plate has a lump on it, one that fits into the recess in the receiver. That keeps it from turning when assembled. Also, the retaining plate has a guide key in it, a stub that rides in the groove you see machined in the threads of the buffer tube.

At this point you are in much the same place as with the A1/A2: retrieve the takedown spring, thumb down the buffer retainer and unscrew the buffer tube.

Once it is all off, you can dis-assemble the stock. The retaining plate slides off the front. You do this if you are replacing the original plate with one stamped with loops for a sling swivel. Also, you can spin the castle nut off. You do this if you have to clean it up and remove the Loctite residue.

Reassembling the tele-stock is involved, and at times approaches being a three-handed job. First, if you took them out, get the rear takedown pin and its plunger back in, as you did in the A1/A2 process. Then, screw the castle nut back on, big notches toward the rear. Spin it on all the way back. Slide the retainer on, with its anti-rotation tab to the front. Screw the buffer tube into the receiver until you have enough threads caught that it won't fall out on its own.

Have the takedown pin spring and the buffer retainer and spring handy. When you get to the point where the lip of the buffer tube will over-run the buffer retainer, install the spring and retainer and turn the tube until it holds the retainer but doesn't trap it down so far it can't hold in the buffer. Basically, over the edge of the retainer, but not binding against the post of the retainer.

Turn the tube and retaining plate just enough to get a clear shot at the takedown pin hole, and insert the spring. Turn the tube so it is straight up and down, and then press the retaining plate

One thing the mil-spec guys are right about, the allen-head pistol grip screws are wrong. Wrong. And always use the lock washer.

forward. As with the A1/A2, make sure you press the spring into the hole and don't bend it or trap it outside. Now, holding the retaining plate against the receiver, spin the castle nut down to lock the retaining plate in place.

This is your chance to stop and give your hands a rest.

At this moment, the buffer tube is holding the buffer retainer in place, and the castle nut is holding the retaining plate in place, but nothing is tight. Look at the alignment of the stock. Is the stock (or the fin) straight up and down? If not, you can tweak it a bit to the right or left to get it straight. You want to do this before you torque the castle nut down.

Once everything is straight and the castle nut is hand-tight, place the lower receiver on the bench top, right side down, top toward you. Hook the stock wrench onto the castle nut, and brace your left hand (right-handers) on the pistol grip. Tighten the castle nut as much as you can. Once it is tight, take another moment to check straightness of the stock.

Once everything is tight and straight, use a spring-loaded centerpunch to stake the castle nut. To do this, place the tip of the punch on the retaining plate, next to one of the small notches of the castle nut. Press down, and when the punch loads and then snaps, it will strike the steel of the retaining plate, and kick a burr or steel into the notch. Now, it is rare, but I have run into retaining plates that were so hard it wasn't possible to stake them. This is not good, and one of the few exceptions where Loctite might be called for. Also, the ones I have run into were not standard plates, but the looped ones for slings.

There you have it, complete disassembly and re-assembly.

Now, if the task you are faced with is a box of parts, and a receiver set, and you need to assemble a rifle, no problem. Re-read this chapter, and pick up at the point where we re-assemble. Since you already have it apart (that's what a box 'o parts is) you can just jump in there.

CHAPTER 6
FIELD CLEANING

THIS IS THE LEVEL of cleaning you do in a class or during a weekend spent burning through more ammo than you can afford or find at the local big-box store to replace. The idea is simple, you aren't going to detail strip and lovingly scrub and re-lube all the parts. You want to keep the rifle running and you want to do so without spending any more time at it than you need to.

We have two approaches and two levels of cleaning to consider. The approaches are Neo-brutal and Cautious-brutal, and our two levels are "break for lunch" and "day is done, get ready for tomorrow."

Let's mix and match, shall we?

You've got an hour, maybe less, and in that time you have to hit the restroom, get lunch, slather on sunscreen/insect repellant, re-hydrate so you don't pitch over face-first into the dirt in the afternoon, dive into the vehicle to get more gear or ammo, and do some cleaning of your rifle. All the rest, you have to figure out on your own. Here, I'll just talk about the rifle cleaning.

NEO-BRUTAL, LUNCH BREAK

"Neo," a prefix from Neanderthal meaning before modern, and not as used in Neolithic. "Brutal" would be to simply neglect it until something breaks or stops working, and then fix it. We'll go

up a step in caveman hierarchy, and actually tend to a few, very few, things.

You unload (if the class or range day is at a "hot" range) and pop open your rifle. Pull out the bolt/carrier group and set it aside. Take your chamber brush on its "T" handle and scrub the chamber and locking lugs. Poke a patch, wet with either oil or copper solvent, down the bore. Set the upper aside. Use your plastic brush to knock off the bigger chunks of carbon from the bolt and carrier. Wipe the bolt and carrier with a shop cloth. Lubricate the extractor and ejector. Squirt some oil back into the bolt at the carrier tunnel, and into the gas port holes on the carrier.

If you have the time, energy and paper towels, wipe the gunk out of the upper.

Drop some oil onto the springs of the fire control parts of the lower, and the disconnector pivot point.

Slap it all back together, and get on with the lunch break.

"But, but, but!" I know, you've been told to run the AR dry. Almost completely B.S. Unless your class is in the arctic, in the winter, you need lubricant. You've also been told that the powder residue, mixed with oil, will turn into a lapping compound and grind your rifle into nothing. Again, B.S. If you go to the auto parts store, or browse Brownells, you will find lapping compounds. You will not find one that is marketed as "a top-quality mixture of carbon/powder residue in grease."

Is the carbon residue in your receiver awful

stuff? Yes it is, but it isn't valve-grinding compound. Are you using axle grease to lube your rifle? (I hope the answer to this is "no," but you never know.) If not, the lubricant is not holding the suspended particles against the surface, they are simply sloshing around in there, kind of like the particles of your lunch, in the glass of water you've been drinking. They aren't hard enough, and not pressed firmly enough to the surface, to do any grinding.

So, scrub the chamber, knock the big chunks off, and hose it with oil. When you get to the point that you have enough oil in there that you are splattering the shooter to your right, you've over-done it. (He will probably say something.)

I have gone through multiple classes, from several days to week-long classes, doing nothing but this. As long as you get the build-up out of the chamber so you don't get a round wedged in there, and you keep at it with the lube, your rifle (assuming it is properly-built) will keep on running.

This level of maintenance has also been described as emergency cleaning, fighting clean and combat clean. Oh, and in a pinch, if you find yourself lacking lubricants, don't despair. Is there a vehicle nearby? One you can get under the hood

of? Great. Use the end of the dipstick, or the dip from the transmission, to apply lube. Motor oil, even used, and transmission fluid are both great lubricants. In fact, a lot of the pricey, "special" gun lubes you can buy in cute little one-ounce bottles are repackaged motor oil or ATF, and some even have a special dye in them to make them an attractive-to-shooters color. If you have a plastic bottle of synthetic motor oil, you are good for a long time.

Would a Sergeant or inspecting officer, military or law enforcement, have an attack of the vapors if they looked at your rifle, in such a state? You bet. Will it keep working, despite their protestations? Surely.

CAUTIOUS-BRUTAL, LUNCH BREAK

Here, we're taking a bit longer, because we can, because we have the time or because we just can't stand the thought of "abusing" the rifle we are using. A quick clue: if you are in a class where you are shooting through 1,000 rounds in a few days, or 1,500+ in a five-day class, you are abusing the barrel more from shooting it than from not cleaning it. The heat is worse than the wear. And yes, I realize that in the "new normal" of expensive ammunition and limited supplies, blasting a thousand rounds in a few days can be painful.

For Cautious-brutal, you start with the Neo-brutal and add a few steps.

Once you have it apart and chamber-brush the chamber and locking lugs, push a copper-solvent patch down the bore and get out a roll of paper towels or a can of aerosol cleaning solution. Wipe the interior of the upper with the paper towels. If the range has the gear, or lacks concern for the environment, hold the upper, muzzle up, and spray the interior with the aerosol. Spray with lube and wipe with paper towels. Ignore the exterior.

Do the same with the bolt/carrier assembly. Knock the big chunks off, aerosol spray, lube and wipe.

Do this over a trash can, if the range has one.

Spray the lower, holding it over the trash can. Lube.

If you are going far for a class, or you will be taking care of more than just one rifle, something like the **Otis** team kit will serve you well.

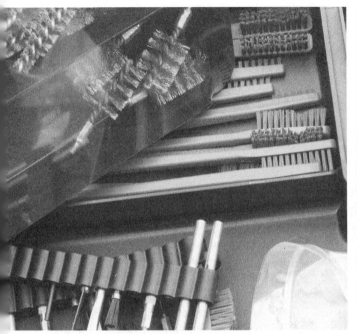 

Left: The Otis team kit has multiple brushes, in a variety of calibers, and no end of pull-through cleaning cables. Right: If you are going to have the means to clean a bunch of rifles, you'll need all the adapters for patches, brushes, etc. Otis has you covered.

Push another patch down the bore, make sure everything is properly lubed, and re-assemble.

Now, in using the aerosol spray can, you are not being gentle or conservative. You are not looking to spray, then wipe gunk off. You are hosing the gunk off with the spray cleaner and letting it air dry.

NEO-BRUTAL, END OF DAY

Those who have been to a class know the drill; class is over, everyone throws off their gear, cases the guns, throws it all in the car, and disappears to the hotel to clean up and get dinner before collapsing for sleep until the next day. You can't.

The end-of-day Neo-brutal is simply the Cautious-brutal with one extra. After you've done the field-strip, hosing, knocking of carbon chunks and re-lubing, you then take a clean and dry cloth (a red shop cloth is perfect) and wipe the mud, dust, dirt and whatever else off the exterior. You also check to make sure everything is still tight and correctly-located.

Then you put it in the rack and let it sit there for a few minutes while you gather up your gear, pack the vehicle and get ready to leave. Then, check your rifle to see if any oil has oozed out, wipe it off, put the rifle in your case, in the car, and drive off.

One thing I've learned to do, at the end of the day and before leaving the range to the hotel, is put my empty rifle case on the hood of the car. That way you can't drive off, leaving your rifle in the rack oozing oil.

At the hotel, haul the gear out, lock the rifle case to something solid, take a shower, get dinner and then collapse for the night.

CAUTIOUS-BRUTAL, END OF DAY

Obviously, you do all the Neo-brutal, end of day steps, but then you do another check once you get back from dinner. (A note; a training class is time for you to train, to learn and to work on your firearms skills. It is not time to socialize. Do not drink. If you have a drink at dinner, there is no

Cautious-brutal cleaning session for you, post-dinner. There is *nothing to do with firearms* until the next morning. Absolutely *nothing*.)

Once you get back, unlock the case and haul the rifle out. Keep all ammunition and loaded magazines away from your work area.

Use your shop cloth to wipe the exterior. Check the tightness of anything bolted on, such as BUIS, optics, sling hardware, etc. Inspect your sling, to make sure it is secure and un-worn. If frayed, replace it. Separate the upper and lower and give them a quick once-over.

Inspect your charging handle. Make sure the front end isn't peened or cracked. Check the upper, make sure the barrel is tight and the handguards are secure.

Inspect the bolt and carrier. Make sure the firing pin is correctly installed, and that there are no obvious cracks in anything.

Look inside the lower, and make sure your hammer and trigger springs both have two legs and that they are properly located.

Put it all back together, in the case, and go to bed. You have a long day ahead of you.

WHAT ARE WE DOING HERE?

The idea is simple; we do everything that keeps the rifle running, and we don't do anything that would take more time, effort, supplies or daylight.

This is a cleaning regime I learned shooting at Second Chance. For those who have read me on the match, feel free to skip ahead. (There *will* be a test. If you fail, don't blame me.) The match was nine full days, with as many as eighteen different events you could enter. My maximum ammo consumption happened in the end days, the last seven or eight years of the match. My ammo load-out, for the drive to Central Lake, was something like two eight-pound powder tubs, empty of powder (loaded into ammo) and filled with reloaded .223 ammo, on the order of 3,000 rounds. Plus extra, factory ammo, just in case I ran over and needed to keep shooting. Two cases of 12 gauge buckshot, two cases of 12 gauge slugs. Another eight-pound powder tub, filled

with reloaded 12 gauge, "warm-up" ammo. Two .50 BMG ammo cans filled with .45 ACP ammo, two more filled with 9mm ammo. One .30 ammo can filled with .38 Super ammunition, and another filled with 9mm ammo. A "brick" of .22LR.

The guns consisted of three AR-15s, three 12 gauge shotguns, three .45 ACP pistols and one .45 ACP revolver, two 9mm pistols, a .38 Super pistol and a .22LR Ruger 10/22 rifle. Complete with a bushel basket sized box of magazines, and another of cleaning supplies.

And to be clear, I was not going to spend a moment longer than necessary keeping them any more clean that they needed to be to work. They were not going to be lovingly stripped down to the last part, scrubbed, wiped, lubed and reassembled. I would be spending all my time shooting and warming up to shoot, and time spent cleaning was time wasted from sleeping or shooting.

So the two cleaning procedures are designed to keep a rifle running, regardless of the volume of shooting or training you are doing. (Modified for the specifics of the firearm involved, they also work for handguns and shotgun.)

They will not put you in the good graces of the training authorities if you are in some official training system. To be plain, The Sergeant will not be happy.

However, most training, military or law enforcement, is not the least bit concerned with actual function, marksmanship or gun handling. It is to reinforce rules of engagement, practice reaction drills, and satisfy training-time requirements. In those circumstances, firearms cleanliness is the only thing a trainer can "gig" you on, and so they will.

Now, a steady diet of this kind of "cleaning" will probably shorten the service life of your rifle. However, and not to contradict or negate the advice above, anyone who sends a rifle through 8,000 rounds continually in this state deserves to have a couple of thousand rounds worth of service life deducted from the total. But, your skills will be all the better for the "loss."

This is for when you and your rifle are working or training. Once you're done, you do a complete and thorough cleaning, as detailed in the next chapter.

CHAPTER 7
COMPLETE CLEANING

T'S TIME TO GET this puppy clean. Clear off your bench, get out the cleaning tools, and get set for an hour, at least, of cleaning time. No interruptions, no TV or other distractions. Also, no ammo nearby.

MATERIALS

You'll need a military cleaning kit, at the minimum. While it will suffice, you will find more/better tools to be a big help. Also, a cleaning system like the Otis is good, but you'll probably be better off keeping it in its field case, and using it if you need to, in the field. (Although, some bench practice with it, to learn the ropes, as it were, is not a bad thing.) A solid rod would be better. A bore guide is good, but not absolutely needed. You'll need cleaning patches, solvent and lubricant. You'll need a general cleaning solvent, such as mineral spirits or an aerosol cleaner, that helps to scrub off large areas that need mud, etc. removed, but won't work for cleaning bores.

You'll need a place to clean and cloths for rubbing or wiping. You need some for drying, some for cleaning up, and some for applying oil. You may be tempted to use paper towels. They are inexpensive, ubiquitous and handy. They also leave impressive amounts of lint behind. Avoid them if you can, except for use in the field or at a

class, and then just on the inside of the upper to wipe out gobs of wet, oily goo.

One cleaning tool for which I have no use is cotton-tipped swabs. They hook on edges and sharp parts and leave behind strands of cotton. They don't pick up much gunk, and you have to use a fistful of them to get anything in an AR clean. And the places they do reach are places you probably don't need to be cleaning anyway. The do not do anything that an aerosol cleaner can't do better.

Having spent many years as a gunsmith, mineral spirits as cleaning solvent always come to mind. They do tend to be smelly. Alas, everything else you'll consider as a substitute that can clean will have some odor or another associated with it, so get used to "smelling like a gunsmith." Even the stuff advertised as "pure and odorless" mineral spirits will have some smell, as the common stuff is often reclaimed/recycled. Only pure, laboratory grade mineral spirits will be odorless, and you will be goggle-eyed at the price of that.

There is no end to the extra, special tools that make cleaning easier. And yes, they do make it easier, but buying and keeping track of them may negate some or all of the ease of cleaning they represent.

If you have a convenient box or case to keep the tools, then having them and a bench to use

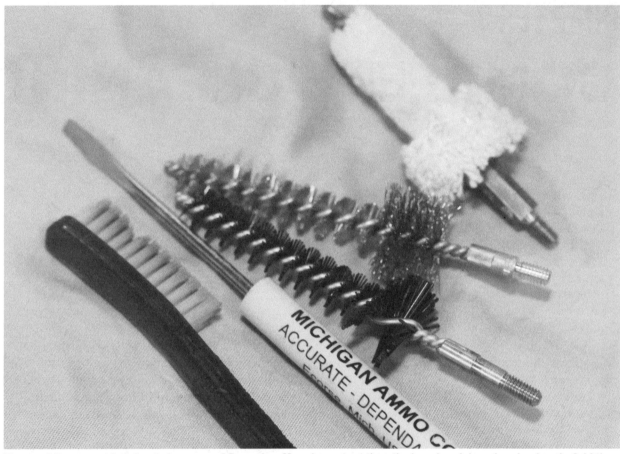

You need the correct brushes to keep your AR running, More important than the bore brush is a chamber brush. Add the GI brush, and a small screwdriver to pry gunked-together parts off, and you're good to go. The bronze chamber brush is the best, the synthetic one is OK. The chamber mop is for swabbing up after you've scrubbed.

them at would be very good. Just don't expect to be lugging a Kennedy box into the field to do a "quick clean" on your rifle. All-told, the collection can get heavy, and a heavy box to store it in just makes things worse.

ULTRASONICS

Before we get into the hand-cleaning methods, let's discuss the power methods, namely, ultrasonics. The name comes from the vibration induced into the cleaning fluid by the mechanism. The high-frequency vibration agitates the solution and loosens hardened gunk, petrified oil and other stuff. If you have painted your rifle, or parts of it, you may find that the ultrasonic system loosens the paint, too. (It depends on the type of paint,

the brand, and how well you cleaned the surface before painting. Also, the sonic solution, heat and time spent cleaning. Don't blame me if your uber-tactical camo job is a mess after a bout in the ultrasonic tank.)

You do not want to submerse any optics, anything battery-powered, or anything with a lack of water-sealing design. No lights, no lasers, no scopes, nothing. That means, to ultrasonically clean an upper, you have to either remove all that stuff or find a way to suspend the upper in the solution while keeping the delicate stuff up out of the wet. Good luck with that.

Ultrasonic are great, but there are a few details to remember.

Your rifle will be clean, but dry. Or, clean but water-wet.

Yes, all the dirt, gunk, scum and smut will be

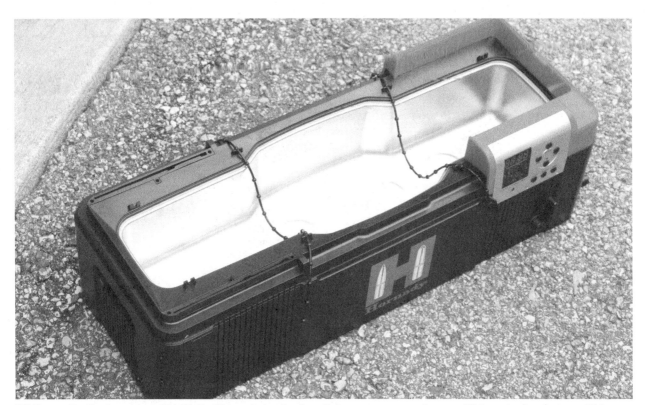

While an ultrasonic system (this is the Hornady Lock n Load) does yeoman work, you still have to do some scrubbing and wiping.

The Hornady L-n-L will hold a 16-inch carbine upper for cleaning.

loosened. You may still have to do some scrubbing to get it off, but it will be greatly loosened and thus easier to scrub. But all the oil will be gone, as well as any grease you might have applied, and perhaps even some of the new "wonder" lubes. You'll have to dry it, making sure you get all the water/solution out of the gaps and joints, and then re-lube. If you use an ultrasonic tank, and you have a preferred lubricant, or lube process, you would do well to write down all the particulars. That way, when your clean upper or lower comes out of the bath and dries, you can re-apply the lube and not miss a spot.

A hair dryer or heat gun set on low will do a good job of drying the water. A good judge of how to get it hot enough, but not too hot, is simple: can you hold it? If it is too hot to hold, you over-did it and need to back off next time.

Gunk will be loosened, but it won't necessarily be removed.

Loose doesn't necessarily mean gone. You'll have to, in some areas, brush away the loosened dirt

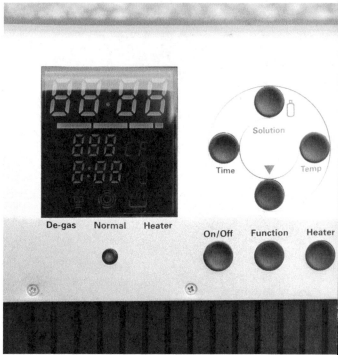

You can set time, heat or no heat, and de-gas the solution, all on the control panel.

Truth be told, I use whatever lube I have. They all work, and the small differences between the best and the worst haven't made any difference to me. If your experience differs, then go with what works. Always go with what works.

and maybe even re-dunk in the ultrasonic cleaner. Once the dirt is loosened and gone, then you can dry. It also means that you will find yourself dealing with gunk that you never had to before. Carbon, dirt and other stuff that worked its way into nooks and crannies will now issue forth.

Resist the temptation to keep cleaning until the ooze from the joints stops happening. You'll be there a long time, with no extra benefit.

While it saves you work, it doesn't save you from paying attention.

A friend of mine once went on vacation, leaving his cartridge case brass cleaner running. Sometime in the ensuing two weeks, it vibrated itself off the bench and fell to the floor. The busted pieces of it were still thrashing around on his return when he went downstairs to see "what that buzzing noise was." You have to keep an eye on your cleaner, or put it on a countdown timer if it doesn't have one built-in, to make sure it turns off.

The proper solvents won't dissolve your receivers, or something like that, but you will risk loosening otherwise-tight fasteners like screws and bolts, and dissolving paint and such. (And here I'm talking two weeks, like my friend, not an overnight "oops.")

Timers are good, and Uniquetek makes a countdown one that you can set for time, if your ultrasonic tank doesn't have one built-in.

It requires room and power.

You need bench space and an outlet. It is a clumsy thing to take along with you on a hunting trip. And if your "gun room" is a corner-of-the-garage portable workbench (with the door closed, please) then having an ultrasonic cleaner set up all the time is not going to happen. You'll have to decant the cleaning solution, clean and dry the cleaner, and store it all away somewhere.

Now, as a gunsmith I had a dedicated cleaning tank with built-in pump to provide a stream of mineral spirits, plus a compressor to blow the parts dry. Unless you have a barn, outbuilding or other structure

dedicated just to gun stuff, you won't have that luxury. So build into your routine the time and effort to set things up, pour in the solution, clean, dry, decant and put it all away. Otherwise the hassle and mess might outweigh the advantage, and you'll be selling your cool, new, ultrasonic cleaning tank to someone at the gun club.

Oh, and ultrasonic, or power, cleaning is not unknown outside of the hobby arena. At a patrol rifle class a short while ago, we ducked into one of the buildings on the NG base to escape the heat and sun. Inside, we found rows of cleaning cabinets. They looked much like stainless steel commercial dishwashers, but up on stands so you didn't have to bend over to use them. Each was big enough to hold a dozen M4s or M16s, and the process was simple: take off optics, lasers, etc. Rack the rifles in the cabinets. Close and lock, turn on and cycle though the cleaning cycle. Remove, oil, re-install optics, lasers, etc. and get on with training.

No, they wouldn't let us use them.

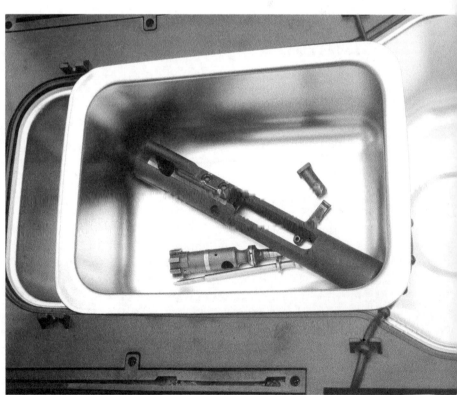

There is a tray for parts (as well as a basket for brass, different solution though) that lets you clean the bolt and carrier and other part.

The Hornady L-n-L ultrasonic cleaner is a bit large, but it stores compactly, and is worth the storage space.

CLEANING

Now, for the hand-cleaning part of it.

Chamber-check. Separate the upper and lower. Remove the bolt/carrier from the upper. On your bench, you'll have the following: upper, complete; charging handle; bolt/carrier assembly, complete; lower, complete.

CHARGING HANDLE

Let's do the easy part first. Inspect it to see that it is straight, uncracked, and unpeened. Check the latch to make sure it pivots, and isn't bent. See that the roll pin is in and flush, and the latch hook is solid. Wipe the gunk off, scrub with a brush if you need to, and wipe with an oiled cloth. Set aside.

UPPER

Inspect the tightness of your sights, iron or optics. Are they where they are supposed to be, and tight? Good. If not, tighten them. Do it now.

If you wait, you'll likely forget, and that won't be good. If you have regular handguards, check to make sure they are solid and uncracked, and correctly installed in the delta ring and front plate. If you have a free-float handguard, make sure it is tight. Also check the tightness of any extras you may have bolted on – lights, lasers, vertical foregrips, etc. Painting-in is good for this, as the paint (assuming it survives the ultrasonics) helps you check.

Use your chamber brush to scrub the chamber and locking lug recesses. If you have one, use a chamber mop to swab out the scrubbed-off gunk. Also, if you have one, use a "star" felt cleaning pad to clean the gunk out of the recesses.

Run a copper-solvent patch down the bore. Let the bore sit while you wipe/scrub the gunk off of the interior of the upper.

If you have the elbow room or the ventilation, you can use an aerosol cleaner to strip off the gunk and degrease at the same time. Otherwise it is a matter of wiping with a solvent-wet patch

The **USGI** barrel nut isn't completely useless. It is always there, in the bottom of your toolkit, and you can use it as a small hammer if you need one.

or cloth, softening the gunk, and then wiping it off with a paper towel. (This is perhaps the one time I will suggest paper towels as a good option for cleaning. They will get incredibly filthy, and you can toss them in the trash when done.) If you really have the time, or your training Sergeant insists, you can use q-tips to get into the corners and wipe out the last bits of it. Just be careful you don't leave stands of cotton behind.

Every five minutes or so as you go through the thorough cleaning process, run a dry patch down the bore, and then follow with a patch with copper solvent on it. We'll get detailed about bore cleaning in a bit.

Check the spring action of the dust cover. Flip it up and let it spring back. It should snap back with a brisk little bit of authority. If it is sluggish, check to see if something is binding the spring, or if the foot of the spring has unwound itself from the shaft half a turn. (Fixing it is pretty involved. If it still works, you may want to just leave it alone.)

Check the forward assist (if your upper has one). Press in the button and look inside the upper to make sure the tip of it pokes out into sight. If it doesn't, it may have broken off, and will no longer work as designed. Replacing it is not a hassle, but

you'll find it requires buying the whole set. It is difficult to buy just a part of it, so resign yourself to the fifteen dollars it will take to buy a complete assembly. (Unless you simply have to have the Colt assembly, and then resign yourself to paying $40, plus shipping. Welcome to the world of mil-spec.)

As you clean, you'll find an amazing amount of carbon gunk oozes out of the various nooks and crannies of the upper. You may wish yet again for an ultrasonic cleaner.

Inspect the front sight assembly for tightness, and the flash hider or other muzzle device, too.

Wipe the exterior with a clean, dry cloth, and get ready for bore cleaning.

If you have been to a particularly difficult class, you may find that a laundry tub and scrubbing with hot, soapy water is a needed first step to get the caked mud and gunk off your rifle. If you do, keep a few things in mind.

The water and soap will strip all the oil off the exterior. You will have to be thorough in re-oiling the exterior, including the black-oxided surface of the barrel.

Hot soapy water is not good for electronics, lights and optics. If you can seal them, great. A plastic bag and gaffers tape can serve. If not, take them off before you dunk the upper.

If you do not thoroughly clean your bore afterwards, it will rust. "But my barrel is stainless/chrome plated." Stainless steel is better-called "slow-rusting steel" and chrome plating, if you have fired your rifle at all, will have cracks in it that will let rust start and attack the steel underneath.

You need to brush and swab your bore clean even if you have used some power-cleaning method, as you can't count on even ultrasonics to get the gunk out. It may well loosen it, but when you dry, it might just dry right back where it was.

CLEANING THE INSIDE

Clean the chamber first. If you don't, you will just have to clean your bore all over again, as we'll see shortly.

For this, use the chamber brush, the one with the stainless steel "goth" collar on it. You need this brush mounted (pretty much permanently) on a section of rod long enough to reach the chamber, and with a "T" handle on it. Push the brush down into the chamber until the collar is fully into the

barrel extension, brushing the locking lugs. Turn the brush (clockwise or counterclockwise, doesn't matter, just do it that way every time) for a couple of full rotations, then keep turning it as you pull it out.

Do not reverse-turn it. If you back up, all you'll do is prematurely wear your brush, and even break off bristles that will hang around and cause problems later. If you are right-handed, it will be natural to turn it clockwise. Always do it that way.

When you press the chamber brush in, you are flexing the bristles back, toward you. As you turn, they will lay down, trailing the direction of your turn. If you back up, you are bending them as they try to fit inside the hole, a hole they were made much larger than. Bent bristles don't clean well. Bent bristles that have been bent at their base will break, sooner or later.

The brush scrubs the gunk loose but doesn't remove much of it. For the next step, either hose the chamber clean, letting the residues you've loosened and sluiced pour down the bore, or use a cotton mop shaped like the chamber brush and scrub. Even the cotton mop won't clean up the loosened stuff that fell down into the bore, so

Left: This is another relatively new breaking event. You'd think this was from a high-mileage rifle, but they are commonly on low round-count rifles. Maybe in the military they see these at 10,000 rounds, but for the rest of us, it happens in a couple of thousand, if at all. Right: Look, things break. This is a relatively new thing, and was not a common breakage in the past. But it happens.

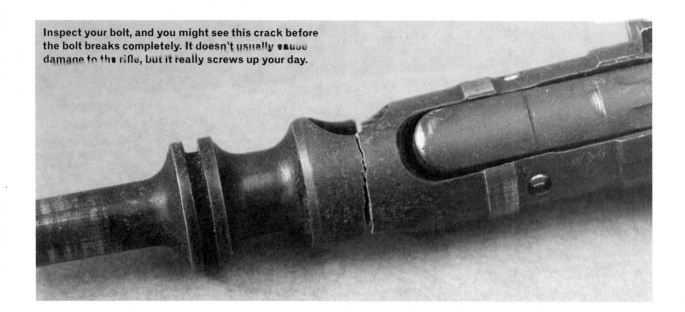

Inspect your bolt, and you might see this crack before the bolt breaks completely. It doesn't usually cause damage to the rifle, but it really screws up your day.

clean the chamber first, then the bore.

Another mopping tool is a bar-shaped section of cotton felt, shaped to pass through the gaps in the locking lugs, but clean behind them and inside the barrel extension. There is also a star-shaped cotton felt wad that cleans in much the same way.

BORE CLEANING

Your efforts to clean the bore will work through two means: scrubbing and chemistry. The scrubbing will loosen powder residue. Only chemistry will remove copper.

Start with a patch with copper solvent on it. Push it down the bore, from chamber to muzzle. Once it pokes out the muzzle, take it off the patch holder, and pull the rod back. Wipe the rod clean. Do something else for five to 15 minutes, and then push a dry patch down the bore. It will come out black and blue. The black is powder residue, and the blue is the chemically-dissolved copper. You can run another dry patch down if you wish, but it won't do much good.

Repeat the process. The condition of the patches will inform you of your progress. The first few times you do this, you'll see less and less black, and more and more blue. Then, the black will disappear and the blue will taper off. When you see no more blue, you have a clean bore.

Interestingly, if you then switch to a powder-fouling solvent, you'll get more black out of the bore. Some will tell you this is powder fouling that had been "trapped" under the copper, and that there is more copper under the powder layer. Until a chemist with a qualitative analysis of the patch tells me it is powder residue (that is, carbon), I'm not buying it. What is it, then, and where does it come from? My suspicion is that it comes from the cleaning tools themselves. Unless you sterilize the brush, rod and patches, you are likely to continue to get false positives, false "there was gunk in there" indications, for as long as you care to poke a brush and patch down the bore.

But, you can get more something out if you swab the bore dry, switch solvents, and clean some more.

You can also clean a bore until you keel over from exhaustion.

Me, I scrub until the blue goes away, switch to powder solvent, clean, then go back to copper (dry-patching in the transitions). When there is no more blue on the patch, I'm done.

Oh, and do be careful in your choice of brushes. Using a brass brush and copper-dissolving solvents may lead to endless cleaning. The trace copper scrubbed off the brush will react with the copper solvent, and you will see blue-traced patches until you run out of solvent, patches or energy.

 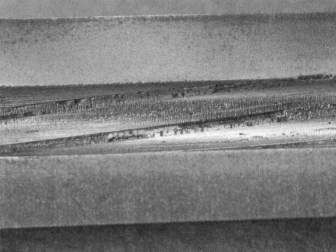

Left: This is amazing gas port wear. This is the kind of wear you see in select-fire rifles and carbines that have received lots of mag dumps. Right: Run a lot of ammo down your bore and, no matter how diligently you clean it, it will wear. And gradually lose accuracy. When accuracy is gone, replace the barrel.

BRUSH VS. PATCH

If you look down a bore with a bore scope, you will in most instances be horrified. The first chance I had to peer down a barrel came on an AR I had been using for a while, but hadn't really done much to baby it. With it, I was still able to easily drop the 300 meter targets at the National Guard base, and that with iron sights. It still delivered accuracy in the MOA region, despite having had more than just a few thousand rounds sluiced through it, and some several thousands of those had been in high round-count classes or courses in hot weather. In other words, your typical AR barrel.

When I looked, I saw sheets of copper plating, rust in the corners of the grooves, and "alligator skin" cracking in the throat. Ouch. A quick dry-brushing removed the rust, but the copper remained.

So, should you brush, or patch? There are advocates for both. The brush loosens the bulky stuff and scrubs off the rust as well as some of the powder residue. But to truly remove plated-on stuff, you need to use patches and dedicated solvents.

One thing to not do is use a stainless steel brush. Some barrel makers do not care, or have an

opinion, but those who do are almost uniformly in agreement: don't use stainless brushes. It is just too aggressive, and wears the bore more than the shooting you just did.

That leaves plastic or bronze. Plastic brushes are not as good at loosening the fouling, but a bronze brush will give you a false positive. That is, if you copper-solvent patch your bore clean, or nearly so, and then use a brush to "loosen the powder residue," you'll rub traces of bronze into your bore. The next patch will come out – you guessed it – blue. You could, especially if you were sloppy with the copper solvent, be "cleaning" your bore forever, trying to remove the final traces of copper, copper left there by you, the last time you shoved the bronze brush through. (And yes, it does bear repeating, as I've seen people do just that, even to the point of dipping a bronze brush into a bottle of copper solvent, before "scrubbing" the bore.)

SOLVENTS

Which solvents? A few years ago, it might have mattered. A generation ago, you probably would have had to mix your own to get something that did more than just scrub out the powder residue. As fondly as I remember the smell of the old

Hoppes #9 (and this isn't to pick on them), I really wonder if any of them did any better than soap and water. These days, it hardly matters because they all work. All the makers of cleaning gear offer specialized solvents, solvents for powder residue, copper, lead, plastic, you name it. Any brand-name copper solvent will attack the jacket residue left in your bore. There are popular home-brew solvents, and some very aggressive commercial ones, too. Just be aware that there have been reports of pitted barrels from people leaving the more-aggressive solvents in the bore too long. By "too long," we typically mean, "I left my bore soaking overnight, and the next morning I could see pitting in the puddle-bottom of the bore."

If you only do the five-to-fifteen minutes routine, you can use the aggressive solvents. But do not leave anything soaking overnight, even the less-aggressive solvents

Does this matter?

Some say yes, some say no. It matters for some because they want repeatable accuracy. An NRA High Power shooter needs a rifle that will shoot to the same point, hot or cold, clean or fouled, and with a high level of precision. If a particular barrel has one point of impact when clean, and then shifts in a few rounds to a different one when fouled, that barrel is not of much use to them. For the rest of us, who will rarely clean a bore, that barrel could be golden.

The High-Power guys need a one-MOA barrel with the same POI, clean and dirty, hot and cold, for as long as it lasts.

Someone who is doing nothing but CQB training doesn't care if the POI shifts like that, they won't notice it at 50 yards. (The POI shift that would make an NRA High Power shooter crazy would be something like five or six inches at 600 yards, clean to dirty. That same barrel, at 50 yards, would shift half an inch. Woop-de-do.) Prairie dog shooters want a barrel like the High-Power shooters do: clean or dirty, hot or cold, it has to deliver. What they will settle for is one that remains accurate even when hot, even if it shifts a bit from cold-and-clean to hot-and-dirty. After all, the 'dogs won't notice.

For most of my rifles, I do nothing or almost nothing. For the beaters, the loaners, the take-to-a-class guns, as long as I can see daylight when I look down the bore, they are left alone. The actions, the bolt and carrier, the trigger mechanism, get lubed, but the bore is left alone. The exception would be if I scrub the chamber. Then I'll poke a rod with patch down the bore, just to shove out the chamber crud that fell down the bore. I may be reluctant to scrub, but I'm not abusive.

The barrels that I do clean get the full scrub then copper solvent, then powder solvent and repeat process.

The loaner guns I carry to a class, to let an officer use while I fix his, don't get cleaned, or get cleaned maybe once a year. But something like my Alexander Arms 6.5 Grendel will get scrubbed after a range trip. The whole raison d'être of the Grendel is pinpoint accuracy at long range, and you keep that by keeping the bore clean.

I just don't want bore cleaning to consume all the time I could be spending doing other, more useful things.

BARREL EXTERIOR AND FLASH HIDER

If you have done any volume shooting you will have "cooked" the oil off of the exterior of your barrel. This will leave it dry, and there will be a white residue on the barrel. Do you scrub that off? If the Sergeant says so, yes. If you really have to, yes. Otherwise, just wipe the exterior with an oiled cloth to re-oil it and protect it, and you're done. Or not, since you'll just bake it off again. This is a case where the climate you work in will dictate the care you take. If you live in the desert, you may not need exterior oil at all. If you live in the swamps, then oil on the outside is your friend.

The flash hider will collect precipitated carbon from the combustion gases cooling as they leave the muzzle. If you have been trained (aka; conditioned) in a white-glove environment, you may want to clean this off. Fine, just don't go attacking it with anything aggressive. Scrubbing the crown with a brush to clean off the carbon is a no-no. The crown is very sensitive to changes, and you can harm accuracy by over-enthusiastic scrubbing with a metal-bristle brush.

Now, in some uses you'll find scrubbed-off paint and such on the barrel, forward of the handguards. This can come from a class or competition, where you've had to aim around a barricade or obstacle. The way to clean that off is with 0000 steel wool (known at the hardware store as "four-aught" steel wool) and oil. Oil the paint. Tear off a small clump of the steel wool and scrub. The oil both lubricates the steel finish from the steel wool, and floats the scrubbed-off paint away. With care you can scour the paint off and not harm the finish.

When done, wipe clean and get on to other things.

BOLT AND CARRIER

Disassemble the bolt and carrier, scrub all the carbon off, and hose liberally and repeatedly with your aerosol cleaner. You cannot, short of actually scrubbing of the Parkerizing, get your bolt and carrier too clean.

Lube, as described in the lubrication section, and reassemble.

UPPER INTERIOR

There are specialty brushes to scrub the interior. You can use them if you like, or if your job is to clean a rack (or several racks) of rifles. As much as I have to admire the folks who develop and offer them, you don't need them. The upper can be cleaned by using the regular toothbrush-like brush and a bucket of cleaning solution.

Scrub the interior, using the cleaning solution to hose the gunk off, and let it drain into the bucket of cleaning solution. There will be a lot of it.

Another method is to spray the interior with something like WD-40 (not as a lube, but as a solvent) and then wipe out the softened carbon with a cloth or paper towel.

You can get the interior as clean as you want, or need, but know that it truly has to be on the level of briquettes of carbon before fouling will interfere with the cycling of the carrier.

Lube, getting the surface dark again, and be sure to put a drop of oil in all the takedown pin pivot holes.

LOWER CLEANING

A thorough cleaning of the lower involves at least taking out the hammer and trigger. Hose the interior with an aerosol cleaner, and scrub with the GI cleaning brush. Hose and brush clean the hammer, trigger and disconnector, taking care not to squirt away the various springs.

Yank the buffer and spring out, wipe them down, and get a brush and cloth down into the interior of the buffer tube.

As with the upper, the lower may need an initial garden hose and scrub brush attack, to get the accumulated mud and such off, if the class you've been in created such a situation.

Lube, getting the surface dark again, and be sure to put a drop of oil on all the takedown pin pivot holes and their springs and plungers. Reassemble the lower, lubing as you go.

BAD CLEANING METHODS

If you want to get lots of bad advice, listen to a lot of veterans. (Nothing personal, but the amount of bad advice from ex-service folks can be staggering.) And if you want no advice at all, listen to law enforcement.

Bad advice from the military? To get a grasp of this, you have to consider the environment the military is in. It is not possible to clean a firearm to "clean enough" simply because of differing opinions. What one Sergeant thinks is clean enough, another would scoff at. And there's always someone who thinks there is no level of cleaning that is "clean enough."

Also, the NCO in charge of the armory is responsible for the weapons in his/her care, and will get savaged by an officer who inspects, if the firearms in there aren't "clean enough" in the opinion of that officer.

So the default is not "clean enough," but "totally clean." This means "white glove" clean, and therein lies the problem. It is not unheard of for soldiers, sailors, Marines and the rest to spend inordinate amounts of time, scraping, scrubbing, wiping, degreasing and otherwise getting every speck of "dirt" off of a rifle, before turning it in. Scraping with everything from toothpicks to dental picks, sharpened screwdrivers, brushing with brushes of all kinds, and even taking rifles into the showers and using hot water, as hot as possible right out of the shower heads, to get them "clean."

A white glove inspection, conducted on a properly-oiled rifle, will come up as "dirty." That is, the inspecting officer's glove will get a dark spot on the tip because of the oil, and you'll get a black mark on your record.

That is why rifles are stored bone-dry, because otherwise, the oil will leave a stain on the glove.

As a result, it is also not unheard-of for soldiers (etc, etc, etc.) to use all kinds of aggressive chemical cleaners. Things like Easy Oven cleaner, Lime Away, spray cleaners meant for kitchens and bathrooms, and other grease-dissolving mixtures, to strip all the oil not just off of, but suck it out of the surfaces.

Oh, and oven cleaner? I have heard, not that I plan to do any testing, that it removes anodizing. That's right, it takes the protective and hard surface off your aluminum parts, leaving them soft and white.

Bad, bad, bad.

And since the inspecting officer/sergeant can be counted on to have very pointy fingertips, those subjected to such abuse will use whatever is at hand (or "gets the job done") to scrape oil, grease or carbon out of corners, crevices and joints.

All that scraping wears a rifle much faster than actual use.

I have heard from recruits who remarked that the rifles they were issued were so worn as to almost be silver, as the finish had been worn off by previous recruits. That is abuse, driven by excessive attention in inspections.

Then there are the bad cleaning methods or processes that came about from good intentions. For instance, the Marine Corps ideal of cleaning a bore, "on three successive days after firing." That came from the early days of the Springfield rifle. Until the mid-1950s, all cartridge primers were corrosive. (Except for M1 Carbine, but that is a minor detail for us here.) That is, the combustion products of the priming compound were hygroscopic, the residues of which attracted moisture.

The only way to keep a bore from rusting back

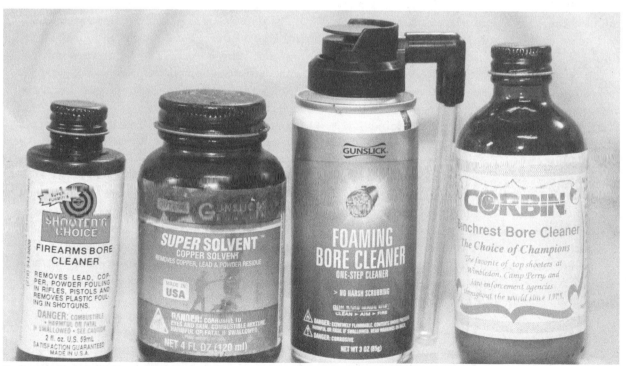

If you must scrub the bore, use a bore solvent, but be sure to swab it out after you are done. Leave the bore dry, not solvent-damp.

then was to clean it. (No hard-chromed bores for American rifles until much later.) In the earliest days, the matter of bore maintenance was a level of knowledge barely more evolved than voodoo. It was common (and incorrect) "knowledge" that the rust was formed by acids created by the powder combustion, acids that "got into the pores of the steel" and had to be scrubbed out. The list of cleaning solutions was impressive, but no one knew at the time that the only one that really mattered in the process was water. Wash out the primer residue, re-oil the bore, and you were good. Many of the favored bore cleaners of the time used lanolin, which was thought to counteract the acidity of the powder residue. What actually did the most good was the water in the lanolin mixture.

The only way to really be sure (because nuking the site from orbit wasn't an option back then) was to clean until it couldn't rust. So, the Marines cleaned the bores of their Springfields three days running after practice or qualification. One, thorough day with hot water would have sufficed.

To this day, more bores are probably worn out from over-cleaning than from neglect and rust. All the friction of cleaning rods zooming in and out of bores wears the throat, wears the crown, and wears the bore more than the bullets passing through.

And on this I will take a radical stance: if it makes you happy to clean your bore, go ahead. If you clean the bore of your rifle more often than every 500 rounds, you are in my opinion doing it too often. And by "clean" I mean anything more than poking a brush down the bore, followed by a patch, dry or wet. Now, you can do a thorough clean, scrub the gunk off of and from the inside of your rifle and chamber-brush the chamber. None of that will harm your bore.

In that, you chamber-brush the chamber, clean the upper, and at the end, brush and patch the bore. And that is it. If you do more, you are likely wearing the bore more with the rod than you are by shooting.

I can hear the howls of outrage. "You can't leave a bore alone, the bore will get clogged with copper fouling, accuracy will go away, pressures will skyrocket, and civilization as we know it will

end."

It may well happen that a rifle that was happily plugging along at 1 MOA, if not scrubbed clean, will drift up to 1.5 MOA after a few bazillion rounds. What won't happen is that not cleaning it turns it into a 10 MOA rifle. We see that in every class. We take 20-30-40 police officers, and spend three or five days working them hard. By the afternoon on the third day of a three-day, they will have a thousand rounds through their rifles. If they thoroughly cleaned it Monday night, they sure didn't do it Tuesday night, and by lunch on Wednesday it will have several hundred rounds through it since the thorough cleaning. By Wednesday afternoon it will be 4-500 rounds past that cleaning, and will be (if they are paying attention) still dropping the 300 meter targets. Accuracy has not noticeably changed.

On the afternoon of the fifth day in a five-day class, they are up to 1,500 rounds and probably haven't given the bore of their rifle a "decent" cleaning since Tuesday morning or that lunch break. Again, there is no apparent change in accuracy.

Which leads me to law enforcement and cleaning.

The default status of clean in law enforcement firearms is often, "I still have it, in case the armorer wants it back." That is; no cleaning whatsoever has been done. Benign neglect is another term for this. They haven't cleaned it, but at least they haven't actively abused it. Once the cool factor of being issued an AR wears off, the rifles pretty much stay in their locked case, in the trunk of the squad car, until it comes time for the qual course, or trouble.

This is also not a good example to follow.

If you hang around police officers long enough, you hear of shotguns with gum wrappers, cigar butts and who knows what else in the bore. If, in that kind of environment, you want to do a proper, thorough and bore-scrubbing clean on the rifle just issued to you, I understand. And since the department will likely never issue enough ammunition to wear out the bore, it may well be that the bore is worn out from cleaning long before wearing out from shooting. Such is life.

CHAPTER 8
INSPECTION

THIS MAY SEEM simple, but it isn't. In the course of teaching and being a gunsmith at a number of law enforcement classes, I've learned that you cannot simply assume that everything is there, and everything is tightly attached. More than once, and even with big-name brand rifles, I or one of the other instructors has started in on solving "the problem" only to find that the real issue is that something is missing, loose, installed backwards or otherwise wrong.

Also, you may be inspecting a rifle to buy it. The gun shop, or the gun show guy you're working with, has a rifle, but you want to make sure it works before you plunk down cash. Fair warning, some shops and some gun shows won't let you cycle the bolt or do things like let the bolt crash home. Just be sure of what the return policy is, before you buy and leave.

So, here's the rundown for checking out a rifle, short of actually stepping to the line and firing it. This could be your pre-purchase inspection. This could be what you do to a rifle that has just been handed to you for use on duty, in a match, or "the zombies will be swarming over that ridgeline in thirty seconds. Gear up."

If the rifle is loaded, unload it before proceeding. If it is unloaded, check. (Check anyway.)

If someone got overly vigorous in malfunction drills, they could bend the charging handle. You want to know this before buying.

BASIC INSPECTION

Here's the basic, "you've just been handed a rifle" inspection. The idea here is to make sure that what you are about to sign for, or pay for, is as it should be.

External, Visual

Check to make sure all the expected parts are there, sights, optics or irons or both. If optics, and they are battery-driven, turn on the sight and see if there is a dot or if the reticle lights up as expected. Flash hider, handguards, stock, pistol grip. Are the lower and upper a good fit to each other, or does it feel as if it will fall apart just from handling?

Next, take a closer look at a few details.

Are the sights vertical? A tipped front or rear is a bad sign. Is the rear sight centered, and is the front sight at the correct level? That is, are they mechanically zeroed, or close to it?

Are the hammer and trigger pins flush on both sides?

Top: The hammer sear hook needs to be clean, un-altered and left alone. Polishing it to "improve" trigger pull is asking for trouble. Bottom: This hammer hook has been heinously altered, in search of an improved trigger pull. The owner may have learned something along the way, but the biggest lesson was the cost of a new hammer.

Extractors can break, bend, crack, and wear. And, you can buy one that was too cheap, too much of a good deal. Inspect and replace if needed.

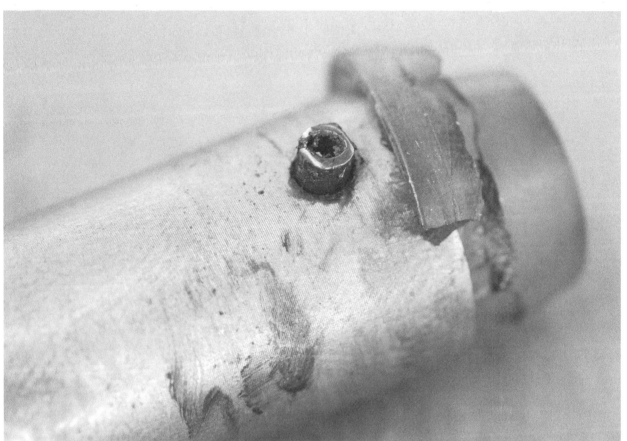

This buffer not only broke the plastic butt end, but the roll pin that was supposed to hold it together started drifting out.

Left: Yes, shaving off the offending ring of plastic with your Rambo survival knife might be a short-term solution. A better one would be to replace it with a good one, and not buy parts so cheap again. Right: The poorly-made magazine catch, on the right, held magazines so marginally that they could be yanked out without even having to press the magazine release button.

The plastic pieces, getting tied up with the buffer spring and causing problems.

A poorly-fitted buffer tube allowed this buffer retainer to escape. The parts rattled around in the lower until they managed to bind the action, and the rifle stopped working.

If the stock is fixed, is it tight? If it is a tele-stock, does it slide smoothly, without a gritty sound and feel?

Next up, the fire controls. Work the bolt. Does it move smoothly, or is there a gritty, grinding or "catch-y" noise or feel? Did the ejection port cover pop open when you worked the bolt? Does it latch back up, when you press it back into place?

With the chamber empty, close the bolt. Work the safety lever. Does it click back and forth with crisp precision, or is it muddy in feel, unsure in setting?

The correct orientation of the hammer spring, on the hammer.

Function Tests

Close the bolt on an empty chamber. Set the selector to Safe. Press the trigger. It should not move, or move only a small (very small) amount. Let go of the trigger.

Flip the selector to Fire, and press the trigger. The hammer should fall. Keep the trigger pressed back, and cycle the bolt with the charging handle.

Slowly (as slowly as you can) ease the trigger forward. You should hear a light "click" as you get near the end. This is the disconnector letting go of the hammer, and handing it off to the trigger sear surface. The trigger should not move much farther after this click.

Leave the selector on Fire and press the trigger. The trigger pull should feel the same as it did before.

Leave the selector on Fire. Either lock the bolt to the rear (which is the first test of the bolt hold-open), or pull the charging handle fully to the

Once found, the buffer retainer had to be pried out from under the hammer, which was attempting to smash it into the trigger.

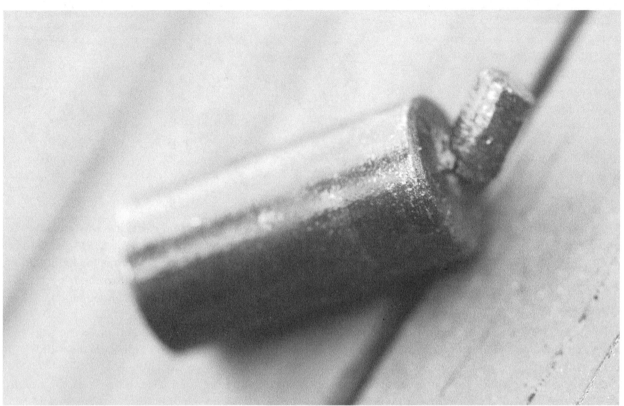

The buffer retainer was damaged in all this and had to be replaced, along with the mangled buffer retainer spring.

The rifle this buffer was in was giving problems. Until we stripped it and inspected it, the problem was mysterious.

This buffer retainer is doing its level best to escape. This is marginal engagement.

Here we have a buffer weight that is not only poorly assembled, but badly made. It should not be a single steel weight on the inside. It should be a series of steel and tungsten weights.

Don't be too worried about wear on the buffer weight face. It happens, and it takes a lot more than this to make a buffer weight unserviceable.

rear and let go. If you have locked the bolt back, press the release button. Let the bolt crash home while the selector is on Fire. Then press the trigger again. The hammer should have stayed cocked, and the trigger pull should be the same as it was originally.

If the rifle won't fire, try turning the selector.

At this point one of two things will happen. You either can or can't push the selector to Safe. If you can, the trigger mechanism has worked as it is supposed to. If you can't, the hammer has probably followed the bolt down, and is right back where it started, pressed against the firing pin. This is bad.

Again, send it back.

At this point, at least one of you is grumbling, "This is an AR gunsmthing book, tell me how to fix it." Again, you paid good money for a rifle that was supposed to work without needing extra gunsmithing on your part. There will be plenty of time to practice your gunsmithing skills, just not now.

OK, you know the safety works when it is on,

and the hammer and disconnector work when you slam-cycle the action.

Let's back up and re-run the tape.

Work the charging handle and cock the hammer. Put the safety on Safe. Pull the trigger. Nothing happens. Let go of the trigger, and press the selector to Semi. Pull the trigger. The hammer should fall.

Hold the trigger all the way back. Cycle the charging handle again, cocking the hammer.

Now, slowly ease the trigger forward. Do it as slowly and incrementally as you can. What if the trigger never catches the hammer? Or, the disconnector never releases it?

Now, the bad result is if the disconnector releases the hammer so soon that the trigger has not yet pivoted up to catch it. You'll know that happens when the result of this test isn't a "click" but a "crash" of the hammer slamming into the rear of the bolt and the firing pin. If it does this, you know what to do: return it. If the disconnector never releases, then it also needs to be returned.

Run a class, and you see a lot of extractors. Run a lot of classes, and you see more than a few broken extractors.

Buy cheap, and you risk this. However, even the best will sometimes do this, as even the best gear will break once in a million times.

Work your gear hard, and you'll break stuff.
Fail to inspect it, and you'll miss something like this.

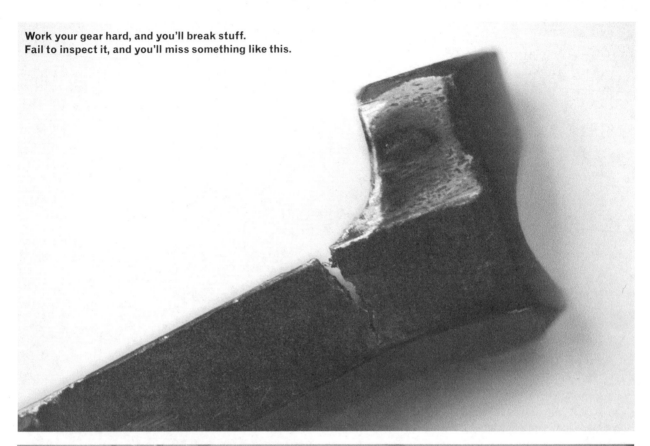

Here you see the correct assembly of the hammer and trigger and their springs, in the lower.

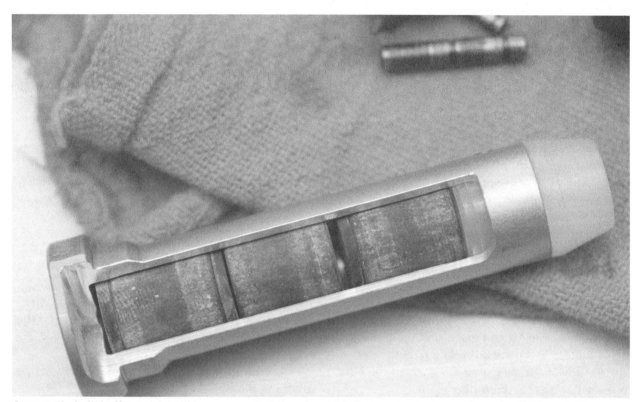

A correctly-built buffer weight will have separate internal weights in it, some steel, some tungsten if it is an "H" or heavier weight.

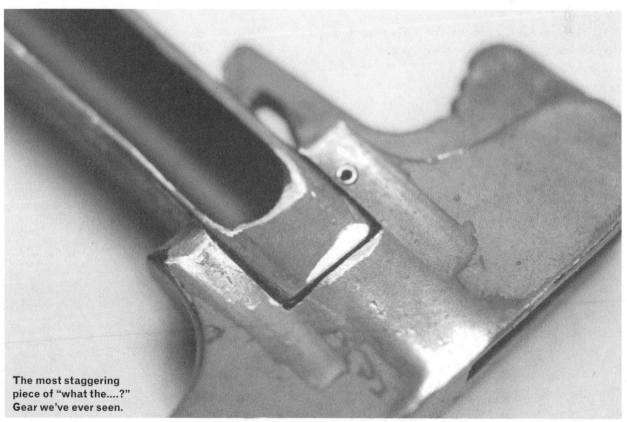

The most staggering piece of "what the....?" Gear we've ever seen.

Internals Check

Open the action and remove the bolt-carrier assembly. Remove the upper from the lower.

Inside the lower, look to see that the springs (hammer, trigger, disconnector) are all there. Confirm that the legs of the hammer spring are outboard and present, and that the hammer spring is correctly installed on the hammer.

Check the buffer to see that it is present and relatively free from wear.

Inspect the bolt and carrier. Is the gas key tight? Is the cotter pin correctly installed, and the firing pin retained? Inspect the bolt lugs. Are they all present? Look closely for cracks, and inspect the extractor to ensure it is not chipped or broken. Look at the ejector to make sure it is above the boltface.

Look at the breech and make sure there is no debris, gunk, lost parts or broken fragments of parts in the locking lug area. Look down the bore. Is there daylight? Is there rifling?

Magazine check

For this you need a selection of known-reliability magazines. Use only the lower. Insert each of them and make sure they lock in place. Then press the button and see that they fall out of their own weight.

Reassemble the upper and lower.

With the bolt forward, insert your magazines again. Can they be pressed up to lock without undue pressure? Do they fall free?

MORE IN-DEPTH INSPECTION

If you have time, pull the bolt out of the carrier. Inspect the cam pin to see if there is heavy wear.

Inspect the gas rings to make sure there are three of them.

Look at the cam pin hole in the bolt, to see if there is a crack or if it might already be broken.

Pull the buffer and spring from the lower, and inspect the buffer. Make sure it isn't cracked, that the synthetic bumper on the rear is intact, and that the spring is correct and has the right number of coils.

Beyond this, you have to test-fire to know anything more.

Not only is this castle nut not staked, it is assembled backwards. The small notch side should go against the retaining plate. The large notches are for the castle nut wrench.

Here is a correctly-assembled, and properly staked castle nut. If yours doesn't look like this, you should correct it. Tighten and stake.

Yes, this bolt does have three gas rings. And yes, it passes the stand-up test. But you really can't say it is properly assembled, can you?

CHAPTER 9
LUBRICANTS

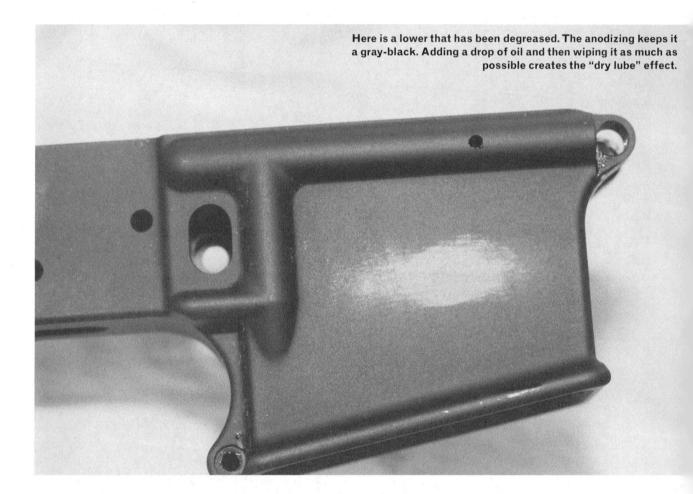

Here is a lower that has been degreased. The anodizing keeps it a gray-black. Adding a drop of oil and then wiping it as much as possible creates the "dry lube" effect.

F YOU OPEN any firearms magazine, you will be pummeled by the attributes of the latest wonder lube. It solves all problems, keeps your rifle running and smells as fresh as a spring day.

No, it doesn't. No lube does.

In a nutshell, they do three things: reduce friction, create a film that seals the surface against oxidation, and keep powder residue, dirt and grit loose, so they can't wedge moving parts in place.

That's it. Anything else is a bonus, or superfluous, or non-existent.

When people ask me what lubricant I use, the only truthful answer is, "Whatever I have handy, whatever I got for free." I really don't care which. What I do care is where and how much.

Lubrication comes in four levels: dry lubed (not to be confused with dry lube), wiped damp, gleaming and wet. No one level is appropriate for all parts of your rifle. Each has its own needs, its own requirements, and you have to treat them as they need to be treated.

DRY LUBE

For an example of dry lube lubrication, take your upper receiver (just because it is handy) and degrease it. You started with a black upper, and now you have a charcoal gray upper. Spray the upper with a lubricant (not WD40, please) and wipe it with your bare hands until the surface is evenly coated. Now, take a shop cloth and wipe the surface until all the excess lube has been wiped up and the surface is evenly coated. It will still be black, but it will no longer be dry. In this instance, the oil is trapped in the interstices of the anodizing on the surface of the aluminum. The anodizing creates a sponge-like layer, only a couple of thousandths of an inch or so thick, and when you degreased you stripped that out. Now that you've oiled, it is back, but you have wiped the excess off the surface, while leaving the oil in the "sponge" layer.

Steel parts that have been black oxided or parkerized present much the same situation. Surfaces that are oiled and then wiped with the stereotypical "oily cloth" are dry lube surfaces. The lubrication serves mostly as a bar to oxidation, while providing a small amount of friction reduction.

WIPED DAMP

Wiped damp is a similar situation, except when you wipe the receiver, you do not use the oily cloth. You only use your hands, and you only wipe as much off as you can with your bare hands. The surface is visibly oiled, but it does not drip oil if left upright.

GLEAMING

Here, you wipe with your hands, but you do not try to squeegee off the excess oil. The surface is visibly oiled, and may even drip if left unattended for some time, or left in the heat or direct sun.

WET

A wet-lubed surface has a visible layer of lubricant on it. If you, for example, take a bottle

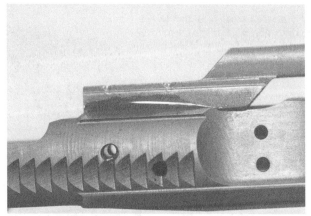

This is a couple of drops of oil, soon to be wiped to the wiped-damp or gleaming stage.

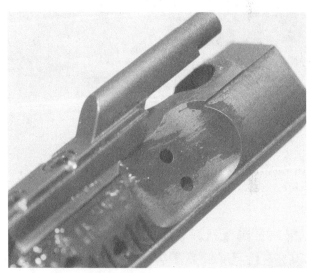

The oil drops wiped to make it gleam.

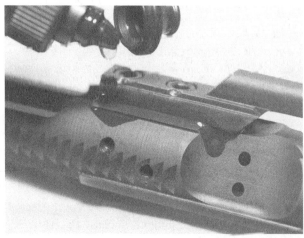

This is wet. When the lube can run off, it is past damp, it is wet.

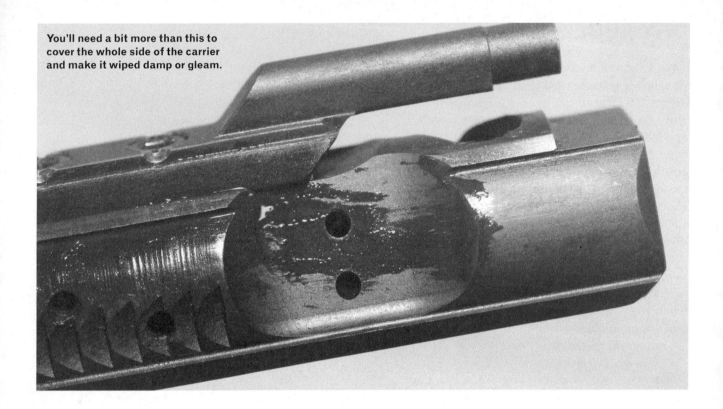

You'll need a bit more than this to cover the whole side of the carrier and make it wiped damp or gleam.

of oil and run a bead of lube down the side of the receiver, the bead is the wet lube.

WHEN DO YOU NEED WHAT?

Dry Lube

The barrel, flash hider, buffer tube on a tele-stock carbine, iron sight housings, free-float forearm if aluminum – these all get the dry lube treatment. The receivers, upper and lower, inside and out, get the dry lube treatment. You need to simply bar oxidation from their surfaces. If you over-oil the barrel, for example, then when you heat it up in a shooting string, you will evaporate and oxidize the oil on the surface, and you'll have a smoking barrel even before it is smoking hot. Now, this is subject to adjustment. In the desert, say living in Arizona or New Mexico, you may not even need to put this much oil on the barrel. And you may want to keep the exterior of the buffer tube dry so as to not attract dust, dirt and grit. On the other hand, if you live in the bayou, you may need to apply a heavier amount of oil to the barrel to control rust, and then just live with the hot barrel smoking.

Wiped Damp

This is what the buffer weight, the buffer spring and the carrier need, with an extra step on the carrier in a moment. The buffer and spring need a small amount of lube, as they rub back and forth inside the tube. The body of the carrier needs only enough lube to keep carbon from adhering to it. However, the guide rails, the raised portions of the carrier need to be lubed wet.

Gleaming

To make a part gleam, you need a drop of oil applied directly to it. The drops go into the plunger that keeps the front sight locked in place, but not the front sight itself. It should be dry lube. The rear sight windage screw threads get a drop. The rear sight gets a drop at the edge of the adjustment plate

(A1) or drum (A2) and the A2 also gets a drop on the threads of the elevation adjustment wheel. The plunger for the buffer retainer gets a drop. The plunger for the takedown pins, front and back, get a drop. The bolt hold open pivot gets a drop. The takedown pin tunnels on the upper get a drop each.

The hammer pivot and spring loops each get a drop, as do the trigger spring loops and their pivot pin. The disconnector gets a drop at its spring. The safety/selector gets a drop on each end, where it goes into the inside wall of the lower receiver.

Wet

What gets wet? Simple: the bolt and cam pin. The bolt, at the rotation band, and once assembled in the carrier, at the bolt/carrier junction. Hose the extractor and ejector and the locking lugs. Get oil into the cam pin slot, and put a drop into each of the gas vent holes on the side of the carrier.

Now, you can over-do this. If your first shot produces a splatter of oil that looks like a drilling rig spill on the side of your shooting bench, you've over-oiled it. This can be a particular problem for left-handed shooters, as the oil splatters out directly at them.

WHAT DIDN'T GET LUBED?

Before we dive into the "should I or shouldn't I" discussion, let's take a look at a few places that have not been mentioned. One, the gas tube and gas key. You can lube the outside of the key to control carbon and make it easier to clean off, if you want to. You not only do not need to lube the gas tube, you don't want to. It is a direct recipient of hot gases and will self-clean. Adding lube just provides more carbon-containing product to be scorched and dried and then blown out when the pressure gets high enough.

The bore has not been lubed. There is no need, unless you have a barrel that is not stainless or not hard-chrome lined. A carbon steel barrel, in some climates, needs to be swabbed with oil to protect the surface. But outside of that limited requirement, no lube in the bore or chamber.

SHOULD I, OR SHOULDN'T I?

Some of you reading this are becoming increasingly skeptical because your local gun show expert, the guy who "knows a guy who knows a SEAL," says to not lube your AR. Run it dry.

He is wrong. In some very limited circumstances, as in Arctic conditions, dry air and tens of degrees below zero, lube is a bad idea. It will freeze, unless it is specially formulated. He'll tell you of his buddy-of-a-buddy and the experience of being in Iraq/Afghanistan/that special op in Iran, and the dust-clogged rifles that had been lubed.

Lube flushes away grit. Lube holds grit in suspension, so it can't build up and lock into an immovable mass. "But, the grit and carbon stays in the oil, and acts as a grinding compound." Ahem. Grinding compound is a specially-formulated mixture of super-hard grit and grease. Not oil, grease. The grease stiffens the mix, and keeps the grit pressed against the surface to be ground. Lube does not stiffen, and the grit in it then floats, not grinding the surface it is next to at the moment.

WHAT LUBRICANT, THEN?

I have a few firm opinions on this. One is that you should not be using WD40. WD40 is the fortieth mixture, or formula, developed to be a water-displacing oil. It is meant to get water away and keep it away. However, the more volatile constituents of the mixture will evaporate, leaving a surprisingly lacquer-like film behind. When I was a full-time gunsmith, I'd regularly see rifles and shotguns brought in, with their various smaller parts glued together by age and heat-hardened WD40.

One common lubricant is CLP. The military bought it by the trainload because they could use it to both clean and lubricate. It does both reasonably well in the original formula that the military bought, but if you want to clean, clean. If you want to lube, lube. Don't expect one thing to do both. If it is what you have, use it. But don't expect anything magical to happen just because your bottle is mil-surplus and holds CLP.

Various motor oils, both distilled petroleum and

It is August, in the Midwest and in farm country. Hot, dry, under a blazing sky, and you're in the fifth day of a high-volume class. If you don't use lubricant, you won't make it this far, your rifle will have quit on Tuesday afternoon.

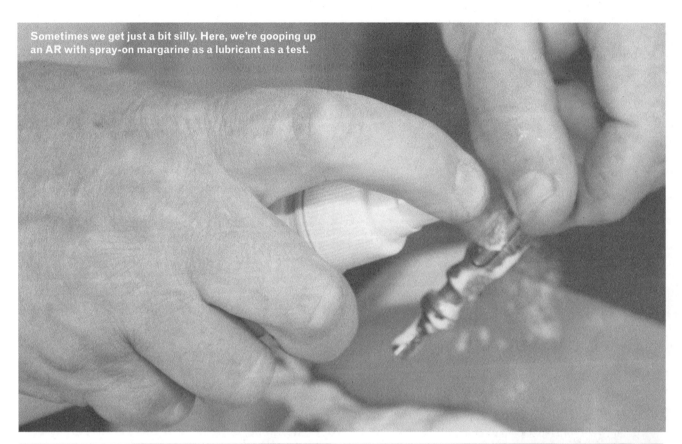

Sometimes we get just a bit silly. Here, we're gooping up an AR with spray-on margarine as a lubricant as a test.

The bolt and carrier should be wet with lubricant, in this case, margarine.

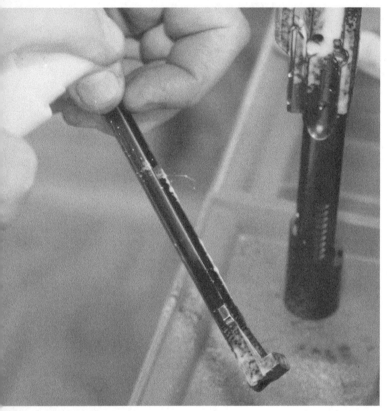

Everything gets sprayed with margarine.

synthetic, can be used as lubricants. Your engine goes a minimum of three thousand miles between oil changes, if you go by the most aggressive schedule. That can easily be ten million cycles of the engine. Ten million, and your shooting buddies scoff that motor oil isn't "good enough" to be used as a firearm lube?

The big problem with motor oil is that you can't buy less than a quart, which is a decades worth of lubrication for most owners of an AR.

In the realm of the "let's get strange," I've been involved in testing where we have used sunscreen as a firearms lubricant and managed to go a whole day without a malfunction. Then there was the episode where one of the guys used margarine in his AR. What you use isn't nearly as important as using it properly, in the right place, and in enough volume.

Now that doesn't mean that there aren't really good lubes out there. I know some of the inventors, and they are earnest in their attempts to make something that is better than what exists. It's just that none of them are perfect.

Get some, use it, and clean when you are done.

After a magazine of ammo, your rifle smells like a bucket of popcorn. Mmmm.

CHAPTER 10
ZEROING

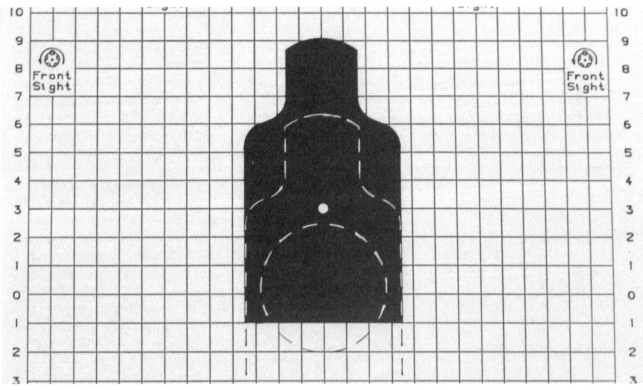

The Army 25-meter zero target. The dotted line is for when the aiming point is the bottom edge of the silhouette.

NO MATTER HOW good your lawyer is, you aren't getting out of obeying this basic law of nature: gravity works. A bullet hurled out into the air will, at the end of its journey, called the trajectory, fall to the ground. How long it takes for it to reach the ground depends on how fast it is going, the angle it leaves at, how well it shrugs off the drag air puts on it and, one factor that people overlook, how far down the ground is. You cannot throw or fire a bullet fast enough to avoid the ground. You can, if you accelerate it sufficiently, miss the ground entirely. This is called reaching escape velocity. If you are trying to reach escape velocity from Earth, that happens to be 25,000 miles per hour. Your rifle isn't going to do that, as it equals 36,745 feet per second.

Hurled into a vacuum at an angle, a bullet would follow a circular arc from the point of origin to the ground. However, the effects of air will enter into the problem, and the result is the curved path the bullet takes, one called a parabola. At long range, the curve of the back half of the trajectory has markedly more curve than the front half. That is a parabola.

One of the design characteristics of the AR is that the barrel is directly in line with the buffer tube, which is also the part that bears on your shoulder. This creates a poor lever for the forces of recoil to act on, resulting in the straight-line recoil you experience. However, your eyes are not in your shoulder, and in order for you to aim, the sights (iron or optical) have to be up where your eyes are.

The design of this ends up with the sights of the AR-15 2.6 inches above the center of the bore. The end result is that you have to arrange the sights so that your line of sight, which is a straight line, and the parabola of the trajectory intersect at some point. This is referred to as "zeroing" your rifle. Additionally, you have to know what that point is or points are. Now, if you are shooting at a target, and you don't shoot at any other distance, you can adjust your sights so that the point of aim (POA) and point of impact (POI) are one and the same at that one distance. Problem solved. If you shoot at different distances, say as a varmint hunter, or you are using an AR for defense, you have to know more than just that one distance.

The arrangement also means that at close range, regardless of your zero (and we'll cover that in excruciating detail in a bit) your point of impact will be below your point of aim. This is something that has to be learned and practiced if you are going to use the AR for defense. If you do not remember, or practice, a close-distance shot will have the bullet striking an inch or two *below* where you were aiming.

So, the line of sight is straight. The bullet arcs up, reaches its highest point, arcs down, and then finally falls to the ground. You have two choices; you can have the trajectory cross the line of sight once, or cross it twice. Well, you can have it not cross at all, but that isn't much use, as you will always have your iron sights or red-dot scope and the aiming point, above where the bullet will strike. And the farther away the target, the greater the difference. Fat load of good *that* does you.

To do all this, regardless of what distance we wish to shoot at, we begin our work at twenty-five yards. Why twenty-five? In part, because we are lazy and don't have time to waste. Yes, we could do our sight-in and zero at 100 yards, but we'd spend more time just walking down there and back than actually shooting and adjusting. At twenty-five yards you are far enough to get good info, but close enough to see the bullet holes without having to walk to the target. (Not that that keeps us from doing the walking any way. Sometimes you've just got to go down and look.) Plus it actually saves ammo. I've lost count of the times I'd be at the gun club and see a club member trying to sight-in his rifle at 100 yards. He couldn't see, through his 3-9X scope on his .30-06, that his shots were missing the target. He'd have to walk down, guess, adjust and shoot more. If he had just started at 25, he would have seen he was off to the right, and gotten close enough to be on paper at 100.

Here's the part that is difficult to grasp for some shooters: the POI at twenty-five yards is not always your POA. That is, at twenty-five yards, in some zero methods, the bullets will still strike below the point of aim. In this particular instance, useful, and not a contradiction of my snarky comment above.

And in a clever move, the Army had the sight correction rotations placed on the target, in the location they would be needed. (I probably shouldn't be snarky, it is a good thing to have done.)

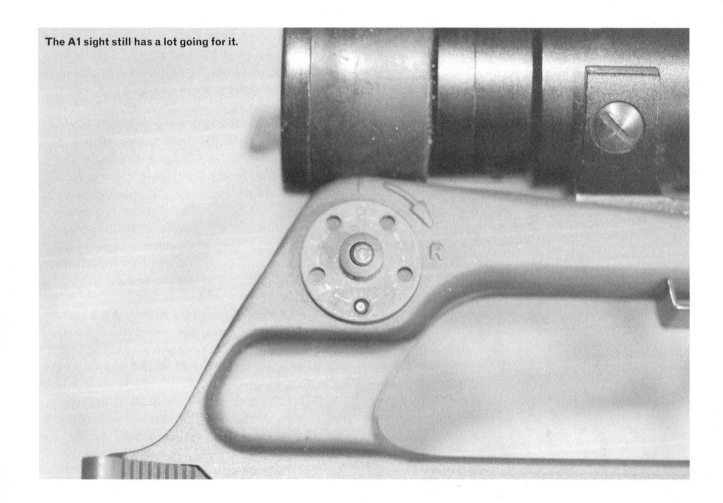

The A1 sight still has a lot going for it.

SIGHTS

Before we get into the details zeroing, we have to get square on what sights are, and what we do with them. Your AR has one of four types of sights. You have two iron sights, the A1 and the A2. And you have two optical sights, the red-dot and the magnifying. Yes, some optical sights can be both red-dots and magnifying, but we'll deal with that when we get there.

A1

The A1 sight has only windage adjustments on the rear. The adjustments are made by pressing in the plunger you can see in one of the openings in the flat wheel on the right side of the carry handle. With the plunger pressed down, you can turn the wheel to make windage corrections. The sight itself is an L-shaped plate, with the windage screw passing through it and an aiming aperture in each of the flat plates. Rotating the sight adjustment plate turns the threaded shaft, and the sight moves right or left along the shaft.

The L plate of the sight can be flipped so you use one or the other sighting aperture. The two apertures are the same size, but one of them, the one with an "L" marking, has the center of its aperture higher above the adjustment shaft than the center of the other one. This is the long-range aperture, hence the L.

This was the height of military aiming technology, circa 1969. Gone was the click-adjustable rear sight of the M14, derived from that of the M1 Garand. Unless you want to be plinking at sandy hillsides out past 350 yards, you will have no need of the L sight, and will do all of your work and aiming with the other aperture.

Vertical adjustments will be made with the front sight.

Once the A1 sight is zeroed, you do not make sight adjustments while firing. That is, if you find you are dealing with a wind from the right while shooting at your target 200 yards away, you will not be turning the adjustment plate. You will have to hold off, that is, into the wind.

Our fathers and grandfathers fought with rifles (this is an M1 Garand) that had adjustable sights worthy of a target rifle. That's what the **USMC** wanted to get back to when they pushed through the A2 improvements.

A2

The A2 is click adjustable for windage and elevation, but it requires that once you have zeroed your rifle, you have to re-adjust the sight adjustment wheels so you have a zero starting point. More in a bit. The sight apertures themselves differ from those of the A1. The L plate of the sight still rides on a threaded shaft, and moves when the adjustment wheel is changed. It also flips up so you can use one or the other. However, the sight apertures are markedly different.

There is a large one, marked "0-2," and a small one. Many new shooters assume that the large aperture is your aiming aperture for shooting from zero to 200 yards. Close, but no cigar. The 0-2 aperture is meant to be used as an aiming device in low-light, night-time or bundled up in chemical protection situations. It's not a regular-use out to 200 yards sight.

You will zero your rifle using the small aperture. Unlike the A1 sight, the centers of the large and small apertures of the A2 are intended to be the same distance above the adjustment screw. Thus they will have the same POI. Given the vagaries of mechanical fabrication and human eyesight, they are close, but not always exactly the same. Plus, the larger aperture produces a larger group on target, at any range, and with any ammo, than with the same ammo at the same range using the small aperture.

So, zero with the small aperture and leave it set to the small aperture, unless it is so dark you need the larger aperture. (And I have to ask, if it is that dark, what are you doing shooting?)

How iron sights work

If you have done any handgun shooting, you know the way those sights align – top edges level, front blade centered in the rear notch, and the bullet will strike at the optical top center of the front blade. Rifle sights of the same design work the same way. The aperture sights of the AR do not.

To aim, you look through the rear aperture. If you relax and let your brain work without overly supervising it, it will find the optical center of the aperture. Now place the tip of the front sight in the center of the aperture, with the protective wings (if you can see them) evenly spaced on the right and the left.

Now, place this whole assembly on your target. The bullet will strike at the tip of the front sight.

The smaller the aperture (because it is smaller, or because you have positioned your face further away and made it appear smaller), the smaller the group you can shoot. But also, the slower you shoot, simply getting things lined up. The larger the aperture, the faster you can shoot. If you expand aperture size, you reach an aperture diameter so large your brain can't precisely determine center, and you then shoot bigger groups than you would otherwise.

With practice, the aperture sight can be very fast

A bit of mis-alignment of the rear sight in its housing is not cause for alarm. If you have to crank it all the way over, front sight housing work may be called for.

and very precise.

They do, however, have some drawbacks. Your eye can only focus at one distance at a time. Your brain can only have one center of attention at a moment. It can, however, perform some operations automatically, if they have been practiced enough to make them semi-autonomous. (This is not multi-tasking, it is simply shuffling through the operations fast enough to be close enough.) But you can still only focus at one distance.

So, the act of aiming has your eye bouncing back and forth – between target, front sight, rear aperture, sight, target, and so on. The classic teaching aid is to tell the shooter to "focus on the front sight, make it sharp, and let the target and rear sight fuzz out." This works well when the target is a stationary, distinct and non-threatening piece of paper or cardboard. In the real world, you have to spend at least some time on the target, if only to determine where it is and that it still qualifies for target status.

Learning iron sights isn't easy, and can be quickly forgotten.

Red-Dot Sights

The red-dot sight began with the Aimpoint back in the very late 1980s. It appeared in the U.S. in competition at the 1990 USPSA Nationals, on the pistol used by Jerry Barnhart. The first reaction was, "No way will that work." After Jerry cleaned everyone's clocks, Doug Koenig had one on his pistol a few months later at the IPSC World Shoot, where he became world champion.

As soon as national-level 3-gun competition began, rifles had red-dots on them. They were derided as "impractical" and "not real combat gear." In the beginning, yes. But the reliability imperative of practical shooting competition (your gear is your problem, once the clock starts, and if it fails you do not get a do-over) meant all competitors using them were always looking for more reliability, durability and utility.

By the second Iraq war, red-dot sights had been adopted and proved their usefulness. It was mildly amusing, seeing photos of M4s in Iraq, rifles that were equipped to have made decent but not match-winning Open class 3-gun rifles back in the 1990s.

Red-dot sights work by projecting a red dot, reticle or other pattern onto a screen inside of a tube or housing. The miracle of optical physics presents the dot to you as if it were on the same optical plane as the target. That is, it appears to be "out there" and not a dot a few inches from your face. This means your eye has only the one focus job, dot and target together. Your brain has only two things to deal with, dot and target.

You place the dot on the target and press the trigger.

But wait, there's more goodness: the dot is, essentially, parallax-free. That is, if the dot appears

A red-dot sight, like this **EOTech**, can also be teamed up with a magnifying adapter, and thus get you the best of both worlds.

to be at the edge of the field of view, the bullet will still strike at the dot. Moving the dot does not change the agreement of dot with bullet.

The bad news is simple, dots need batteries.

Magnifying Optics

Magnifying optics were not new when they began to be adopted on rifles in the trenches in WWI. Since then, they have increased in durability, light-gathering, clarity and reticle designs. What they do is let you see better, but not necessarily shoot better. The choice of magnifying optics comes down to a matter of balance. That is, size and weight against increased magnification and fragility. Increased performance increases cost,

where a top-grade scope can cost more than the rifle it is mounted on. And with variable scopes, there is a need to shift from one power to another, as any extreme is useful only for a specific purpose. A 3-9X scope is great, at 9X, if you are shooting at something at extreme range. Let a target of opportunity pop up ten yards away, and 9X is very much the wrong power to be on.

ZERO PROCESS

You should do all your zero work from a solid bench, with supports such as sandbags, or prone, with sandbags or supports. You cannot zero a rifle shooting offhand. No one is that good.

To start, shoot a five-shot group. Measure closely

The **USMC** bought truckloads of the Acog, and did good work with them over in the various sandy places of the world.

Optics need not be expensive. This Millet **DMS-1** is plenty good enough, and won't break the bank.

the distance from your aiming point to the center of the group, and consider how much adjustment you need to move the group to the aiming point. When we do this in classes, it can take forever. Some shooters have rifles already zeroed. Some don't. And some take several magazines of practice to shoot a group smaller than the target paper, typically a target run off of a copying machine.

If you need to make a correction, make it. Don't do half the estimated number of clicks, do them all. Then shoot again.

When we have had the instructors zero rifles (at least enough to make sure they are close), the instructors will shoot two or three, make a full correction, and shoot two more. We're often "in the circle" (the circle used for the desired zero setting) in five shots. Sometimes it takes more.

The different zero settings go by a variety of names, but what I use are 100 yard, 50 yard and 25 yard zero. All my calculations will be done here

with a 55 grain fmj bullet, at a muzzle velocity of 3100 fps. Changing bullets will change the trajectory in minor ways, but this will give you a good grasp of what a zero is and what it does. For instance, those of you with SBRs will find the drop to be greater, since you'll be starting off with less velocity. Those who can afford the Mk 262 load, with 75 or 77 grain bullets, will see less drop, as the bullet has a larger ballistic coefficient than the lowly 55 fmj.

Here's how they work.

100 Yard Zero

Use the small aperture on an A2 sight, or the unmarked (not the "L" aperture) on an A1 sight.

Use your twenty-five yard zero target and adjust your sights so the group is an inch and a half below the POA. The result is that the bullet will still be rising up to 100 yards, where it will reach its maximum height, and ride close to the line of sight for about ten yards before starting downwards. At 200 yards it will be 2.23 inches low (a convenient memory aid) and at 300 yards it will be a foot low.

So what you have is a zero setting where, from the muzzle to 200 yards, your bullet is never more than the differential between the line of sight and the parabola of the trajectory, and the bullet is always below the line of sight when they differ. Inside of 200 yards, you are not more than two and a half inches off. And out past two hundred yards to three hundred, a high center chest hold will get you a solid hit on a miscreant.

This zero has the benefit of being simple and straightforward. You have a close association of the line of sight with POI, and at no time is the bullet above the line of sight. The 100 yard zero is the one method where there is only one crossing, one point where the line of sight is crossed (or in this instance, met) by the trajectory.

All the other methods have the trajectory crossing the line of sight twice, the near zero and the far zero. All the other methods also have details between the A1 and the A2 that you have to attend to.

50 Yard Zero

In this process, the zero target is again at twenty five yards. Here, the point of aim is at twenty-five yards, and the point of impact there is 1.2 inches low. The result is an improved medium-range trajectory.

At fifty yards, the bullet is at zero. At one hundred yards, the bullet is now 1.6 inches high, an amount that could only be seen or used through a magnifying optic. Iron sight and red-dot shooters won't notice a thing, unless they are very good, and shooting from a supported prone.

Between 130 and 150 yards, the bullet will be 2.0 inches high, as high above the line of sight as the bullet will get.

At two hundred yards, the bullet will still be half an inch high. That is more than even the magnifying optics users can see.

At 300 yards, the bullet is now 5.9 inches low.

25 Yard Zero

Here, point of aim and point of impact are the same at 25 yards. The results are dramatically different. At 100 yards, the bullet impacts 6.3 inches high. Roll that around in your head for a bit, half a foot over your point of aim.

At 200 yards, the bullet is ten and a half inches high.

At 300 yards, the bullet is still eight inches high, with the crest of the parabola having been reached just a bit past the 00 yard markers, at 1.6 inches in height over the line of sight. The bullet does not come back down to the line of sight until 385 yards.

In the vernacular; what the frak?

The 25 yard (or in military use, 25 meter) zero is meant to replicate the trajectory of old, the rifles of yore. The intent was simple, a century-plus ago: use the belt buckle on the enemy soldier as an aiming point, and you will get an abdomen or chest hit all the way out to 400 yards. Clearly, today, no one will stand still, or even move in the open, with 400 yards of clear space between them and the enemy. Plus, we aren't in a military context. I'm not sure you can coherently describe a situation where you need to be shooting at someone 400 yards distant with a rifle.

So, What Zero?

For the longest time, I used the 100 yard zero. It presents an easy and straightforward system of aiming. At close range, hold off to account for line of sight. Beyond twenty-five yards, out to as far as I plan to ever be shooting people, line of sight and point of impact are closer to each other than the group size I'm likely to shoot.

However, the 50 yard zero does have some advantages, if I plan on shooting in matches with

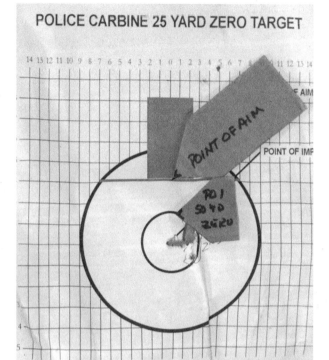

With the 100-yard zero, your bullet will strike the target well below the point of aim.

The 50-meter zero moves the initial point of impact up, as well as pushing out further the second point the trajectory crosses the line of sight.

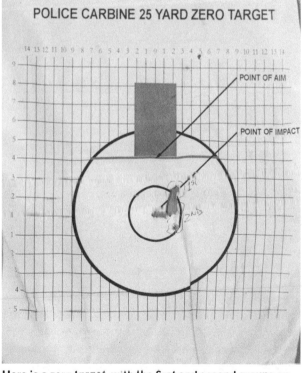

With the 25-yard zero, the point of aim and the point of impact are the same at 25 yards.

Here is a zero target, with the first and second groups on it. This upper came off the bench pretty close to being zeroed as-is.

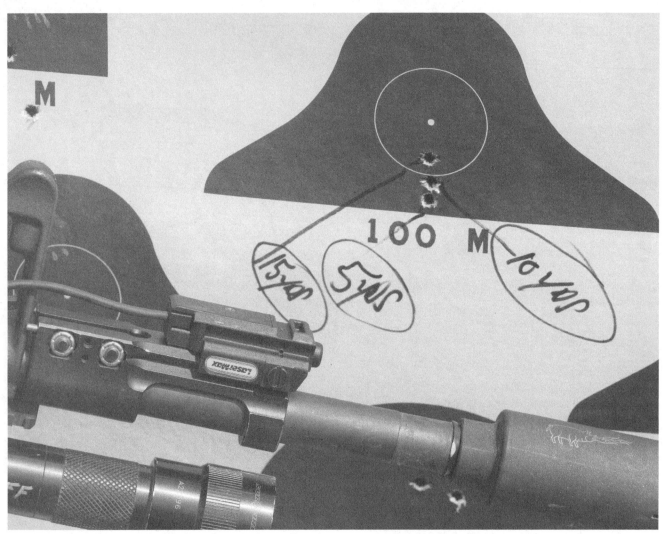

Here, on one target, you see the effect of moving closer, which moves the point of impact lower and lower below the point of aim.

rifle stages beyond CQB distances.

25 yard zero? No use for me, at least none that I can see for now.

Last Step

Now, if you use a solid bench and a rest to shoot from, or shoot prone with a sandbag support, you can get very well zeroed. Even an average shooter, with indifferent ammo and a rack-grade rifle with iron sights and not-egregious trigger, should be able to shoot a group of one inch at twenty-five yards. A good shooter, even with irons and a good rifle and ammo combo, should be able to shoot five shots that touch.

The best should be able to shoot a one-hole group.

Once done, go to the 100 yard line and verify. Don't shoot just one group and adjust. Do several and take the average, or take the last half of more than a few groups.

CHAPTER 11
TEST & LEARN

YOU HAVE A NEW RIFLE, or a new-to-you rifle, and you want to make sure it is correct and ready to go. We've covered that in Inspection. Then, you want to test-fire it and see that it functions correctly. Or, you've just assembled one, and you want to wring it out. Cool. You will need the following items:

- Cleaning kit, to include brushes, patches, rod, chamber brush, lube and disassembly tools.
- Sight adjustment tools. The military manuals will tell you that a bullet tip is enough to change your sight settings. They lie. Well, perhaps it's not an outright lie, but certainly a gross exaggeration. If you depend on the bullet tip method, you will certainly mar your rifles finish with scraped brass markings, and likely bark your knuckles. You may even break something. Get the right tools and have them with you.
- Tightening tools. Take along a screwdriver that fits the pistol grip screw, for example. And a screwdriver or allen wrench that fits the sight or scope-base screws. It's no fun driving an hour to the range to find out that something essential is loose in a magazine. It is even less fun if you lack the tightening tool, and have to pack up and drive home.
- Ammunition. Do not test-fire a new, freshly-assembled or new-to-you rifle using questionable reloads. In fact, don't use reloads at all. Use factory-new, name brand ammo, of the appropriate type. For example, if you are testing an M4gery, with a 1/7 twist barrel, feeding it 45 grain Blitz/varmint ammo will be

frustrating at best. The bullets will be spun too quickly, will likely disintegrate on the way to the 100-yard target frame, and you will have no hits to measure.

- Magazines. Use magazines of known brand, quality and testing. Do not use heavily-worn "range" magazines.

Set aside enough time and range space to do the job properly. Rushing through the process is only going to result in having to do it all over again sometime later.

There are a few things you do not want to do.

Do not jump right in practicing drills and working on your various tactical/competition/defense routines. This isn't about you or your skills, this is about making sure the rifle works properly.

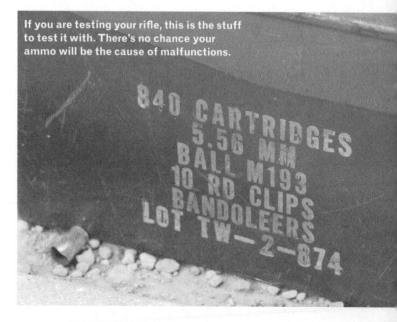

If you are testing your rifle, this is the stuff to test it with. There's no chance your ammo will be the cause of malfunctions.

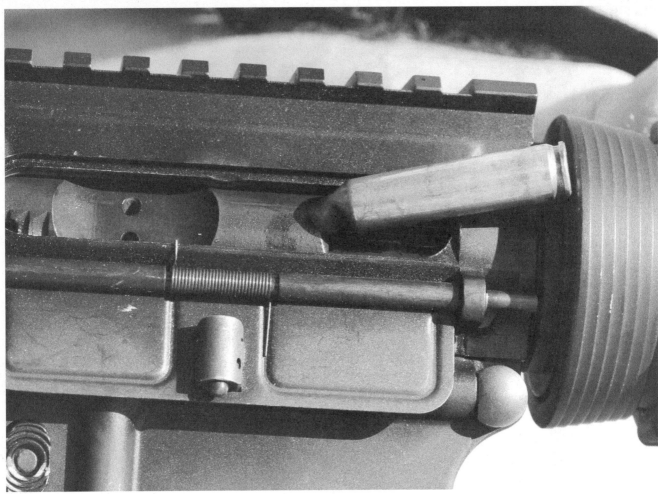

Use new, factory ammo, and of good quality. If you used reloads, you wouldn't know what caused this malfunction.

Do not immediately bolt on all the cool-guy "contractor" gear that your buddy at the gun shop tells you is "essential" if your AR is to be Tactical/Operator proper. At the very least, if there is a problem and you have to send it back, you'll have to unbolt all that stuff. Worse yet, the gear itself may be inducing the problem. Last, how would you feel if a rifle you made was returned, and it had bits of paint, Loctite, and marks from lights, scopes and other gear, along with a letter saying, "It doesn't work"? You'd be a bit put out. You may even wonder if someone is trying to pull a fast one on warranty work. Don't put yourself in the position of sending back a rifle that someone else has to fix, a rifle that you've obviously spent some time with.

Clean it, and make sure everything that is supposed to be there is there, and properly attached. Don't function-test a rifle lacking sights, for example. Yes, it may work 100%. But lacking sights, you'll be hard-pressed to tell if it is accurate or can be zeroed.

Take it to the range, along with the ammo, magazines and tools. First, perform a dry-fire function test.

DRY-FIRE FUNCTION TEST

Repeat the function test we covered in Chapter Nine. Yes, you did it at the gun shop or the gun show, and it passed. Do it again, both to test the rifle and remind yourself how things work.

In the old days, a "short-stroke" malfunction like this would have the barely-clued breaking out their power drills to open the gas port. Now we know such things are usually the ejector being bound, or the extractor lacking tension.

LIVE-FIRE TEST

Load a single round. Aim and fire. The recoil should seem normal. The bolt should lock back. Look for the empty. It should be some six to eight feet away. Inspect the case. Is it dented, scarred or otherwise mangled? Look at the base. Is there a shiny dot from the ejector? That is a bad sign, usually that you have a .223 leade.

Some people get entirely too involved in the direction their brass gets thrown. My take is simple; as long as it isn't too far forward or too far back (with exceptions), it is good enough. Worrying that your brass is going to two o'clock instead of four o'clock is a sign you are losing perspective.

Load two rounds and repeat.

Why not just load up and shoot? OK, you've

If you own a lot of magazines, mark them. Yes, you want to keep yours, yours, but also if one of them starts to act up, you want to know which one.

just bought your AR, and at the range you load a 30-round magazine. Is this the moment you want to discover that the shop owner's son has been learning how to do AR-15 trigger jobs? And that yours will go through all 30 rounds in a couple of seconds?

So, your rifle shoots the first round, ejects and then chambers the second. Let go of the trigger, let the disconnector hand off the hammer to the trigger, and fire again.

FIVE-SHOT TESTS

Load your reliable magazines with five rounds each. Fire them. This test is to make sure the magazine spring has enough oomph, and the bolt not too much speed, to handle rounds. A weak spring can lead to bolt-over-base failures. Also, a bolt that is cycling too fast can cause problems if the rounds haven't had time to settle down in the feed lips. (With the vibration of the rifle on firing, things jump around. A lot.)

Next, load your magazine full, but only fire five rounds. This again tests the magazines, but also test the system by seeing that the bolt has enough force to strip off rounds from a fully-loaded magazine.

BRASS CHECK

Are your empties in more-or-less the same area? If they are, then things are good. If they are scattered all over the place, this could be an indication of a changing gas system, a clogging ejector or a weakening extractor. (Or, it could be the ammo, which is why you want to use good stuff to test with.)

BOLT CHECK

Unload, and strip your rifle. Look at the bolt face. It should be a bit grubby, with some brassing, but not heavily brassed. A heavily-brassed bolt face typically means excessive pressure, usually a .223 leade.

If all is good, then start working on drills, bolt on your goodies, and have fun.

Left: So, the extractor tore though the rim. Too much gas, bad load, crusty chamber? Cut donw the variables, use good ammo. (Which this was.) Right: Not only is this cause for inspecting the rifle, but also inspecting the other empties. One in a carton is a hassle, but one per magazine is cause for real concern.

CHAPTER 12
SPARES & EMERGENCIES

WHAT DO YOU WANT to have on hand in case something breaks? What spares do you need, want, desire or will you be able to use?

The last part of that is the first to consider. If you do not have the tools or expertise to deal with a problem, having the spare part to solve the problem isn't much of a solution. Having a spare ejector and spring won't help if you don't have the bolt tool to take the bolt apart, or the pin punch you need to drive out the ejector pin.

Another example is a spare barrel. Let's say you find a smokin' hot deal and can get two excellent barrels at a really good price. So you buy them both, and keep the second as a spare. If you don't have the tools to install it, it is really a spare for your gunsmith. And in any case, you are not going to be schlepping the second barrel with you on a prairie dog shoot or a tactical class.

So, what should you have, and what can you expect to manage in a reasonable timeframe, on a hunt, in a match or in a defensive situation?

BREAKS AND LOSSES

The spare parts you can use are those that might break (even if the odds are remote) and those that you might lose, in cleaning, disassembly or other maintenance.

If you are cleaning your AR and have the bolt stripped, whatever you drop you will probably never see again. Well, if you are cleaning it in a bare concrete room maybe you'll find it. But in grass, sand, dirt, water, weeds, etc. it will be gone, whatever it is/was.

So we plan not just for breakage, but droppage as well.

EXTRACTOR

Extractors are not so expensive that you can't afford a spare. A spare for each one, perhaps stored in the pistol grip. And while you're at it, don't be cheap. Your spare extractor should already be equipped with spring, internal buffer

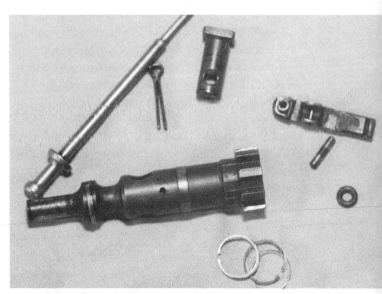

The spares you might be able to use in an emergency, or without extensive tools. A complete bolt, extra extractor, pin and o ring. Firing pin, cotter pin, gas rings.

and D-Fender or O ring. "Hey, if my extractor breaks, I'll just strip the spring and such out of the old one." Uh-huh. And if you have dropped it? Have the new one fully equipped.

As extra insurance, I'd put a spare extractor pin in the kit, maybe two. (Hey, if you drop one, you'll drop another, right?)

FIRING PIN

They hardly ever break, but again, they aren't expensive and they don't take up much room,. Besides, you can always use the spare firing pin as a disassembly assistance tool. Oh, and the firing pin should have its own cotter pin, too, or maybe two.

GAS RINGS

They are small, light, cheap, and easy to bend or lose. So you should have three spares. Why three? As I said, they are small, light, cheap and easy to bend.

SPARE BOLT

The current tacti-cool fashion is to have a spare bolt someplace, typically inside the pistol grip. In the past I really wasn't a fan of this. A bolt, fitted with rings, ejector, extractor, tested to your barrel, and stuffed in the pistol grip, costs you from $75 to $150. And in the past, bolts were not a problem.

Well, we've been seeing enough broken bolts lately that having a spare bolt, ready to go, seems like a lot better idea than it did back then.

If it is going to do you any good, it has to be right there, so the Magpul pistol grip designed to store a bolt is a must-have.

The bolt must be headspaced to that rifle (and if you have more than one rifle, make absolutely sure the spare stays with the tested rifle), fully-assembled and test-fired.

BATTERIES

If anything on your rifle is battery-driven, and you depend on it for more than entertainment, spare batteries are essential. Sealed, so rain, snow or a spill into water won't short them out.

Pistol grips used to just be pistol grips. Now you can adjust them for size, angle and storage capacity.

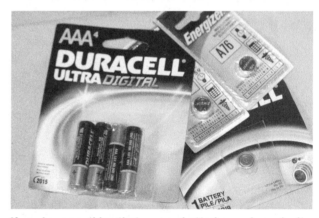

If you have anything that runs on batteries, and you don't have spare batteries, it will die and you will be out of luck.

TOOLS

A toolkit to go with the spares is good. In it, have a screwdriver to fit the pistol grip screw (or one of those horrid allen wrenches to fit), something to push the takedown pins if your rifle is a tight fit, and either a broken case extractor, a cleaning rod or, better, both. A compact cleaning system like the Real Avid or the Otis, with a broken case extractor tossed in, will do the job. Remember, this is the emergency kit, not the maintenance kit.

The rest of the tools are in your gunsmithing gear kit, or maintenance kit, not on your belt or in your bug-out/fighting bag.

CHAPTER 13

REAL-TIME TROUBLESHOOTING & CLEARING

WE ALL WANT a rifle that works 100% of the time. We all want to be good looking, rich, smart and charming. What we get is what we get. Sometimes we end up owning a rifle that needs some extra TLC. Or we find out selves in a situation where we need to do a bit more because the rain, snow, ice, mud, whatever is just so deep or thick that the rifle says, "I'm outta here."

Sometimes we can be careful, cautious and considered. Other times we need to get it fixed just as quickly as humanly possible, or suffer the consequences. Let's cover the first one, which I call the Gunsmith's Mindset.

"Hmm, that's interesting." Everything is a puzzle to be dissected, sorted out and solved. This is the mindset you want to be in, on the range, testing a new AR. It doesn't fire? Interesting. It fires, but the magazine drops out? Very interesting. Each time it fires, all the nearby car alarms chirp? Very interesting.

Nothing that happens is something that has to be taken care of in a hurry.

So, the gunsmith testing an AR will note the direction and distance each empty is tossed, and what dings it might have on it. What is recoil like, what is the muzzle blast like, and none of it is immediately corrected.

One of the amazing aspects of the AR-15 is that even when it blows and parts fly off, the shooter is rarely harmed.

The second approach is what I'll call the Tactical Mindset. In the Tactical Mindset, everything is a problem that has to be solved in the shortest time possible. And, it has to be solved also while dealing with the problem that precipitated the use of the AR in the first place. That is, you've just used half a magazine to deal

Left: This looks like the bolt broke, and then the gun blew up. It was the other way around, the gun blew, and the bolt broke in a way that duplicates other breakages. Right: No amount of **SPORTS**, or **T-R-B**, no matter how vigorously applied, will solve this "wedgie." You have to follow the simple malfunction plan: unload, clear, reload.

with a small group of mutant bikers/zombies and your rifle stops working. You have to get it working again, as quickly as possible, but also you need to be dealing with the biker/zombies. If that means communicating with your team members while moving to cover, then do so. If it means running like the wind because there are no team members (i.e., you're on your own), then get running. Let's look at the two more-or-less traditional methods, before I tell you what actually works.

SPORTS

First up is S.P.O.R.T.S. That is the Army acronym for "Slap, pull, observe, release, tap, shoot."

The idea is simple. When you have a malfunction, you slap the bottom of the magazine to make sure it is seated. You pull back the charging handle, you observe to see if something comes out, or if something is blocking the bolt. You release the charging handle, tap the forward assist, and then you shoot. With all due respect, B.S.

The Army system depends on a host of variables, almost all of which you will find insulting. First

of all, it depends on you, the rifleman, not having a sidearm. Until recent experiences in Iraq and Afghanistan, handguns were officers-only, with some issued to NCOs, machinegunners, RTOs, etc. I read that at the end, the Army was issuing a sidearm to everyone, since some bright light had discovered that rifles aren't always handy. (Especially when the SOP calls for them to be racked, unloaded, by the door, instead of leaning against each desk in an office.)

If you are not military and are armed and in a shooting situation, I suspect there is a high probability that you have a handgun. If so, the first step is to get behind cover, draw your sidearm, and deal with the problem well enough to correct your rifle's predicament.

Second, it calls for you to have the time and space to do all this. Now, if you are part of a Fire Team and the rest of your crew is slinging lead at the bad guys, throwing grenades, calling in artillery or air support, and generally killing people and breaking things, well then you can get behind something and spend some quality time bonding with your problem child. Alas, most of us do not have a fire team at hand, and have to solve problems ourselves, either in the world or on a range in a competition.

Third, this calls for daylight. How are you going to observe anything that comes out of your rifle at night? Tell your buddy "Hey, shine a light over here?' That's not really clever, in the middle of a nighttime altercation.

Fourth, it assumes you, the end-user aren't smart, motivated or educated enough to do more than cycle the charging handle back and forth. You bought this book, clearly you're above that level.

And finally, it doesn't solve any problems. Just racking the bolt, when you have any problem other than a dead primer, just makes things worse.

TAP-RACK-BANG

This is a sub-set, a variant of the SPORTS system, one that came about as a result of competition. TRB came from a very special set of circumstances – practical shooting competition.

OK, you've signed up for a match. You step into the box to shoot a stage and the RO tells you to "load and make ready." On the buzzer you draw (or present your rifle) and when you pull the

If you have fingers slender enough to reach in there, then you have fingers lacking the strength to do anything useful.

trigger, you hear a click. Or, on the second, would-be shot, you hear a click.

What has happened is simple; you haven't seated the magazine hard enough to lock it in place. The first-shot click comes from the magazine riding low and not chambering a round when you made ready. Sometimes the mag rides high enough to feed, but not be locked. The recoil of the first shot causes it to drop lower (or out entirely) and there is no second round chambered.

In this situation, slapping the mag to seat it fully and working the charging handle will get a round chambered. The malfunction was not with the rifle, but you. Or to be precise, your procedure.

Only in this situation will the TRP, or even SPORTS for that matter, solve your problem.

WHAT ARE WE DEALING WITH?

There are a number of problems your AR could have fallen heir to, from a simple dud primer, up to a sub-critical detonation that causes parts to fall off.

Failure to Extract

This is usually an extractor problem (gee, ya think?) and needs an extractor fix. No amount of slapping, tapping, racking or cursing will solve it.

Failure to Eject

Would it be too obvious, or insulting, to say "see above" and use the word ejector in place of extractor?

Failure to Fire

This could be an incorrectly-installed firing pin, a dud primer or an incorrectly-assembled hammer spring. At the latest class, we had a very curious situation. The rounds being used by the officers in question were factory-new. And yet, the case shoulders were shorter than .223 should be. As a result, the rounds (there were 3-4 in a case of 1,000) would chamber too deeply to let the firing pin set off the primer. But also, the extractor couldn't reach the rim.

Lock the bolt back. Strip out the magazine. Get your fingers in up through the magazine well, and fiddle the wedged brass and round free. Then reload.

Double Feed

Two rounds trying to feed at once, this is almost always a magazine issue.

Faux Double Feed

Here, the round feeding can't get past the ejecting empty. Usually the root cause is gas leak, and the key has to be staked. It's often an extractor issue, and almost never a gas port incorrect-diameter issue.

THE SOLUTION

A quick summary of the solution is simple: unload, finger-fight the problem, reload and continue.

The process is simple. When you have a problem like this, you'll know it because bullets stop coming out of your rifle. Some teach to look, others teach to not look. Me, I look. If I can see it, I can solve it. If I can't see it, then I can still solve it.

Lock the bolt back. Remove the magazine.

Stick your hand or a few fingers up the magazine well. Yes, the problem is something

going on near the ejection port, but your fingers are slim enough to reach in there. But two rounds, or a round and an empty case, wedged into the feed area, can be un-wedged if you jab them with your fingertips from below.

Let them fall out.

Cycle the bolt a couple of times.

Re-load a magazine, work the charging handle, and get back to work.

Have you solved the problem? That depends on how you define "the problem." If the clock was ticking, yes. If the zombies were still coming, yes. If you were practicing at the gun club, yes and no. Yes in that you practiced how to solve it, but no, in that it will happen again until or unless you get to the root cause of the problem.

Oh, and while you are doing this, maintain situational awareness.

On the range, either at the club, practicing, or in a match, keep the muzzle in a safe direction. Failing to do so at the club might just get you a social admonishment. In a match, failure to respect the 180 plane will get you DQ'd. In the real world, sometimes called the two-way range, failing to notice what is going on around you can lead to terminal penalties.

If they are so-wedged that fingers won't work, you'll have to use tools. Just remember, there's a primer in there, with a very sensitive nature. Don't go annoying it.

CHAPTER 14:

DID YOU BUY A GOOD RIFLE?

I F YOU TRY TO navigate your way through the digital swamp known as the internet, you will find plenty of places where you will be told, "No, you didn't." If you did not buy a rifle that conforms in every detail to the hive/collective's idea of what is "best," from name brand uppers and lowers, to mil-spec barrels, to purchasing a bolt/carrier assembly that came wrapped in gold-plated titanium foil, you have bought junk.

The advocates of each type will, if pressed, tell you that the sure way to acquire a good rifle is to make sure you buy only known, top-quality brands, and that by doing so you are safe from low-quality gear. There are a couple of problems with this. First, while there is still a bunch of bad stuff out there, it isn't like the "bad old days" where there were a whole lot of crappy parts to be found. I remember sorting through a box of disconnectors back in the 1980s, ditching the ones that were poorly stamped and keeping only the ones that could be made to fit, before buying what I grabbed. Back then, it was good gear/ parts, or utter crap. Today, we have the premium, top-quality stuff, then we have lots and lots of good-enough stuff, and a little bit of crap, and the really bad stuff is easy to spot once you have a bit of experience.

The second problem is what the top-quality parts people do; they inspect and hand-fit. Now, as we discussed earlier, there are some tests you can't

If you are going to do this right, you will need tools. On the left, a chamber brush, to start your chamber check. On the right, the M-Guns 223/556 gauge.

Some gas blocks are held on by friction and set screws. Once you have it straight, and the screws tight, paint them in so you can see if they move.

do. For instance, you probably can't high-pressure test and magnetic particle inspect your own bolt. You can, however, do the inspection that the name establishments do, and ensure your rifle is as up to snuff as it is going to be.

In some instances inspection is not correction. A case in point, my friend Ned and I once worked on a particular rifle at a class. The officer involved worked for a department that had tried to get patrol rifles for the cars at the absolute lowest cost. Not surprisingly, the rifles just didn't want to work. We went through the list of usual problems and solved the issues we could, one after another, but two rifles refused to cooperate.

We finally tracked down the problems by swapping uppers and lowers from (other brand and build) rifles of known performance. What we found was stunning; the cylindrical bore of the upper, the tunnel the carrier rides in, had been machined off-spec. That, and the location

of the bottom of the upper, the part that bears against the lower, had been machined in the wrong place.

There was nothing to be done but replace the upper, installing all the old parts into new uppers.

Inspection will tell you that is the problem (in this example), but inspection won't correct it. However, there are things you can inspect and correct on your own.

A rifle assembled from decent parts, that you have subjected to the following inspection and correction process, is the equal of a name-brand rifle in performance. Your choices in specs may hinder that. If you select, for instance, a 1/12 barrel that is made of bare steel, it won't stand up to as much abuse (or be as happy with heavy bullets) as a chrome-lined 1/7 barrel. And, to a top-end competitive shooter, your rifle may fall a bit short in some areas. Again, a less than premium barrel in the hands of an NRA

High Power High Master may not shoot as well. However, we're talking points and X-count at 600 yards. Just to make High Master you have to shoot over 97%, and in that rarified air, every point counts.

How do I know this works? Because I've taken unreliable rifles, rifles that at the start of our classes won't even work 100% of the time, and by applying this process I (or the officer who brought it to the class) shoots a passing or perfect score in the qualifications and drops a satisfying number of targets out to 300 meters on the computer pop-up course.

Here's the process.

INSPECT AND CHECK

You've got a brand-new, or a new-to-you used rifle. What do you do? Clean it. Unload and disassemble for a field cleaning. Run a brush and swabs down the bore. Get a chamber brush in the chamber, then a mop. Pull the bolt out of the carrier, and clean and lube everything. Give all the various external parts a look, and then hand-wrench them to make sure they are tight. If they are not tight, tighten them.

Simple things like the pistol grip, or a fixed stock, being loose, are not reason to box it up and send it back to the manufacturer. They are, however, a reason to be suspicious.

Check the flash hider, pistol grip, stock and forearm/handguards to make sure they are tight. Or, in the case of the handguards, not more loose than they should be. If they are loose, tighten them. Last, inspect the sights. The rear sight should be vertical (if it is a bolted-on BUIS) or not bent or tilted. The front sight should be vertical, and not at all tilted to one side or the other.

A front sight that is tilted is cause for alarm. If it is a front sight secured to the barrel, this can be cause to send it back. A pinned-on sight, tilted, can only be fixed by the factory or a gunsmith with the right tools. This is not an occasion to show off your hand-held power drill skills.

If it is bolted to a handguard/free-float rail, then the handguard/rail may be installed not-square. This is a dicey situation. It could be easily re-installed to be square, but why should you do this,

when the maker should have gotten it right?

Once you have checked it all, it is time to load up. Set aside a range day. Take only good ammo, ammo that is either factory, or reloads you have loaded and know for certain are 100% proper. Take only your best, fully-functional magazines. You'll need about 200 rounds.

Oh, and do not, I repeat, do not, start bolting on gear, scopes, lights, accessories and such. If your testing determines that you will have to get your rifle serviced, you'll have a double task – determining if the gear caused the problem, and un-bolting it all. Leave it as-is for the first sessions.

Now, in this day of expensive ammo, that much ammo may seem like a lot. And it is a hit to the wallet. Also, your barrel has a limited service life. Depending on how you use it and what you expect of it, that service life could be as little as 5,000 rounds, and as many as 15,000. At the low end, you are using four percent of your barrel's potential service life, just checking to see if it works. That's life.

This is not a blasting/plinking session, this is work, and detailed work, at that. The good news is that you can do all this in conjunction with your iron and optics zeroing, and your magazine

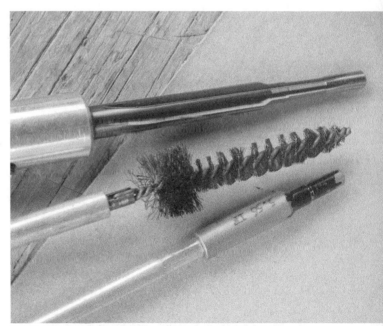

The brush is for cleaning, the gauge is for measuring, and the reamer is to correct a leade that was 223 to 5.56.

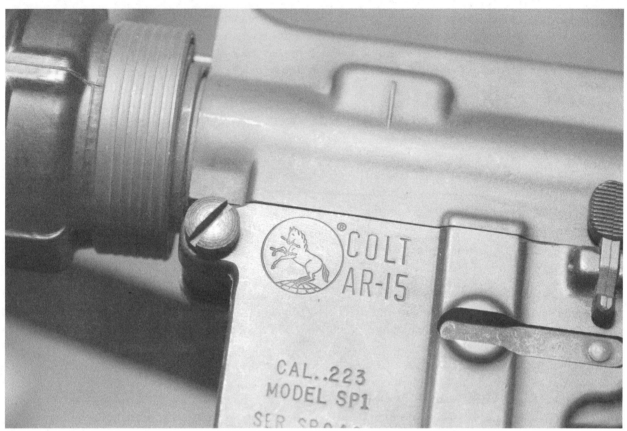

Only Colt can call their rifles "AR-15" and you'd better believe it that they protect it. Oh, and this is an early SP1, with the two-screw front takedown pin.

and function test live-fire checking. It isn't just mindless blasting into a hillside.

First, load only five rounds in each magazine. Use a target, 25 yards is a good start, and shoot from the bench. Your check points are simple: does the rifle lock open when each magazine is empty? If not, you've got a problem. If it does, move on.

Next, load up your magazines full, and fire five rounds each. A thirty-round magazine is working hardest when it is full, and if your rifle has a gas problem or a feeding problem, it will likely show up from full mags. Each five, pull the magazine out, top off, and repeat. If you have feeding problems, you can diagnose, or simply note and ship back.

Oh, and while you're doing this, check groups on paper and adjust your sights to zero the rifle.

If, at this point, you're saying to yourself, "This sounds a lot like what we just did in Chapter Twelve," you're right. Gold star for paying attention. Except here, instead of learning about

yourself, you're learning about your new rifle.

If, at 25 yards, you cannot shoot a group smaller than an inch (and you are a good shot), this could be bad. It may be that your rifle just doesn't like that ammo. It happens. At 25 yards, from the bench, you should be able to, with good ammo, shoot a group you can cover with a thumbnail. If, despite your best efforts you cannot get factory ammo to shoot that well, and you paid for a good barrel, one that was supposed to do better, try one more thing: get a better shooter. If the best shooter at your gun club can't do any better, then you need to ship it back.

Also, you should be able to zero your rifle at 25 yards without having to crank the sights too far. If you find you cannot get it centered despite adjusting the rear sight hard against the inside of the sight housing, your front sight is installed tilted, or the barrel alignment pin is in the wrong spot, or the slot in the upper to align that pin is in the wrong spot. None of these are things you

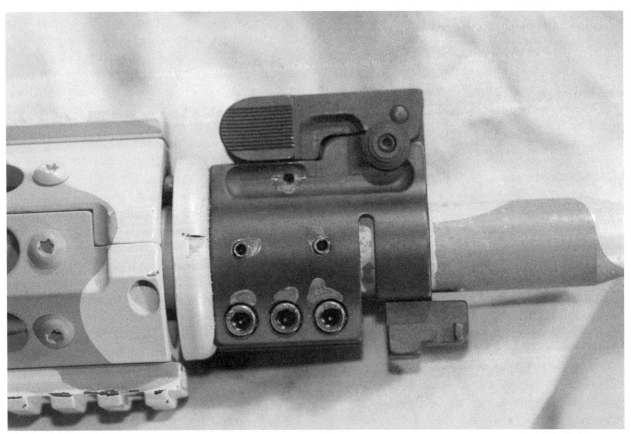

Screws do not belong on rifles. If you have to use a screw-secured part, paint the screwheads once you have made it all tight. It helps lock the screw in, and offers evidence of movement.

can easily fix, nor should you. Save a target, box up the rifle and ship it back. Unless, of course you want to fix it yourself.

If you cannot get a vertical zero without turning your front post so far up it risks falling out, or so far down if is almost hidden in the housing, you have the wrong one on the barrel. It is either an M4 on a non-M4 upper, or a non-M4 in an M4 upper. Or, it is a gas-block folding front sight installed on a free-float handguard, or vice-versa.

Needless to say, failures to feed, from stubbing rounds or rounds stopping angled, sideways or bent in the feedway, are all cause for shipping it back.

And then there are the things you can fix. Before we jump right into fixing things, why should you? And why are we going to all this trouble? Fixing in a lot of instances is faster and easier if you do it, than if the factory does it. Yes, they will not get the feedback that lets them correct the problem in-house (if they care) but that's not your problem.

Shipping a rifle back costs time and money. You have to find a box (hopefully you saved the cardboard sleeve the rifle came in), pack the rifle, seal it, label it, schlep it down to the local shipping hub, and then explain to them that yes, you can ship a rifle, and no, they don't need to inspect it. Then after you've educated them on their own regs, you pay them to ship it.

Doing the fixing yourself saves the time and money, and ensures it gets done right.

As an example, we're still struggling with manufacturers over the carrier gas key problem. The key needs to be staked, and staked securely. Some still do a lackadaisical job, and if yours is poorly done, shipping it back may not get you satisfaction. If that's the job they do, they'll just ship it back with a note that says, "That's the way we do it."

If your rifle works 100% through the tests, then you can go right to the final touches part of this chapter.

MECHANICAL WORK-OVER & UPGRADE

Every rifle I own has had the following things checked and if need-be, tended to.

Chamber check for 5.56 leade, with Mguns gauge. If not 5.56, it gets Mguns 5.56 reamed. (I long ago gave up checking headspace, as the problem has not been a problem for so long, it wasn't worth the effort. Someday that will "bite" me, but until then….)

As explained previously, AR-15 rifles with .223 Remington leades have caused more problems than anything else with the exception of the next step. The only barrels not to be reamed are those which have treated to the Melonite process. This makes the steel surface so hard it will take the edge off the leade reamer.

The carrier key is staked, double-staked, and if I thought it would help and still had the tools, I'd tack-weld the thing on. Gas blow-by from the carrier key is the cause of many other problems, problems that have in the past been erroneously attributed to other sources. This calls for use of the MOACKS, after disassembling, cleaning and then applying Loctite.

If the stock is a fixed stock, A1 or A2, I make sure it is tight. The A1/A2 gets the screw removed and checked. If it has a nylon locking section, great. If it has a smear of blue Loctite, fine. If not, I use blue and tighten it down. If it is a tele-stock, I make sure everything is tight and aligned, and I then stake the castle nut.

I take of the pistol grip, remove the spring that activates the selector plunger, and apply a small wedge/diamond of masking tape to it. I then jam the spring back down into the pistol grip, tape end first. The tape makes sure the spring doesn't fall out when next I disassemble the pistol grip.

I do all the inspections I've described, to make sure all the parts are there, tight, straight, and properly secured. I then paint-in the various parts that might try to move, such as BUIS, and then I'm done. Well, done until the next round of experimentation, adjustment, trying-new-gear, etc.

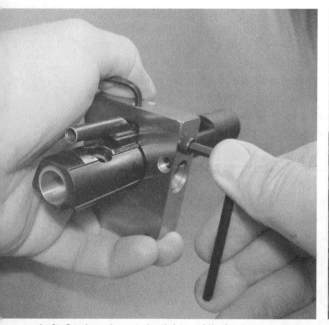

Left: Gas keys have to be tight, and the best way to make sure they stay tight is to stake the screws in. That means a **MOACKS**. Right: This forearm uses a top rail, clamped on the flat-top, to hold on tight. The locking screw, in addition to being Loctite-d, is painted in.

CHAPTER 15:

HOW TO STAY LEGAL

F YOU LET yourself be influenced by the news, pundits or politicians, you'd believe that you'd have to hold regular exorcisms of your AR just to keep it from coming for you in the dark of night, evil thoughts ablaze. It is, however, merely an inanimate object, and can't do anything on its own.

What it can do, however, is get you sideways with the law if you aren't careful with your choices or actions. The very modularity of the AR can result in the wrong parts being bolted on (by you or someone else) with the result of a legal violation.

Out of the box, you're highly unlikely to run into problems. The people who manufacturer or assemble ARs for a living know what is allowed

An AR hammer on top, with the firing pin catch notch, and an M16 on the bottom, with the rounded corner. Both work just fine.

and what isn't, and don't want to get in trouble. It is when owners start changing things that trouble can ensue.

There are two arenas where you can get into trouble, state/municipal and federal. Since the feds, curiously, are clearer and easier to describe, we'll cover them first.

Your AR, for the purposes of categorizing at the federal level, falls into one five slots: rifle, SBR, machine gun, pistol and "any other weapon." When you are discussing the law, you cannot mix terms. A federal definition may have little or nothing to do with a state definition, and vice-versa, and you will only confuse things if you are not clear.

The AR, due to its modularity, allows for mix-n-match combos. An assembled upper or lower that does not have a mate is termed an "unassigned" upper or lower. If you have one lower and two uppers, the uppers are clearly assigned to that lower. If you have two lowers, and three uppers, and you leave them as two assembled rifles and the extra upper, that third upper is an unassigned upper. Throw an un-assembled lower in the safe, and some spare barrels, and you now have a potential minefield. Which upper, currently not on a lower, goes with which lower? It can matter, as we'll see.

RIFLE

A rifle, in federal terms, is an AR with a barrel longer than 16 inches, and an overall length greater than 26 inches. This is easy, as any buffer tube makes an AR carbine thirty inches or more in length. Overall length is easy, measure the

AR or M16? An M16 trigger, which to be used in an AR (semi-auto-only) rifle you should weld or silver-solder the rear slot closed.

length, parallel to the bore, from one end to the other. Barrels are measured by the distance from the bolt face when closed to the forward-most part of the barrel that is permanent. Keep that in mind – permanent. Your flash hider does not count for overall length unless it is permanently attached. It doesn't matter how tightly you have it torqued on. The ATF does not view any thread-locking compound as being permanent, regardless of brand or strength rating. Soft solder is not permanent. They will not settle for anything less than a high-temperature silver-solder job or welding.

This matters because there are a lot of barrels to be had at gun shows, over the internet and at the gun club. Most of them will be 16, 18 or 20 inches in length. However, there are always "deals" to be had on shorter ones, alleged 14.5-inch M4 "takeoffs" (the government does not yank off perfectly good barrels or sell them by their weight as scrap steel) and 11.5-inch "commando" barrels of dubious origins.

So, your smokin'-hot deal on an M4 barrel that is 14.5 inches long can get you in trouble. If you install it on your rifle/carbine, it will be too short to be legal. You have to permanently attach a flash hider or suppressor mount to it, one that adds at a bare minimum of 1.5 inches to the barrel's length, better a full two inches. If you do not, you cannot use it to build an upper, even an unassigned one, because it is the work of a moment to slap it onto a lower and make an unlawful rifle.

You can own the spare barrel at 14.5 inches, but you cannot assemble it to an upper. In fact, it would be prudent to not own that barrel and an un-assembled upper. The ATF views such things through the legal lens of "constructive intent." You owned all the parts to make a prohibited rifle, you hadn't (yet) assembled them, but you could have in five minutes. More on this is a bit. Just keep in mind, you do not want prohibited parts floating around your gun room.

SBR

A short-barreled rifle is a semi-automatic rifle with a barrel shorter than 16 inches. To own one you have to do the NFA-34 dance, as an SBR is treated as if it were a machine gun. (It isn't a machine gun, and you must also be clear on that.) You have to apply to the ATF to get the Tax Stamp by paying the $200 tax, and then be happy. There are, however, a few things to keep in mind.

Federal law does not trump state law on this, or any of the following categories. Just because the feds license it, if your state does not permit it, you can't have it.

Also, the Tax Stamp/SBR is for a *particular* rifle, the one detailed on the form you submitted. If you SBR'd your AR, the rifle known as Bob's Guns #123, then *that* rifle is the SBR. You cannot simply plop your short-barreled upper onto any other AR you own and call that one your SBR for the day. This applies even to police departments, something it has been difficult to get across to some administrators. The SBR is the serial-numbered lower listed on the Tax Stamp, and only that one can be the recipient of a short-barreled upper.

If you, the departmental armorer, are instructed to build up any old lower as the "departmental SBR" because the department has received permission to build an SBR, or you are ordered to do something similar, something you know to be against the law, I offer my condolences. Your

These are barrels too short for a regular rifle or carbine. They are **SBR** or pistol barrels, and you'd best have the right paperwork and firearm to own such a barrel.

choices are simple: tell the Sergeant. Deputy Chief, Chief, Sheriff, whomever, "no" and risk a career-interrupting event, or obey the order knowing you are breaking federal law. One of those choices will land you in prison.

The safe way to own an SBR is to keep the SBR upper on the SBR lower all the time except when cleaning. And not have other rifles apart for cleaning, on the same bench, that aren't SBRs. And, if you have several uppers for that lower, keep them all in one large hard-sided case. And never leave an unassigned lower lying about.

For departmental armorers, it would be prudent to somehow mark the upper with the serial number of the SBR lower it is assigned to. That way there can be no confusion, and if a superior orders a bad thing, you have the "the uppers and lowers are serial-number matched" as a temporary dodge until you can get the departmental attorney on your side.

A hazardous time for SBR owners is a fun day at the range with friends. One of your buddies

thinks, "Hey, that SBR thing is cool, I wonder how that would work on my lower?" When you aren't looking, he swaps your SBR upper onto his lower to try. That, my friends, is a federal felony, an unlawful construction, and you could get in trouble. Is the law irrational and stupid? Yes. But it is also very clear, and you should know better.

THE SBR PROCESS

You apply to the ATF to have your rifle SBR'd. (And yes, the term has been used enough now to be a verb.) You get approval, buy the parts, build the rifle and mark it according to the regs. (Yes, you have to mark it, as the builder of the SBR.) You shoot it for a while, then get tired of the whole thing and decide you want out.

In order to transfer it to your buddy, he has to apply for his own Tax Stamp, pay his own $200 and receive approval. Then, and only then, can you transfer it to him. Or, you can sell it to a

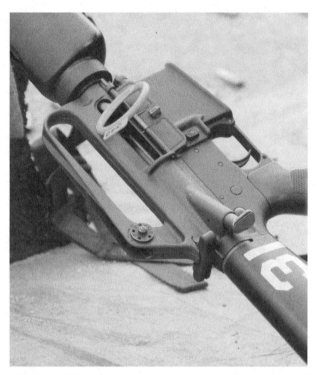

This is an M16 (an A1) and will always and ever be so. The ATF rule is simple; "Once a machine gun, always a machine gun." Were this transferable, it would be worth close to $20,000. It isn't, and thus is worth ten years in Ft. Leavenworth.

dealer in such things, known in the trade as a "Class Three" dealer. He does not have to pay the transfer tax, but the person who buys it from him does.

You could just re-build it with a 16-inch or longer barrel and ignore the SBR status it still has. That would be fraught with peril. If you take your still-SBR-status AR across state lines without filing the correct travel papers, you're in violation of the law. And if you forgot it was still an SBR and sold it, the new owner would be in violation (actually, both of you) for owning an SBR for which he hadn't paid the tax.

You can, however, simply write to the ATF and ask that your rifle be removed from the registry. You do not get your $200 back, but you now have a plain rifle again.

MACHINE GUN

This is a select-fire AR, called an M16, and you buy it through the same process as the SBR: Tax Stamp, $200 tax, license. As a machine gun, it can be whatever you want it to be. You can put

There is no part on this rifle that meets mil-spec. Everything on it is better. Also, there is no need to use anything M16-ish inside, as it would actually hinder performance. Buying M16 parts for a rifle like this is false economy.

an SBR upper on it without any extra paperwork, as the machine gun status trumps the SBR status and paperwork.

If an MG is superior to an SBR, why go the SBR route? Cost. The current cost of a transferable M16 is in the region of $13,000. That's right, a transferable M16 runs as much as the cost of a small car. The NFA Registry for machine guns was frozen in 1986 and no new ones have been built since. SBRs have not been frozen, and buying one simply costs you the price of an AR, the $200 tax and the conversion costs by you or your gunsmith.

If the numbers have been frozen why can you see them all over the internet, in videos? And how do police departments have them? The first part is simple: a manufacturer built them. You can, if you wish, apply for a manufacturers license, and begin building select-fire AR-15s. You cannot, however, sell them. They are not transferable except to police departments, the group excepted from the ban on newly-made machine guns.

Oh, and if you do decide the expense of a manufacturers license is too much, all your M16-like ARs must either be sold to another manufacturer (and they will offer a dime on the dollar for them, at your original cost) or turned in to the ATF for destruction. That's a hobby best left to lottery winners.

The best way to store your transferable M16 is in a locked, hard-sided case, in your locked gun room, in the locked safe, with all the uppers it uses. In the case of a question, you want there to be no uncertainty; the M16 is as secure as the launch codes for the nukes.

Oh, and don't be a moron – insure it for full value.

PISTOL

An AR pistol is one that does not have a stock. As a pistol, it can have a barrel of any length, including less than 16 inches. However, simply sliding the stock off of your buffer tube does not make it a pistol. The defining characteristic of an AR pistol is that it has a buffer tube which lacks *any* provision whatsoever for attaching a stock. It is a bare tube, lacking both the rear, threaded hole to bolt on an A1/A2 stock,

and the lower spine to adjust a slider for the telescoping stock.

To make an AR pistol, you either buy one that was made that way from the start, or you build from a bare lower that has never been a functioning firearm. You assemble it with the pistol buffer tube, and it is then a handgun. (It is also a handgun under state law, and you'd better be covered there, too, or you're in trouble. Make sure you know your local laws and follow them.)

If you decide that you are tired of an AR pistol, you can then make it a rifle. You cannot, however, make it a rifle with the shorter-than-16-inch pistol barrel on it. And it would probably not even be smart to keep the shorter pistol barrel. Sell it, buy a 16-inch barrel, then re-build as a rifle. Can you re-re-build it as a handgun again? I'd say no, but some say you can. No one really knows, because the ATF hasn't issued a ruling nor have the courts weighed in on it. They've weighed in on a different, similar case, but a similar court case may not impress them. They would insist on a *particular* court case. The question here is, do you want to be the one in the middle of that new, particular, court case? I thought not.

It is common to mark an **AR** handgun thusly, even though you don't have to. Well, you might by state law, but not for the feds.

AR handguns are fun. A pain to get and keep running, but fun. Just make sure you keep the pistol upper on the pistol lower, and everything will be fine.

Be smart and if you decide to go back to an AR pistol, start over with a new, bare, lower. The AR pistol is a one-way street, pistol to rifle, but never back again. Not until the law is clear.

AOW

"Any Other Weapon" is the catch-all term that the ATF uses to sweep up everything that doesn't fit neatly into the other descriptions. Actually, they have been forced into it by moronic legislators who really don't know anything about firearms, but who have passed laws anyway. You see, by the "reasoning" of some lawmakers, any handgun with a vertical foregrip is a particularly evil and deadly firearm. You can put that foregrip on any of the

other categories of AR – rifle, SBR, machine gun – but not onto a handgun. If you do, it is an AOW. The good news is that the Tax Stamp to own an AOW can be as little as $5.

CONSTRUCTIVE INTENT

Let's go all "Breaking Bad" here. You have this kewl idea for a Halloween party: you get all the gear, all the precursor chemicals, and you find the formula for making crystal meth. You have all your guests show up in hazmat suits and wear respirators, and you play episodes from the Blu-Ray Collectors Edition, Directors Cut DVDs in your collection. Cool party, eh? Yes, and a perfect example of constructive intent. You didn't have

The firing pin area has been altered over the years. The M16, on the left, has a shrouded firing pin. The AR-15 on the right is open, to prevent tampering and conversion.

the intent to make it, but if anyone mixes two chemicals, you are then in the process of making crystal meth. You're in hot water.

So, don't go buying all the parts needed to be making yourself an SBR (for example) and leave them lying about. The process of getting an SBR takes some time, and you'll have plenty of opportunities to acquire the parts you need once the approved Tax Stamp returns. Plus, if you are having someone build it for you, they won't even start until they see your approved form. If they do, and you get denied, they are in possession of an un-approved SBR, a felony.

Similarly, if you plan to build an AR pistol, don't collect the parts until you have a lower on which to assemble them. And then, keep all the parts together in a locked case, box, whatever. You want there to be no misunderstanding if someone sees the parts.

How could that happen, you ask? Hmm, let's see, how can people be in your house? Guests at a party, and you forgot to lock the spare bedroom, the one where you do your gun work. Or, guests at a party and a fight breaks out. Or an accidental fire. Or a heart attack. The resulting police or fire response puts your house under scrutiny. If there is a fire, the firemen are not going to respect locked doors in their quest to keep the place from burning to the ground. What has been seen cannot be un-seen.

Save yourself risk, heartache, legal expense and perhaps a "vacation" in orange. If you're going to do this, do it right.

HOW MANY M16 PARTS CAN I HAVE IN MY AR?

The simple, easy, and unlikely-to-get-you-in-trouble answer is none. The ATF doesn't really care how many parts you have, what they care about is, "does it act like a machine gun?" The big question for a long time was the carrier. An M16 carrier is heavier than the AR-modified ones, and the extra weight does have a functioning advantage. The ATF has come out with the opinion that the carrier is now no big deal, and now some AR manufacturers ship their semi-auto only ARs with M16 carriers. The rest of the parts are still problematic.

The hammer, trigger, disconnector and safety/selector are all relatively common parts. You could if you wanted, acquire a full set of M16 internals, but why would you want to? Back in the early days of AR building, the M16 parts were far more common than the AR-15 parts. (Only Colt made AR-15 parts. Military surplus parts were all M16, and common and cheap at gun shows. A set of proper Colt AR-15 parts could cost you four or five times as much as the mil-surp set.) It was not uncommon for someone to buy the M16 parts, assemble a rifle and make sure it worked correctly, then de-fang the M16 parts. That is, grind off the extra hooks, tabs, etc. that made them M16 parts, and to solder-up the gaps in the selector so it wouldn't work except as semi-auto parts. Why assemble first, then modify? If a part was defective, you could go back and exchange it. If you had already ground on it, the seller wouldn't take it back. This is now a dangerous practice. Imagine trying to explain to a jury of non-gun people (all the gun people would have been bounced off the jury by the Prosecution during interviewing of prospective jurors) just what "un-M16ing" a part entails, how it works, and why you would bother. Especially since you can buy perfectly good, semi-auto-only parts these days just about everywhere, and for much the same cost.

A friend of mine, a law enforcement trainer, has told me a cautionary tale. (He tells it in every one of his classes.) A long-serving command staff police administrator was accused of selling guns out of the evidence locker to gang members.

Of course, any reasonable person who believed the "confidential informant" would simply get a warrant, and then go down and conduct an inventory of the evidence locker to verify the truth of this rumor.

No, the feds raided his house and confiscated his guns. Finding no evidence-locker guns, they were in a bind. So, they latched onto a competition AR the officer had built, built exactly as described above. Through all kinds of trickery, the ATF was able to get the rifle to fire two rounds on one trigger pull. Ah-ha! A machine gun. It took (and this was a couple of decades ago) several years

An array of disconnectors. On top, an M16, middle an AR-15, and bottom an early Colt AR-15, that proved to be troublesome for Colt. You can make the top one like the middle one by simply chopping off the extra length.

and fifty thousand dollars to fight and win.

More recently, a National Guard sergeant in a Midwestern state was run through the same wringer, but did not win, and served time in prison.

It would be prudent to not mess with M16 parts, unless you actually have an M16. But, you can do it properly, so we'll look into that.

WHAT DO M16 PARTS LOOK LIKE?

In the manufacturing process, some of the parts in your AR-15 were made as M16 parts before the manufacturer took one more step and turned them into AR-15 parts. The hammer and carrier are two common ones. I've also seen disconnectors that were M16 parts in the manufacturing plant, until the last step to make them AR-15 parts. So, in the following example, you are doing pretty much what the manufacturers are doing in many cases.

The parts you need to know about are hammer, trigger, disconnector, safety and receiver auto-sear. Of the five, if you ever encounter a receiver auto-sear, get rid of it immediately. I've been accused of being a bit paranoid about this, but it serves no useful purpose to the owner of an AR, a semi-auto-only rifle, and can only get you in trouble.

The hammer of an M16 has a square lump on the top rear of the hook. This lump, or hammer auto-sear, connects/engages the receiver auto sear I just told you to get rid of (And you did, didn't you? Didn't you?) when the M16 is set on Auto or Burst. To remove the hammer auto-sear (if you insist on keeping this particular hammer), you simply use a bench grinder to grind it off. Grind it completely off. Don't get cute, and just grind off "enough" or leave some there. Grind

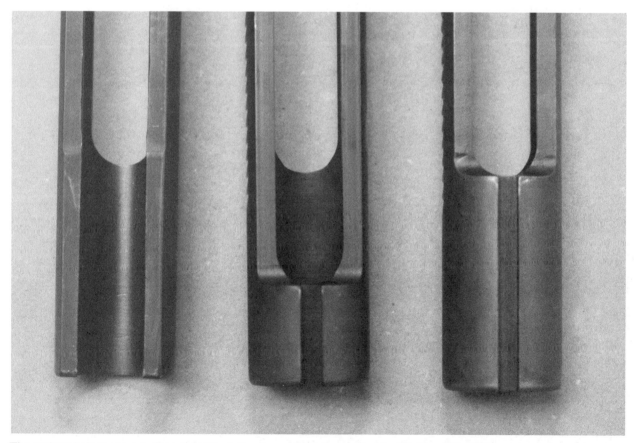

The various bolt carriers. Left to right, the fully-shaved Colt, the semi-auto AR-15, and the M16.

the hammer surface to a flat surface, just as the manufacturers do.

Disconnectors are flat pieces of heavy gauge sheet steel, stamped or fine-blanked out of coils of steel. The M16 disconnector has a longer tail,

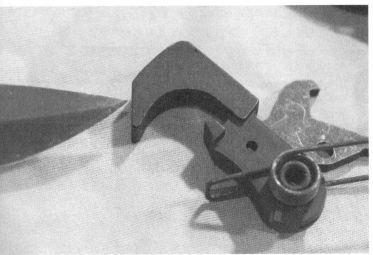

If there had been an auto-sear lump on it, this is where it would have been before the manufacturer ground it off to make it an AR-15 hammer.

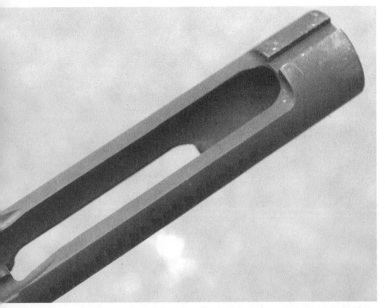

Carrier mods have created all kinds of variants. This is a shrouded-pin, common on M16, trimmed-back autosear shoulder (and thus semi-auto only) carrier, that is common these days. I don't know of any place where this would get you into trouble.

and the tail engages the M16 safety/selector. All you have to do is cut or grind off the tail and it is now an AR-15 disconnector. Again, don't do "just enough" or simply lower the tail, there is no advantage to leaving any of it there. Grind it off. You can do this with a bench grinder, or clamp the disconnector in a vise and use a cut-off wheel. I've even seen people who dealt with M16 disconnectors by clamping the part in a big vise with just the offending part sticking up, and using a big hammer to bend it until it broke off.

Triggers, too, start as M16 triggers in the manufacturing plant, and the last step there is to make them into AR-15 triggers. The trigger has a slot in the middle, where the disconnector rides. The M16 trigger is open at the back of the slot. That opening allows the longer tail of the M16 disconnector to engage the safety. To convert it back to an AR-15 trigger, you have to weld or silver-solder up that opening so an un-altered M16 disconnector no longer fits. A lot of people don't bother, and if you do either in a ham-handed way you can ruin the heat-treatment of the trigger, and it will wear and fail.

Triggers also come with two locations for the disconnector spring, and the two types of two-spring triggers are not the same. When Colt first made semi-auto AR-15s, they radically modified the disconnector. They changed the location of the disconnector spring, and they moved it too far. To correct that, and allow for future parts use, Colt made triggers with two spring holes. Later, the Burst trigger also came with two diconnector spring holes. The difference is, the standard AR-15 two-spring trigger has the same narrow slot as the M16, and the holes are directly in line. The Burst trigger has a much wider slot, and the spring holes are offset. You can't un-Burst the Burst trigger, so you should ditch it, just like the auto-sear mentioned above.

Safeties are hopeless. If you have an M16 safety in your rifle, disassemble the lower, remove the safety, and install a proper AR-15 safety. There is no practical way to un-M16 the safety.

STATE LAWS

Here we have a real mess. Some of the state laws are so irrational, so off-the-wall, that they make the feds seem civil, rational and polite. For example, in Ohio, any magazine over thirty rounds capacity is a machine gun. So, driving to Indiana with your legal, travel-form-approved SBR, you're fine. You're covered. But the extended magazine you'll use in the match is a machine gun under Ohio law, and could get you in trouble. Yes, you read that correctly. The magazine, in and of itself, is a machine gun, not merely a machine gun part, in Ohio.

California is so easy, it is almost embarrassing picking on them, but here we go. Threaded

muzzles. You can't have them, they make it too easy to attach a suppressor. And you can't just silver-solder or otherwise attached a cover, as the threads are still there. Oh, and no flash hiders, either. Magazines that are allowed only if they

<table>
<tr><td>

TRAVELING WITH YOUR SBR OR MG

If you own an SBR or a machine gun, you need to file the proper form with the ATF if you plan to cross state lines with it. You can be very general, saying on the form (they want to know where and when you're going) for example in the travel section "To Indiana in calendar 2015, January to December." That way, when you drive to Indiana each month to shoot in the 3-gun match with your SBR, you're covered. Driving to another 3-gun match in a different state? You need an approved form for that state also.

</td></tr>
</table>

A barrel extension has to be permanently attached to count for length. Screwing on a suppressor doesn't count, and doesn't make an **SBR** long enough.

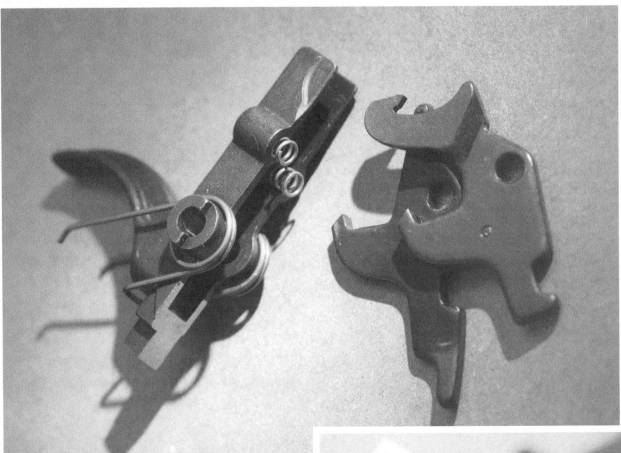

Here we have the burst-fire trigger and disconnectors. Yes, plural disconnectors, and a stupid design, too.

need a tool to remove them, thus the "bullet button" magazine catch for California rifles.

Traveling through, moving to, or simply visiting such states, you do not get any leeway because you don't live there.

So, if you are to own an AR-15, you have to know the laws of your jurisdiction and those where you will be taking it for a visit. The feds won't trump state laws, and you must know them.

In this day and age it is easy to go to the web page of your state, the Attorney General or the state police and read the laws. Your local gun shop probably has a good idea of the broad strokes of the law, but they might be a bit fuzzy on some of the particulars. Read up, frequent internet forums and also have the Rifle and Pistol Association (or whatever it is called) of your state in your bookmarks. Be sure you know

This isn't an M16 trigger, it has been modified by **Colt** to fit an **AR** that has a steel block in the lower.

the particulars and peculiarities in your area. You never know, what you think is the perfect arrangement of parts to create the best AR ever, might just be a technical violation of the law. And when it comes to guns, the authorities in many places are just as happy to hammer down on technicalities as they are real criminals.

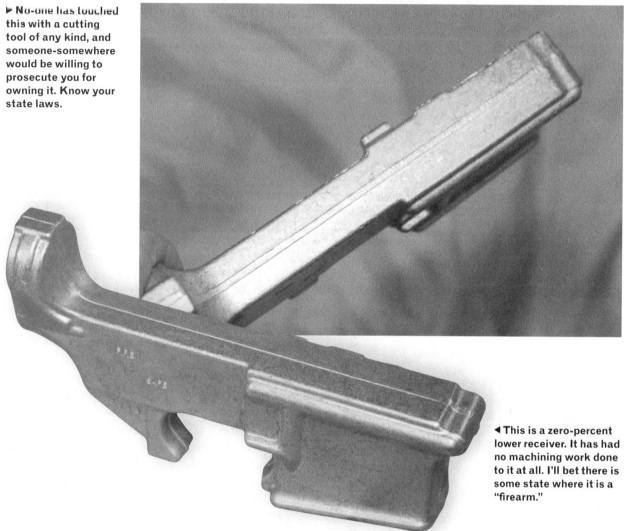

► No-one has touched this with a cutting tool of any kind, and someone-somewhere would be willing to prosecute you for owning it. Know your state laws.

◄ This is a zero-percent lower receiver. It has had no machining work done to it at all. I'll bet there is some state where it is a "firearm."

80% RECEIVERS

What is this eighty-percent receiver you speak of? Simple. The ATF, in order to get a handle on the complex process known as manufacturing, had to draw the line somewhere. Remember, there is a specific license and fee to be a manufacturer. Legislators left it to the ATF, which determined that the machining needed to create a lower receiver did not create something that could be called a "firearm" until it had passed 80% of the work needed. An "80% receiver" is one that stops short of that.

Typically, it is a receiver, in the white, that has had all the work done except carving out the recess for the hammer, trigger and such, and drilling the holes for their pins (and the safety/selector). A receiver at this point is still a lump of aluminum as far as the ATF is concerned. (State laws may vary.) Once you start the drilling/milling, etc., it becomes a firearm.

Some shooters, perhaps not as clever as they think they are, buy 80% receivers and finish the work themselves. As long as they do all the work themselves, and do not do it for profit or to deliver to someone else, all is kosher. But the process is fraught with pitfalls.

You have to do the work yourself. That means you can't hand it to your buddy the machinist with blueprints and come back in an hour, day, whatever. In that case, he does the work, he delivers it to you, he's a manufacturer, and you have taken possession of a firearm from a manufacturer, sans form 4473. You've both just committed federal felonies.

The desire to avoid "paperwork" typically drives

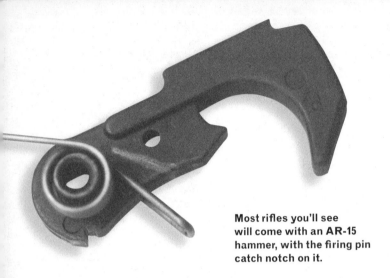

Most rifles you'll see will come with an AR-15 hammer, with the firing pin catch notch on it.

people who are custom gunsmiths. The ATF has tried to get such simple tasks as re-barreling a rifle, or re-stocking, declared "manufacturing." One aspect they are clear about is that a gunsmith cannot order up a slew of parts, assemble firearms, and then sell them at retail, without a manufacturers license. Well, they can, but no more than 50 a year.

So, you cannot go to your local gun shop, one with a gunsmith in the back, and order up a lower, its internal parts, and then ask, "Say, can you guys put this together for me?' That makes them a manufacturer. Not that people don't do it, but if the ATF gets wind of it, oh boy.

What you have to do, to protect both you and the gunsmith, is make a good-faith effort to assemble it yourself. Then, if you fail, take the partially-assembled, inadequately-functioning rifle to the gunsmith, and ask him to fix it for you.

A lot of people are quite lax about things like this, especially since the ATF regs are often unclear. But the basics are clear: you can buy lowers (through an FFL, on a 4473) and assemble them into rifles for yourself. What you can't do is make a business, or even a hobby, of buying stripped lowers, assembling them, and then selling them, lacking a manufacturers license.

The question of "build parties" comes up from time to time. You and a bunch of friends can get together and help each other, working through the process of building a lower, uppers, or complete rifles from parts. But you can't do it at a licensed location, because that would mean the FFL is facilitating manufacturing.

No one can charge for anything used in the build party. Not electricity or hourly time in the shop, not rental on tools, not replacement of broken parts, nothing. I'd even be leery of letting whoever's shop (or garage) it is get free pizza when the group orders. I've been accused of being overly cautious on such things, but, bottom line,   the law says you can't manufacture without a manufacturers license. I'm not going to do anything that even looks like I'm doing that, or saying that you should do it.

This trigger is from a burst-fire parts set. You can't even get it to work with a normal disconnector, and you gain nothing but risk by owning it.

this. One problem: soft aluminum won't stand up to use. So, you have to have it anodized. Guess what? Anyone who anodizes firearms has an FFL and will enter your lower in their records. No FFL? We're back to committing federal felonies for anodizing. That said, some receivers can be had anodized, but you still leave soft aluminum any place you drill or machine. Not as useful as you might think.

Another aspect of the manufacturing process comes into play. The ATF has had an acrimonious relationship at times with the general group of

Stay on target with

GunDigest
THE MAGAZINE

- ⊕ **GUN REVIEWS**
- ⊕ **NEW PRODUCT UPDATES**
- ⊕ **GUNS FOR SALE**
- ⊕ **FIREARMS INDUSTRY NEWS**
- ⊕ **AUCTION AND SHOW LISTINGS**

↘ 3 EASY WAYS TO SUBSCRIBE NOW:

 Order your print or digital subscription at
subscribe.gundigest.com

NOW AVAILABLE ON:

 CALL **800.829.9127**

A3GNLA

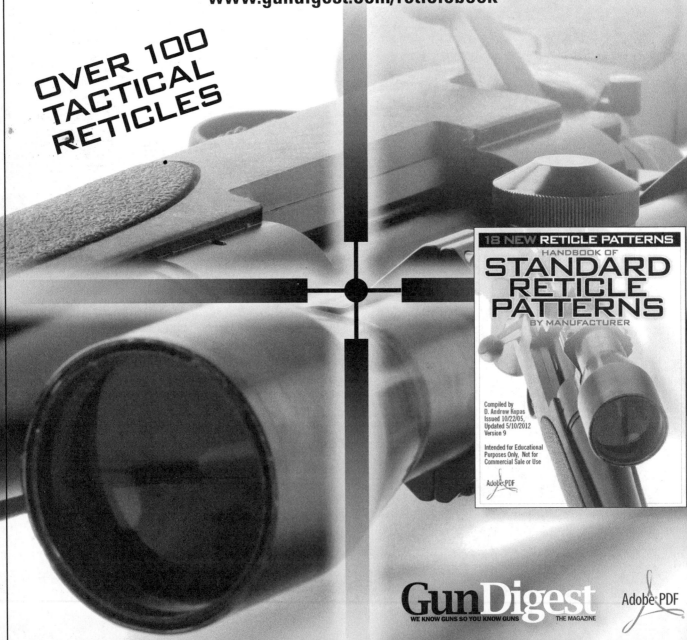